Rise of a Japanese Chinatown

T0339368

HARVARD EAST ASIAN MONOGRAPHS 367

Rise of a Japanese Chinatown

Yokohama, 1894–1972

ERIC C. HAN

Published by the Harvard University Asia Center
Distributed by Harvard University Press
Cambridge (Massachusetts) and London 2020

© 2014, 2020 by The President and Fellows of Harvard College

Printed in the United States of America

The Harvard University Asia Center publishes a monograph series and, in coordination with the Fairbank Center for Chinese Studies, the Korea Institute, the Reischauer Institute of Japanese Studies, and other facilities and institutes, administers research projects designed to further scholarly understanding of China, Japan, Vietnam, Korea, and other Asian countries. The Center also sponsors projects addressing multidisciplinary and regional issues in Asia.

Studies of the Weatherhead East Asian Institute, Columbia University

The Studies of the Weatherhead East Asian Institute of Columbia University were inaugurated in 1962 to bring to a wider public the results of significant new research on modern and contemporary East Asia.

Library of Congress Cataloging-in-Publication Data

Han, Eric C., 1974-
  Rise of a Japanese Chinatown : Yokohama, 1894–1972 / Eric C. Han.
      pages cm. — (Harvard East Asian monographs ; 367)
  Includes bibliographical references and index.
  ISBN 978-0-674-49198-4 (hardcover : alk. paper)
  ISBN 978-0-674-24453-5 (pbk : alk. paper)
  1. Chinese—Japan—Yokohama-shi—History—20th century. 2. Yokohama-shi (Japan)—History—20th century. 3. Yokohama-shi (Japan)—Ethnic relations—History—20th century. I. Harvard University. Asia Center, issuing body.
  II. Title.
  DS897.Y69C553 2014
  305.895'10521364—dc23

                                                                    2013032677

Index by the author
First paperback edition 2020

Printed on acid-free paper
Last figure below indicates year of this printing
29 28 27 26 25 24 23 22 21 20

For my mother and father

Contents

Contents

Figures and Maps

Figures

Maps

Acknowledgments

I first saw Yokohama Chinatown in the summer of 1996. I had no inkling then that I would someday write a book about the district. How could I? I had recently graduated with a degree in molecular biology and had the barest of familiarity with historical research. But this early visit left me with some intriguing questions. What did these Chinese think about the troubled history between China and Japan? Did they see themselves as more Japanese than Chinese or vice versa? These were two questions that eventually germinated into this book, but it would take many years before I had the skills and confidence to write it. Along the way, I received encouragement, inspiration, and support from a great many individuals, without whom I would never have made the transition from the natural sciences to the humanities. I offer gratitude first to the place where the project truly began, the Inter-University Center for Japanese Language Studies in Yokohama. From 1999 to 2000, I acquired the fundamental Japanese language ability that made further graduate study possible. But it was also there that I composed my first reflections on the Yokohama Chinese community.

Before that fateful millennial year, however, many individuals had already shaped my intellectual development. Martin Collcutt of Princeton University first sparked my interest in Japanese history. Next, at the University of Illinois at Urbana-Champaign, I earned an MA in East Asian Languages and Cultures. I built an interdisciplinary foundation through the expertise of Ronald Toby, Donald Smith, and the late David Goodman. I also express my deep appreciation to the International Chinese Language Program at National Taiwan University, whose teachers rapidly elevated my Chinese language competence over the summer of 1999.

My professors at Columbia University, where I earned my PhD in East Asian history, deserve credit for guiding this project through its most crucial phases. I wholeheartedly thank my adviser Carol Gluck, whose tireless editing and searching questions have allowed my project to mature into a dissertation and whose continuing encouragement has led me to publish it. I am also grateful to my dissertation committee members, Adam McKeown, Gregory Pflugfelder, José Moya, and Mae Ngai, whose advice, insights, and critiques helped polish and enhance my analysis. I thank my other professors at Columbia University, foremost among those Eugenia Lean, David Lurie, Henry Smith, Marilyn Ivy, Charles Armstrong, William T. de Bary, and Liu Lening, who have made my years in New York City extraordinarily fruitful.

My fieldwork in Japan was made possible by a 2004 Fulbright Institute for International Education grant, and my research was greatly aided by my adviser at the University of Tokyo, Yoshimi Shunya, the members of his seminar, Itō Izumi and the staff of the Yokohama Archives of History, Li Runhua and Wang Liang of the Yokohama Chinese Association, Fukuoka Yasunori of Saitama University, Lan Pu and the staff of the Kobe Chinese History Museum, Kure Kōmei of Kyoto Seika University, Yasui Sankichi of Kobe University, Kagotani Naoto of Kyoto University, Yamashita Kiyomi of Tsukuba University, Guo Fang of Momoyama Gakuin University, and Chen Tien-shi of the National Museum of Ethnology, Japan. I owe a special debt of gratitude to Fu Xunhe, Zeng Deshen, Niikura Yōko, and to the Chinese of Yokohama. They have welcomed me into their community, opened their personal collections, and offered me a window into their personal and family stories.

I give thanks to the College of William & Mary, where I have been teaching since the fall of 2008, and my marvelous, esteemed, and supportive colleagues. Leisa Meyer, Scott Nelson, Cindy Hahamovitch, Rachel DiNitto, Sibel Zandi-Sayek, Hiroshi Kitamura, Fred Corney, Fabricio Prado, Emily Wilcox, and Matthew Mosca have been extraordinarily generous with their time in helping me to rethink my arguments and source materials. Additional research I conducted in recent years was made possible by two William & Mary Faculty Summer Research Grants. Over the previous two and a half years, it has been a great pleasure to work with Daniel Rivero of the East Asian Institute at Columbia University, and William Hammell and Deborah Del Gais at the Harvard University Asia Center. Their care and patience finally enabled me to bring my manuscript to this stage. I am also grateful to the anonymous reviewers who offered comparative cases and methodological critiques to strengthen my writing in important ways.

I deeply appreciate the camaraderie, generosity, and moral support of my colleagues and friends. I have had the great fortune to share ideas and meals with many extraordinary people, and their presence in my life has enabled me to learn, to grow, and to survive the long years of writing and revising. In particular, I want to recognize my entering cohort of Matt Augustine and Federico Marcon; University of Illinois at Urbana-Champaign friends Kyoko Kondo, Asuka Sango, and Semi Oh; Columbia colleagues Adam Bronson, Adam Clulow, Christopher Craig, Michael Emmerich, Michael Fish, Dennis Frost, Yuka Hattori, Reto Hoffman, Colin Jaundrill, Jun Mizukawa, Tom Mullaney, Alyssa Park, Satoko Shimazaki, Jenny Wang Medina, Steve Wills, and Tim Yang; and dear friends Catherine Bae, Ayako Takamori, Lingyun Tang, Michael Yuan, David Evans and Risa Tanaka, Lena and Ben Grenier, Theresa Liu, and Ron Devilla and Michelle Van Noy. And finally, I offer deepest thanks to my parents. Though they have not always grasped the whys and wherefores of an academic career, I have always felt the solid foundation of their love beneath my feet. It was their experience of war, migration, and survival that provided the original inspiration for this research, and they have influenced the writing of this book in ways deeper than they know.

Abbreviations

AH	Academia Historica
BX	*Bainian xiaoshi*
CAC	Chinese Athletics Club (Zhonghua tiyu hui)
CKK	Chūkakaikan (Chinese Guild)
DDK	Diplomatic Despatches: Kanagawa
DPJ	Democratic Party of Japan
DRMFA	Diplomatic Records of the Ministry of Foreign Affairs
FNWS	*Funühui wushinian shi*
GMD	Guomindang (Nationalist Party of China)
JACAR	Japan Center for Asian Historical Records
JCP	Japan Communist Party
JMFA	Japanese Ministry of Foreign Affairs
JOAK	Tokyo Broadcasting Station
JWM	*Japan Weekly Mail*

KPA	Kanagawa Prefectural Archives
LDP	Liberal Democratic Party
MEXT	Ministry of Education, Culture, Sports, Science and Technology
NACP	National Archives at College Park, MD
OCAC	Overseas Chinese Affairs Committee (Qiaowu weiyuanhui)
PRC	People's Republic of China
RHM	Records of the former Home Ministry
ROC	Republic of China
TNNS	*Tokyo nichinichi shinbun*
YBS	*Yokohama bōeki shinpō*
YDA	Yokohama Chinatown Development Association (Yokohama Chūkagai hattenkai)
YKS	Yokohama kaikō shiryōkan (Yokohama Archives of History)
YSSII	*Yokohama shishi II*

Introduction

Paradoxes of a Japanese Chinatown

Walking south from Yokohama Park, home of the major-league Baystars baseball team, one is immediately confronted by an immense gate decorated in Chinese style, black, crimson, and emerald, with columns topped by ornate gold spires (fig. 0.1). The center-mounted plaque announces that beyond lies Yokohama's Chinatown (Chūkagai 中華街). These blocks are home to more than 150 Chinese-owned Chinese restaurants, clustered in less than a tenth of a square mile.[1] Where did this community come from? And what does it mean to live as Chinese in a Japanese city? A visitor's initial impressions, however, offer little insight into deeper questions of the community's identity. The district's gaudy neon signs, souvenir shops, and young women in Chinese dresses calling out in accented Japanese demonstrate little more than a highly commodified Chinese culture, shaped by the demands of Japanese consumers. A Baystars banner affixed to the gate—sponsored by an association that represents the district's restaurants and other businesses—also reveals the degree of cross-promotion between Chinatown and Yokohama City.[2] It is tempting to judge the district as inauthentic. But, a search for its Chinese lineages—links to an original cultural essence—can only tell half the story. To understand how this community arose and thrived in Yokohama, we need to direct our attention to the evolving relationship—a shared past of conflict and cooperation—with their Japanese neighbors. This enclave is, after all, a Japanese Chinatown.

---

1. Yokohama Chūkagai hattenkai kyōdō kumiai, *Machizukuri kihon kōsō*, p. 9. In 1992, there were 151 Chinese restaurants operated by Chinese, and 7 by Japanese.

2. This organization is the Chinatown Development Association (Yokohama Chūkagai hattenkai kyōdō kumiai), which will be discussed in chap. 5.

FIG. 0.1. The Xuanwu Gate (Genbumon), which marks the northern entrance to Yokohama Chinatown. Photograph by the author.

Japan is not often thought of as an immigrant-receiving country. Its barriers to meaningful integration for foreigners are well recognized: citizenship laws based on bloodline, restrictive naturalization procedures, and since 1945, a popular belief in ethnic and cultural homogeneity. The scholarly consensus, at least through the 1990s, has held that Japanese society consistently effaces or denies the presence of ethnic minorities. However, even though the myth of Japanese homogeneity lives on in prevailing belief, today's bustling Yokohama Chinatown is anything but invisible (fig. 0.2). It is widely recognized as a major tourist destination, and its imagery has enjoyed circulation in a variety of mass media.[3]

---

3. Murphy-Shigematsu, "Multiethnic Japan and the Monoethnic Myth"; Fowler, "Minorities in a 'Homogeneous' State: Japan"; Befu, *Hegemony of Homogeneity*; Weiner, "Editor's Introduction." Fans of Japanese animation may even recall that

FIG. 0.2. The mild bustle of a weekday evening in Yokohama Chinatown, March 2005. Photograph by the author.

This paradox is often explained by the exceptional nature of Yokohama, an argument that holds that the city itself is somehow special, if not un-Japanese.[4] Such an attitude is not new, nor is it limited to Japanese observers. A 1920 publication by the U.S. Navy Bureau of Navigation declared

---

the heroine of the science-fiction classic *Super Dimension Fortress Macross* (Chōjikū yōsai makurosu), Lynn Minmay, hailed from Yokohama Chinatown.

4. Lie, *Multiethnic Japan*, p. 27. This insistence on Japan's essential ethnic homogeneity, so it goes, is "capable of denying the realities of those on the margins, Japan's minorities including Burakumin, Okinawans, resident Koreans and indigenous Ainu" (Creighton, "*Soto* Others and *Uchi* Others," p. 213). The Burakumin are descended from outcaste communities during the Tokugawa period (1600–1868) who worked in such putatively impure occupations as slaughtering animals and leatherwork. Okinawans and Ainu are ethnically distinct groups from the far south and far north islands of Japan, respectively.

Yokohama to be "the most cosmopolitan city in the Empire. It is less typically Japanese than any other city in Japan, being a [former] treaty port, and consequently a foreign trade center."[5] Indeed, having served as Japan's most important port in the nineteenth and early twentieth centuries, this city remains highly active in trade. In 2003, $78 billion of foreign trade was conducted in the city—9.2 percent of Japan's total foreign trade—and international shipping at Yokohama carried 78 million tons of goods to and from foreign destinations.[6]

Yokohama's importance as a port derives from its proximity to Tokyo, Japan's capital and largest city. Yokohama lies only 17 miles away from the capital, along the western shore of Tokyo Bay, and satellite images show Yokohama and Tokyo as a contiguous urban mass. However, Yokohama is a large city in its own right—Japan's second largest, in fact—with 3.7 million residents. And the city's history has yielded a distinct cultural identity, one that sets it apart from its larger neighbor. In contrast to Tokyo's clamor and glamour, foot traffic in Yokohama flows at a less frenetic pace, and one is never far from either a glimpse of the bay or a cool breeze carrying its briney scent. On the one hand, Tokyo is home to the national government and serves as focus of a hegemonic national culture. Yokohama, on the other hand, lays claim to a cosmopolitan and globalized culture built from its port city past.

Yokohama has cultivated a thriving tourism industry from this cosmopolitan history, which contributes to perceptions of the city's exceptionalism. The stately stone structure that formerly housed the British consulate general is now the Yokohama Archives of History (Yokohama kaikō shiryōkan; YKS). A pair of red brick warehouses on the waterfront, built in the 1910s and miraculously intact, now serves as a fashionable shopping venue. Several homes of Western expatriates and diplomats on the Bluff, a forested hill on the south side of the city, are maintained as public attractions. And below the Bluff, the legacy of the treaty port lives on in a bustling Chinatown, the topic of this book.

These sites are emblems of a particular past, but one that should not be considered unique in Japan; the very forces of migration, trade, and cultural exchange that globalized Yokohama are now touching nearly every corner of the country. With the transition to air travel, any community near an

---

5. U.S. Bureau of Navigation, *U.S. Navy Ports of the World*, p. 12.

6. Yokohama-shi, *Tōkei sho* 83:139–144. This dollar value is calculated according to the 2003 exchange rate of $1 = ¥115.

airport can develop into a cosmopolitan "port" city. Herein lies the broader significance of Yokohama's Chinatown. The history of this enclave is the paradoxical story of foreigners finding, in war and peace, an enduring place within a monoethnic state. It is a paradox that explains much about the challenges of integration faced by municipalities all over Japan today, as the country experiences rising foreign migration.

Nation Building and Yokohama

This book narrates the development of a Chinese community in Yokohama, from the Sino-Japanese War of 1894–95 to the normalization of Sino-Japanese relations in 1972 and beyond. Chinese and Japanese nations are not givens in this study; as is now well recognized, nations are "imagined communities" and national identities are relational categories.[7] I seek to show how an awareness of national difference emerged through interactions between Chinese and Japanese. But such a national consciousness was neither inevitable nor final; it was a provisional outcome of historical interactions that also yielded nonnational collective identities. Across this time span, Chinese identified as Yokohama residents as they integrated socially and economically into their host city. The city, in turn, acknowledged them as such. The historical narrative presented in this work aims to analyze the creation of mental categories of belonging, both national and local.

The story of the Yokohama Chinese as a prime example of ethnic diversity in Japan has largely been acknowledged and contained in local, that is to say, subnational identities. Indeed, a multitude of idioms in Japan reflect the articulation of such local identities: *edokko*, literally, child of Edo (the pre-1868 name for Tokyo) denotes a native of Tokyo; whereas *hamakko* refers to a child of Yokohama, a Yokohama-ite. The *hamakko* identity is famously inclusive. As the popular saying goes: "It takes three generations to be an *edokko*, three days to be a *hamakko*" (*edokko wa sandai sumeba edokko, hamakko wa mikka sumeba hamakko*). Many non-Japanese quite proudly and uncontroversially self-identify as Yokohama-ites in this fashion, including Chinese residents.[8]

---

7. B. Anderson, *Imagined Communities*; Duara, *Rescuing History from the Nation*.

8. One example comes from the recently published memoir of George Lavrov, born in Yokohama in 1941 of Russian parents, who declares: "Still, I am a Hamakko, a native of Yokohama, a little bit of charming Yokohama remains forever in my heart" (Lavrov, *Yokohama Gaijin*, p. xiii).

The public acceptance of Chinese *hamakko*, however, challenges the Japanese myth of ethnic homogeneity. But, debunking Japan's monoethnic myth is not the book's central concern; the myth was not the dominant discourse of Japanese identity across the time period covered in this study.[9] It is also of little analytical relevance outside of the field of Japanese studies. Scholars Tom Gill and Chris Burgess point out that the population of ethnic minorities and foreigners in Japan is comparatively small in world context, which has made the myth resistant to factual invalidation over the decades. Gill declares that "Japan is far closer to monoethnicity than to multiethnicity," and Burgess concurs by arguing that "the 'myth' of homogeneity persists because it both resonates with and seems true to people *and* can be verified statistically."[10] More to the point, the myth is not falsified by the presence of the roughly 4,000 Chinese in Yokohama's Chinatown, nor for that matter, 600,000 Koreans in Japan. It is the very process of categorization that has maintained the notion of ethnic purity, and no number of non-Japanese can detract from it.

Accordingly, before we can speak of the local integration of these Chinese, we need to investigate the category of Chinese and how a collective identity as such emerged in Yokohama in the first place. The long historical view shows that the community did not arrive in Japan as a preformed diaspora—that is, a community with links to a singular homeland and a consciousness as Chinese.[11] The traditional locus of affective attachment for overseas Chinese was their so-called "native place," meaning their province or region of origin. The unification of the Chinese into a singular community unfolded post-migration. The establishment of a Chinatown in Yokohama during the late nineteenth century was, in fact, coeval with the larger story of Chinese nation building, which stitched together various regional and dialect groups into a pan-Chinese identity. As several generations of

---

9. Befu, *Hegemony of Homogeneity*, p. 14; Oguma, *Genealogy of 'Japanese' Self-Images*. It is important to recognize that the myth has a history of its own. Although it has enjoyed a heyday in popular and scholarly writings from the 1960s to the 1980s, during the former half of the twentieth century, official discourse on Japanese identity acknowledged a multiethnic imperium. The goal of assimilating Koreans and Taiwanese as Japanese subjects demanded such a formulation of imperial identity.

10. Gill, "Review: *Multiethnic Japan*," p. 575; Burgess, "'Illusion' of Homogeneous Japan."

11. Nagano Takeshi, *Zainichi Chūgokujin*, p. 26.

scholars point out, Yokohama Chinatown was an important stage for this nation-building process at the close of the Qing dynasty (1644–1912). Existing works document and analyze the exchanges between Chinese reformers and revolutionaries in Yokohama and their Japanese patrons.[12] This book addresses the contributions of non-elites—those members of the community who sheltered the expatriate activists, served as an audience for their nationalist messages, and over time acquired a Chinese political consciousness.

This consciousness signified a diasporic identity for these Chinese. The term "diaspora" derives from the Greek, denoting the dispersion and suffering of a people throughout many lands; it was later applied to *galut*, or the exile of Jews from their homeland. These have been the traditional meanings of the term.[13] In recent decades, scholars have deployed the term to cover a wide range of migrations and minority statuses, including the overseas Chinese. According to William Safran, the six features of diaspora are (1) dispersion from a central location; (2) a collective memory, myth, or vision of the homeland; (3) insulation from the host society; (4) belief in the ancestral homeland as their true and ideal home; (5) a commitment to this homeland; and (6) an ethnocommunal consciousness that allows them to relate to the homeland. The diasporic Chinese identity is denoted by the term *huaqiao*, which is a late nineteenth-century neologism that came to signify, according to Wang Gungwu, "a militant commitment to remaining Chinese or to restoring one's 'Chineseness' " among existing overseas communities. This diasporic conceptualization of Chinese identity emphasizes homeland patriotism and downplays attachment to place of settlement.[14]

The diasporic condition is particularly instructive for understanding the processes by which individuals come to accept national identities. The imagination of a national self is never uncontested; as Prasenjit Duara argues,

---

12. Harrell, "Meiji 'New Woman' and China"; Jansen, *Japanese and Sun Yat-sen*; Judge, "Talent, Virtue, and the Nation"; Lu Yan, *Re-Understanding Japan*; Miyazaki, *My Thirty-Three Years' Dream*; Spence, *Gate of Heavenly Peace*.

13. Safran, "Diasporas in Modern Societies," pp. 83–84.

14. G. Wang, "Note on the Origins of *Hua-Ch'iao*," pp. 123–24. I use the blanket term "Chinese" when the group in question is not explicitly defined by a political relationship to the homeland, but rather a range of characteristics that might be seen as Chinese, such as ethnic, cultural, and linguistic features that distinguish them from the surrounding Japanese society. The point is not to presume the priority of the homeland in the formation of their community.

nationalist ideologies seek to "fix and privilege a single identity from among the contesting multiplicity of identifications."[15] Examining nation building outside of the homeland can bring the operations of nationalism into especial relief. In such a setting, nationalist ideology must assert a vertical relation with the nation while denying other collective identities that link the immigrant to his or her host society. Claims of national belonging in diaspora require greater and more conspicuous artifice to be persuasive.

Finally, it bears mention that national identities are imagined, but the point can be overstated. A careful look at the community's history shows that these individuals did not imagine their Chinese identities out of thin air. There were multiple and overlapping versions of Chineseness, many of ancient vintage, including the elite civilizational conception of China, political allegiance to the Qing dynasty, and the shifting set of discourses on blood and lineage that ostensibly set the Han Chinese apart from others.[16] This book tells the story of how a modern Chinese nationalism was reconciled with existing affiliations, interpreted, and put to use by common people, sometimes at odds with the intentions and conceptions offered by expatriate intellectuals. Concretely, this study examines the institutional, social, economic, and legal mechanisms by which these individuals developed linkages to both China and Yokohama. I have sought to elaborate this portrait by reconstructing the texture of everyday lives through local newspapers, official government records and planning documents, published memoirs, and selected conversations with residents. This eclectic approach was necessary because the city of Yokohama was twice burned to the ground, in 1923 and 1945, and lost a great deal of its documentary heritage. These varied sources also allow us to trace the lives of people who left few words to posterity, speaking instead through their choices and deeds.

Yokohama's Chinese Sons (and Daughters)

This historical narrative aims to explain how individuals became Chinese and, at the same time, Yokohama's sons. The social processes of community formation described in this work were gendered and emphatically

---

15. Duara, *Rescuing History from the Nation*, p. 81. See also Duara, "Transnationalism and the Predicament of Sovereignty."

16. For a detailed examination of these latter discourses, see Dikötter, *Discourse of Race in Modern China.*

asymmetrical. Modern Chinese and Japanese identities have been defined as communities of common descent and cultural heritage just as much as legal statuses. Around the turn of the twentieth century, both countries established nationality laws based on bloodline—in other words, the principle of *jus sanguinis* (Latin: right of blood). Until 1985, Japan's nationality law was moreover patrilineal; the children of foreign men did not automatically receive Japanese nationality. Accordingly, Japanese women who married Chinese men lost their Japanese nationality and joined the Chinese community. The following narrative does not slight the roles played by the women of Chinatown, but by necessity keeps certain patriarchal assumptions, which were in play during the period, in focus. The community was kept Chinese, legally speaking, via its sons.

By world standards, Yokohama's Chinatown is not large. As of 2011, Chinese nationals residing in Yokohama City numbered 33,000, second to neighboring Tokyo's 140,000 Chinese. However, only 27 percent (9,085) of these Chinese live in Yokohama's Chinatown and surrounding Naka Ward.[17] Moreover, the historical Chinatown population was but a fraction of this figure. The scale of this community has been obscured in statistical surveys by a surge in new migrants from the People's Republic of China (PRC) from the 1980s. Since the end of the Asia-Pacific War (or Second Sino-Japanese War, 1937–45), the Chinese population of Naka Ward remained in the 3,000 range and only broke 4,000 in the early 1990s. In the prewar era, the Chinese population of Yokohama remained at similar levels, fluctuating in a range between 2,000 and 4,000, and only briefly surpassed 6,000 around 1910.

Historically, however, the Yokohama Chinese population was demographically and economically significant in Japan (figs. 0.3 and 0.4). From the opening of Yokohama to foreign trade and settlement in 1859 until 1911, the Chinese there comprised more than 50 percent of the total Chinese population in Japan, overshadowing the other two historical Chinatowns of Nagasaki and Kobe. Moreover, across the same time frame, Chinese residents of Yokohama comprised close to one-third of the total foreign population in Japan.

Population trends followed the vicissitudes of the Sino-Japanese relationship. As shown in fig. 0.4, Chinese left the city in large numbers during the first Sino-Japanese War (1894–95), the end of an exchange-student boom

---

17. Yokohama-shi tōkei jōhōka, *Daitoshi hikaku tōkei nenpyō.*

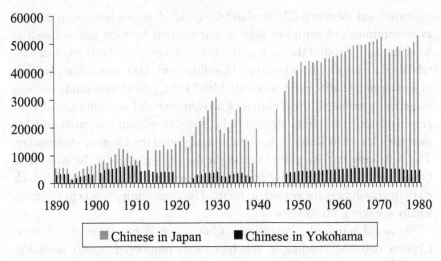

FIG. 0.3. The Chinese population in Japan, 1890–1980. *Sources*: Guo, *Zainichi kakyō*, pp. 47–48; Statistics Bureau, *Registered Aliens by Nationality*.

after the Chinese Republican Revolution of 1911, the Kantō earthquake of 1923, the Manchurian Incident (1931–32), and the Asia-Pacific War (1937–45). In addition, several thousand Chinese naturalized as Japanese after the normalization of diplomatic relations between Japan and the PRC in 1972, depressing population figures until the arrival of a new wave of migrants from the PRC. The history of Yokohama Chinatown is part of the wider narrative of Sino-Japanese relations, and sheds light on the consequences of international conflict for individuals caught in-between.

Historically, a majority of these individuals were Cantonese, that is, from Guangdong Province. Given the province's linguistic and cultural diversity, however, the term is not sufficiently specific. The largest subgroup was from Xiangshan County (now Zhongshan City). This population grew through a process of chain migration—that is, early arrivals facilitated the subsequent migration of relatives and acquaintances. Until very recently, Cantonese-speakers in Yokohama had to speak the Xiangshan dialect to be mutually understood. By way of comparison, similar practices of chain migration in North American Chinatowns led to the predominance of Cantonese from Taishan County, who spoke their own distinct dialect.[18]

―――――――――

18. Yamamuro and Kawamura, "Yokohama zairyū kakyō," p. 13; CKK and YKS, *Yokohama kakyō no kioku*, p. 153. In 1962, among Cantonese, those from Zhongshan

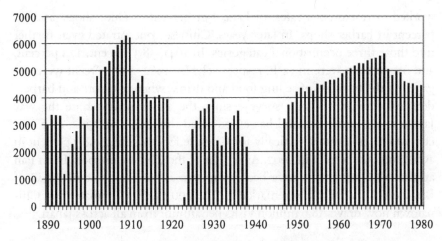

FIG. 0.4. The Chinese population of Yokohama, 1890–1980. Gaps in the record occurred between 1920 and 1922 because of the 1923 Kantō earthquake and again between 1939 and 1946 as a result of the Asia-Pacific War. *Sources:* Itō Izumi, "Yokohama kakyō shakai no keisei," p. 5; Yokohama-shi, *Tōkei sho-.*

These subtleties aside, a survey conducted by the Republic of China (ROC) consulate general at the start of 1923 documented that of the 5,721 Chinese living in Yokohama, 74.1 percent were from Guangdong Province, 14.5 percent from Zhejiang, 8.4 percent from Jiangsu, and 1.7 percent from Fujian.[19] A 1962 survey confirmed the continuity of these proportions, with 53.1 percent of the Chinatown population originating from Guangdong Province, 12.0 percent from Jiangsu, 10.9 percent from Zhejiang, and 10.4 percent from Taiwan.[20]

Yokohama Chinatown's status as a gourmet tourist destination, so manifest today, is of relatively recent vintage. This role emerged from new economic and social arrangements in the 1970s. Nevertheless, restaurants have been an important pillar of its economy since its founding. Merchants and traders established the Chinese presence in 1859, but, much like overseas Chinese communities around the world, the enclave's economy came to rely on the so-called "three knives" (*san ba dao*) of chef's cleaver, tailor's scissors, and the barber's razor. In 1927, 31.2 percent of the Chinese in Chinatown

---

comprised 31.8 percent, those from Gaoming 19.7 percent, and those from Taishan a mere 3.9 percent.

19. Sun, *Huaqiao zhuangkuang*, pp. 6–7.

20. Yamamuro and Kawamura, "Yokohama zairyū kakyō," p. 16.

worked in restaurants, cafes, or bars, 15.1 percent in tailor shops, and 7.0 percent in barber shops. In later years, Chinese concentrated even further into those three occupational categories. In 1941, 38.3 percent, 17.3 percent, and 6.0 percent, were in each, respectively. By 1962, 44.2 percent were engaged in the business of selling food and drink, whereas tailors and barbers declined further.[21] Visitor surveys since the 1980s demonstrate the way Japanese consumer demand has empowered this trend. In 1982, 45.6 percent of visitors came specifically for Chinese food, rising to 58.7 percent in 1992, and 69.7 percent in 2002. As scholar of the Chinese diaspora Lynn Pan argues, all Chinatowns have become tourist attractions to some extent.[22] But the Yokohama case is remarkable. The 2002 survey estimates that Chinatown now draws 18.6 million visits per annum from all across Japan.[23]

Constructing Yokohama Chinatown, "My Utopia"

Succeeding chapters will show how today's Yokohama Chinatown arose from a complex history of commercial and social exchange between the Chinese and the surrounding community. I say complex, because such contact possessed ambivalent potentials. On the one hand, the way Japanese consumers have avidly embraced this Chinatown shows the district to be economically integrated into the city and recognized as part of the local self. On the other hand, the commodification of Chinese culture helps define and reinforce cultural differences and, in that sense, maintained the separateness of Chinese and Japanese identities.

In addition, across this time frame, the characteristics and markers of Chinese self-identity were not static; the meaning of being Chinese in Yokohama shifted along with changing relations with Japanese society and their Chinese homeland. A major theme of this book is the ongoing "social construction" of Yokohama Chinatown as a place and the Chinese as a community. Today, the enclave presents itself as a playful space of Chinese cultural kitsch. It is, moreover, a Chinatown absent the grime, possessing, in

---

21. Kanagawa kenchō, *Warera no Kanagawa-ken*, pp. 522–29; Uchida, *Nihon kakyō shakai no kenkyū*, p. 317; Yamamuro and Kawamura, "Yokohama zairyū kakyō," p. 27.

22. L. Pan, *Sons of the Yellow Emperor*, pp. 305, 310.

23. Yokohama Chūkagai machi zukuri dantai rengō kyōgikai, *Gurando dezain*, pp. 8, 11. In 2002, 45.6 percent of visitors were from Yokohama City or the surrounding Kanagawa Prefecture, whereas 21.1 percent were from Tokyo and 33.3 percent were from elsewhere.

Pan's words, an "almost Parisian chic."[24] Popular literature, the mass media, and the Chinese restaurants that depend on Japanese customers have joined together to create this image. But it is relatively new, and behind this façade lie the layered and often contradictory historical images of Yokohama Chinatown. Like Chinatowns in the American imagination, Yokohama's Chinese enclave has served as a powerful metaphor for the inscrutable other, with both threatening and alluring dimensions.[25]

Two identically titled works of Japanese pulp detective fiction can help us probe the cultural meanings of the site: *Yokohama Chūkagai satsujin jiken* (Yokohama Chinatown murder case) by Saitō Sakae (1993) and Kotani Kyōsuke (2001).[26] Set in 1989, Kotani's work describes a series of murders tied to disreputable real estate dealings and a Chinese-themed hostess club in Yokohama. There are no Chinese characters of import to the plot, and the club's mysterious madam is eventually revealed to be a Japanese woman living under a Chinese pseudonym. The backdrop of Yokohama Chinatown contributes little more than sinister overtones of un-Japanese criminality within law-abiding Japan. The enclave appears to the reader as a source of impurity in an otherwise pure nation. In that regard, the novel's perspective closely adheres to what might be understood as a national problematic.[27] The work displays an obsession, all too common in contemporary Japan, with defining the Japanese nation in contradistinction to the foreign.

The earlier novel by Saitō contrasts with Kotani's work by articulating a local pride born from Yokohama's mixed cultural heritage. The plot describes efforts by Investigator Nikaidō and his fortune-teller wife Himiko to solve a chain of murders that begins at a sumptuous Chinese restaurant in Chinatown. Tellingly, this portrayal of Chinatown lingers on its gourmet attractions, evincing little of the dread expressed in Kotani's novel. Saitō,

---

24. L. Pan, *Sons of the Yellow Emperor*, p. 298.

25. K. Anderson, "Idea of Chinatown." As Kay J. Anderson has shown, imagery and institutional practices in nineteenth- and twentieth-century North America have constructed Chinatowns as uniquely immoral, unhygenic, dangerous spaces. Chinatowns have in this fashion served as concrete embodiments of a system of racial classification.

26. Saitō, *Yokohama Chūkagai satsujin jiken*; Kotani, *Yokohama Chūkagai satsujin jiken*.

27. Abrams, "History, Sociology, Historical Sociology," p. 9. In the writings of Louis Althusser and Philip Abrams, the term "problematic" refers to a method of organizing phenomena that yields problems for investigation and delimits the range of possible answers.

speaking through Himiko, boasts that the district has become the "best Chinatown in the world."[28] Even when the culprit is revealed to be Nikaidō's Chinese acupuncturist, his lengthy suicide note proves his motives as noble and sympathetic. Less national problematic than exotic gimmick, the work characterizes Chinatown as a positive presence for the city, a symbol of its cosmopolitan cachet rather than a warning about cultural contamination. Nevertheless, the dichotomy between Japanese and Chinese cultures remains intact.

These culturally essentialist narratives of Yokohama Chinatown are typical of depictions of the foreign in contemporary Japan and accord with the ethnic-national definition of Japaneseness. But they do point to conflicting perspectives on Yokohama's mixed cultural heritage. A similar tension can be seen in the place making of the Chinese port city of Shanghai, as described by historian Mark Swislocki's analysis of cuisine; from the mid-nineteenth century, cuisine has played a dual role in the city as a highly porous boundary between cultures and as an affective experience of place-based identity. It can serve as a pillar of both autochthonous and cosmopolitan identities for the city, that is, cultures defined by its natives and migrants, respectively.[29] These contrasting views on cultural mixing are typical outcomes of cultural encounter. Moreover, as we will see in later chapters, cuisine has played a similarly important role in defining Yokohama's local cultures.

However, the Chinese of Yokohama were themselves deeply involved in both constructing and critiquing these essentialisms. A third novelistic account offers a rare portrait of the psychology of a Yokohama Chinese resident. It provides a sense of the dilemmas of living hybrid lives in communities defined by rigid and one-dimensional understandings of identity. Akutagawa Prize–winning author Okamatsu Kazuo's 1988 novel, *Umi no toride* (Fortress of the sea), narrates the two-decade friendship between Akigawa and Arima, two men born in Yokohama but of different ethnic heritages. The half-Chinese, half-Japanese Arima struggles throughout the novel to construct his life in local terms—according to an ideal of Yokohama as it could be. But he repeatedly confronts the rigid constraints of national difference, including the Second Sino-Japanese War, which claimed

---

28. Saitō, *Yokohama Chūkagai satsujin jiken*, pp. 20–21.
29. Swislocki, *Culinary Nostalgia*, pp. 2, 104, 232.

the lives of his brothers. The eldest returned to his Chinese homeland to attend medical school, joined the ROC army under Chiang Kaishek (1887–1975) as a military doctor, and perished in battle against the Japanese. The second studied medicine in Tokyo, practiced in a Beijing hospital, was drafted by the Japanese army, and also died in the war. Finally, the third brother graduated from Waseda University and died serving as an interpreter for the Japanese army.[30]

Arima's attempts at self-invention are ultimately thwarted, and in a moment of despair he reveals to the "pure" Japanese Akigawa his quixotic ideal of home: "Well, it's hard to explain, but it was like an ink landscape painting without either Japan or China. When you bring states [*kokka*] into the equation, countries [*kuni*] end up hating each other and people get sacrificed for the sake of those in power. What happened to my older brothers during the war makes me think that I've had enough of that. Inside my head, I wanted to make Yokohama my utopia."[31]

Arima's psychological predicament, as both imperfectly Chinese and Japanese, speaks to the exclusivity and narrowness of Chinese and Japanese identities. As of yet, there is no Chinese Japanese identity analogous to Chinese American or Chinese Australian and no satisfactory terminology to describe Arima's ambiguous position. Arima chooses to self-identify as diasporic Chinese (*huaqiao*) and as Yokohama-ite (*hamakko*). The combination allows him to express membership in local society without claiming Japaneseness. But his choice can be subversive as well. It disputes the priority of attachment to a distant homeland implied in *huaqiao*, as well as the assumption, implicit in *hamakko*, of belonging to a subcommunity of the Japanese nation. It signifies nothing less than a repudiation of national problematics.

This idealized conception of Yokohama as a cosmopolitan space apart from national categories needs to be contextualized against a history of repeated Sino-Japanese conflict. Since the end of the nineteenth century, China and Japan have gone to war three times: from 1894–95, 1931–32, and 1937–45. And in times of war, national affiliation mattered crucially. The fate of Arima's brothers in *Umi no toride* was no mere dramatic fabrication by the author. Okamatsu's characters were based on a well-known Chinatown family and reflected their actual wartime experiences.[32] Bao Tang

---

30. Okamatsu, *Umi no toride*, pp. 17–18.
31. Ibid., p. 153. Author's translation.
32. Okamatsu, "Chūgokujin no bochi," pp. 158–59.

(1854–1905) was a Cantonese immigrant who settled in Yokohama around 1871 and married a Japanese farmer's daughter named Mizorogi Masu. During the Second Sino-Japanese War, two of their sons worked for the Japanese army. One served as an army doctor; the other worked as a Chinese-language interpreter and died in the fighting on the Chinese mainland. The third son crossed over to China to serve as a doctor for the Chinese army. The fourth son, Bao Bogong (?–1958), the one most similar to Arima, refrained from directly participating in the war, choosing instead to remain in Yokohama to manage the family restaurant.[33]

The yearning of Yokohama's Chinese residents to overcome conflicting destinies of Chinese and Japanese blood imbues the city's history with utopian overtones. However, boundary-testing cases—like the Bao family—also show the tragic consequences of the roles countries call on their citizens to play; like Arima, these individuals confronted hard limits to the flexibility of their identities and the difficulty of imagining and inhabiting a utopia.

Beyond the Terminal Community

Ultimate demands of loyalty to a singular nation formed the precondition for the dilemma that confronted Arima (or Bao Bogong) and his brothers. Their predicament is illustrative of some persistent features of the modern world. Since the nineteenth century, political modernizers in both Japan and China have sought to inculcate national and ethnic consciousness among the populace. Government policies institutionalized national identity as an individual's "terminal" community, that is, the largest collective that can claim his or her loyalty "when the chips are down." As Rupert Emerson explains, such a community is expected to override "the claims of the lesser communities within it and those that cut across it within a still greater society."[34]

---

33. Okamatsu, *Umi no toride*, p. 183; Sugawara, *Nihon no kakyō*, pp. 20–21. Okamatsu suggestively introduces an elderly Chinese man toward the end of the novel named Wen Bogong, combining the names of Bao Bogong and Wen Bingchen (1866–1955), another eminent Chinatown resident who will be introduced in chap. 2.

34. Rupert Emerson, quoted in Glazer, "Universalisation of Ethnicity," p. 10. Although post-1949 China and pre-1945 Japan are not and were not conceived as monoethnic polities, their strategies of inclusion have nevertheless relied on bloodline. The "family of nationalities" in the PRC does not imply open-ended inclusion of ethnic others, but rather a fixed set of communities of descent. Likewise, the

This study rejects the assumptions and priorities inherent in such terminal identities; it offers a critical examination of collective identities in Yokohama to show both their historicity and multiplicity. Collective identities—or more precisely, identifications—are relational categories that structure social life, defining friend and foe, native and foreign. They are distinguishable from self-identity, which George Devereux defines as the "absolute uniqueness" of an individual. This individuality, understood by Devereux as humanness, is built from the specific repertoire of identifications each person may access. Collective and individual identities, however, are easily confused in everyday language; the multiplicity of group affiliations that make up a unique pattern of personality are not always apparent. Dissociative situations, events that require differentiation between self and other—for example, war between China and Japan—efface the distinction between the self and one's group affiliation. When taken to extremes, obsession with one's terminal identification can acquire psychopathological dimensions. As Devereux argues, an obsession with possessing ethnic—and he may as well have said "national" with the same degree of justification—identity above all others signifies a catastrophic dysfunction of one's sense of personhood. When an individual reduces his or her multiple social affiliations to terminal one-dimensionality, the result is the annihilation of true identity.

For some scholars, the concept of diaspora has offered a way to counter one-dimensional identification with a territorial nation-state. In their works, the diasporic subject can function as "a figure for double and multiple consciousness, for a split, even dispersed subject-in-process that criss-crosses boundaries."[35] For instance, James Clifford argues that diaspora's primary significance lies in the way it defines itself against assimilationist state power and essentialism. Identification with a diaspora is thus a mode of resistance, serving to articulate "specific cosmopolitanisms" that counter "nation-state/assimilationist ideologies" as well as "indigenous, especially autochthonous, claims."[36]

---

multiethnic formation of the Great Japanese Empire before 1945 was predicated on the assimilability of Koreans and Taiwanese, but was never extended to Chinese from China. In practice then, political affiliation to either China or Japan has depended on ethnicity.

35. Tölölyan, "Rethinking Diaspora(s)," p. 28.

36. Clifford, *Routes*, pp. 53, 250.

Khachig Tölölyan points out, however, that works that treat diasporas as utopian and, for that matter, as wholly discursive objects of knowledge are historically nearsighted; they fail to account for the institutions, cultural practices, and nationalisms that have given many diasporic identities stability and persistence.[37] Similarly, Adam McKeown argues that the contemporary trend to valorize diaspora as a liberatory form of identity is at odds with "those narratives of essentialized, primordial identity that were so important to earlier definitions of diaspora."[38] Historical studies in the latter vein thus investigate how diasporas *did* function, rather than meditate on how they *could* function, and shed light on processes of migration, discrimination, and accommodation.[39]

As I will endeavor to show in the chapters that follow, Yokohama's Chinese community exemplifies both of these conceptions of diaspora. Chinese long-distance nationalism did indeed yield a version of diaspora characterized by "essential and unchanging cultural identities that persist despite exile and dispersal."[40] On the other hand, members of the mixed Yokohama community expressed both national and local identifications. They illustrated how a multiplicity of identifications can arise under diasporic conditions and militate against one-dimensional identity and national problematics.

The wider aim of this book is to consider how people attempted to reconcile a cosmopolitan and inclusive local identity with national or ethnic identities that are exclusive and conflictual. Yokohama is my chosen site for this story, but it is not unique in this regard. In their 2012 book *Pax Ethnica: Where and How Diversity Succeeds*, Karl E. Meyer and Shareen Blair Brysac observe a similar history of migration and an inclusive culture in the French port city of Marseille. Meyer and Brysac argue that a Marseille civic identity

---

37. Tölölyan pointedly argues that "diasporas have become the most recent site of the American celebratory, indeed, Utopian, impulse, which is always vigorous, always disappointed, and always in search of new objects of knowledge that it can invest with positive meanings, hopes and aspirations . . . diasporas are juxtaposed to the nation in a manner that neglects diasporic nationalism" (Tölölyan, "Rethinking Diaspora(s)," pp. 71–72). See also Carter, "Geopolitics of Diaspora."

38. McKeown, "Conceptualizing Chinese Diasporas," p. 309.

39. See Münz and Ohliger, "Diasporas and Ethnic Minorities in Twentieth-Century Europe." At times, though, historically grounded works on diaspora become little more than typologies in world history or comparison to an ideal type.

40. McKeown, *Chinese Migrant Networks and Cultural Change*, p. 12.

bolstered the integrity of the underlying community, and was a crucial factor in reducing ethnic tensions in the city when ethnic riots spread across France in the fall of 2005. The authors cite psychologist Alain Moreau, who argues that "young people from Marseille, particularly those of North African origin, often stressed that in matters of social identity, they declare themselves first and foremost as 'Marseillais.'"[41] The parallel with the way both Chinese and Japanese have identified as *hamakko* is striking.

The past century and a half of Sino-Japanese interactions is remembered more for conflict than for cooperation, and the current state of rivalry between the two countries is as tense as it has been since 1945. Discourses of national identity that are oppositional and mutually exclusive, in fact, have lent past and present conflicts an air of inevitability. The story of Yokohama Chinatown, on the contrary, offers a critical perspective on such discourses of national identity; it allows us to think through the historicity of collective identities—that is, the processes that governed their making and unmaking—and how they both exacerbated and mitigated conflicts between Chinese and Japanese. In reflecting on this history, it is my hope that we may imagine ways beyond the paradigm of terminal national identities.

Synopsis of the Book

This book is organized chronologically and divided according to major shifts in the Yokohama Chinese community's relationships with homeland and host land. The first chapter opens with a discussion of Chinese migration to Japan from the premodern period through the mid-nineteenth century, an era when Chinese immigrants were largely absorbed into their host communities. Permanent Chinese communities emerged after the establishment of treaty ports in Japan, including Yokohama in 1859; these ports were products of global modernity, in the sense that they derived from new diplomatic norms and changes in the relationship between states and their subjects. The Sino-Japanese War of 1894–95 contributed to this shift, bringing the consequences of international warfare to the social life of this cosmopolitan port city. Just as countries were instituting nationality as the principle of inclusion and exclusion, the conflict forced Chinese immigrants and their descendants to see their lives in ethnic terms.

---

41. Meyer and Brysac, *Pax Ethnica*, pp. 109, 131–33.

To the end of the nineteenth century, however, attachment to native place or dialect group remained the primary basis for Chinese social organization in Yokohama. Chapter 2 examines how, in the years before the Chinese Revolution of 1911, Chinese expatriate leaders attempted to turn a sense of ethnic unity into active Chinese citizenship. For men such as Kang Youwei (1858–1927), Liang Qichao (1873–1929), and Sun Yatsen (1866–1925), Japan served as a model for modernization and Yokohama served as a base for their organizing activities. Working among the Chinese residents there, these activists established nationhood as an aspiration and discourse through publishing and education. They also intervened in a Japanese debate over permitting "mixed residence" for the Chinese outside of the treaty ports, by advocating for the same rights of settlement and commerce to be given to Western nationals. These nation-building activities, however, unleashed significant political partisanship and revealed persistent subethnic divides of religion, class, and native place. Moreover, their sought-after rights of mixed residence in the interior also brought more opportunities for interaction and cultural exchange with Japanese. At the end of the Qing dynasty, the Chinese of Yokohama were acquiring a Chinese national consciousness by degrees; but they were also building the basis for a Yokohama local identity.

Chapter 3 traces the institutionalization of Chinese identity in Yokohama from the founding of the ROC in 1912 to the Manchurian Incident of 1931–32. During these two decades of rising Sino-Japanese tensions, the new Chinese state extended its power into the lives of its overseas citizens by registering and educating them to be patriotic *huaqiao*. The shared crisis of the Kantō earthquake of 1923, moreover, pushed the Yokohama Chinese to downplay subnational divisions and to rely more fully on national representatives. Cultural developments also illustrate the increasing salience of national categories in daily life; by participating in baseball tourneys and introducing Chinese cuisine to Japanese consumers, the Yokohama Chinese were integrating into their local community, but specifically *as* Chinese. When creating new institutions with their Japanese neighbors, they increasingly employed the conceptual language of international relations to define their activities. Japan's invasion of Manchuria in 1931, however, dealt a blow to these cooperative efforts, and thereafter, Chinese would construct their national identity against a clarified foe.

The outbreak of the Second Sino-Japanese War in 1937 brought grave anxieties to the Yokohama Chinese, and an additional layer of state intervention;

the Japanese government attempted to co-opt the institutions of Chinese nationalism in an effort to discipline and exploit the community for propaganda and other purposes. Chapter 4 narrates the effects of these wartime developments on Chinese community cohesion in Yokohama. For their part, the Yokohama Chinese attempted to resolve the competing imperatives of local attachment and national patriotism—being simultaneously Yokohama-ite and diasporic Chinese—by voicing support for Chinese collaborationist regimes on the mainland. These expressions were not entirely voluntary, but their complicity with the Japanese state nevertheless allowed them to remain in Yokohama as Chinese, neither forcibly removed from Japanese territory nor assimilated as Japanese imperial subjects. In the end, however, they shared the fate of the city in the Allied firebombings of spring 1945. The social and economic foundations of today's Yokohama Chinatown were also laid during these years. The experience of wartime collaboration made pluralistic separation seem preferable to assimilation in subsequent years. Chinese have continued to publicly identify as Yokohama-ites, and the district's Chinese restaurants became the dominant source of employment during these years of hardship and have remained so ever since.

Chapter 5 traces the development of Yokohama Chinatown into a cohesive enclave and economic niche against the backdrop of the Cold War and Japan's economic rise, culminating in the normalization of diplomatic ties between Japan and the PRC in 1972. These years saw the apotheosis of a diasporic Chinese identity, shaped by strident calls for patriotism from the two Chinese claimant states. Over time, however, their internecine political battles destroyed the institutional unity of the community, which led to a transformation of the community from a homeland-oriented diaspora to a minority population, defined by difference from the Japanese majority. Chineseness, no longer exclusively a political identity, now acquired a strongly commercial orientation as Chinese and Japanese residents joined together to develop Chinatown as a gourmet destination for tourists.

The conclusion examines Chinatown from the 1980s and the district's rising commercial fortunes and further institutionalization as a key pillar of Yokohama local identity. Chinese gained public acceptance as local residents, a status that confers certain citizenship rights. Two comparative cases—the *zainichi* (residing in Japan) Korean population and the quickly expanding population of Chinese newcomers who began arriving in the 1980s—help shed light on the issue of foreigner integration into Japanese society. The study concludes with reflections on the significance of Yokohama China-town according to two overarching themes: (1) the historicity of Yokohama Chinese identities and their implications for Sino-Japanese relations, and (2) Yokohama Chinese contributions to social movements seeking to challenge and to reevaluate existing notions of Japanese citizenship.

CHAPTER ONE

The Sino-Japanese War and Ethnic Unity,
1894–95

The story of how communities of Chinese arose and thrived in Japan does not begin in Yokohama. Yokohama was not site of the first large-scale Chinese settlement in Japan. That distinction belongs to Nagasaki, a port city on the southern island of Kyushu, which developed into a thriving Chinese trade base during Japan's Tokugawa era (1600–1868). In this era, it was the only port open to direct trade with China and Europe, and thus served as an important conduit for cultural and economic exchange.[1] The Nagasaki Chinese population was largely transient, however, coming and going with the trading fleets and scarcely unified as a single community. Moreover, because this early Chinatown was not bounded by modern conceptions of ethnicity and citizenship, those Chinese who chose to remain in Nagasaki were able to integrate into local society. Chinese settlement in Yokohama, which began in 1859, took place under a starkly different social and political framework. Modern conceptions of citizenship based on a global system of nation-states made Chinese and Japanese identities mutually exclusive and enduring personal statuses. In the process, Yokohama's Chinatown achieved permanence across multiple generations, even in the face of intermarriage and economic integration. The community emerged as a by-product of global modernity.

This transformation in the meaning of being Chinese in Japan did not take place in one stroke; it took decades, and the Sino-Japanese War of

---

1. Trade with Europe was limited to the Dutch from 1639 to 1859.

1894–95 was a watershed. Conditions of war demanded unity and patriotism for both Chinese and Japanese, leading to greater consciousness of national interests that superseded occupational, familial, and provincial affiliations. On the whole, this process obtained in both Chinese and Japanese
societies.[2] Where Chinese and Japanese lived side by side in Yokohama,
however, the consequences of the war were felt with particular acuteness and
led to structural changes in local society. Numerous conflicts in the streets
forced the adoption of an ethnic-national optic—an imperative of seeing and
distinguishing each other according to ethnic-national categories—and an
intolerance of ambiguity. The point is not that Yokohama residents sud-
denly became aware of differences; they were almost certainly cognizant of
the diverse origins of their neighbors and associates. Rather, new conditions
forced Chinese and Japanese to experience and to record their lives in ethnic
terms, which were then fixed by new legal and institutional arrangements.

   The overwhelming Japanese victory in the war of 1894–95 brought about
a reevaluation of the Japanese image of the Chinese, reducing them in the
public's eyes from affluent merchants from a proud civilization to cowardly
masses and laborers. They were thereafter regulated as a specially restricted
class of foreigner in Japan. On the other hand, the Qing dynasty's crushing
defeat diminished the regime's legitimacy among leading Chinese intellectuals, who launched reform movements and insurrections to reconstitute
China as a modern nation-state. Many of these leaders modeled their reform programs on Japan.[3] But before these overt attempts to build an active
citizenry became influential in China, the war had already forced the
Yokohama Chinese to confront a shared crisis and, by tying their situation
and institutions to a singular homeland, spurred the acceptance of ethnic
unity.

Premodern Chinese Migration to Japan

This study does not presume the transhistorical importance of nationhood
because in premodern times, Chinese and Japanese were not conceived as

---

   2. For analyses of the cultural and intellectual responses to the war in both
countries, see Keene, "Sino-Japanese War of 1894–95"; Chu, "China's Attitudes
toward Japan."
   3. See Harrell, "Meiji 'New Woman' and China"; Jansen, *Japanese and Sun Yatsen*; Judge, "Talent, Virtue, and the Nation"; and Spence, *Gate of Heavenly Peace.*

bounded political, cultural, and ethnic units. China as a classical civilization was defined instead by a body of metaphysical and political philosophy commonly known as Confucianism. Elites achieved their status through mastery of this tradition, and dynasties legitimized their rule by claiming to be its paragons and authentic heirs. The truths of Chinese learning applied universally, to "all under heaven," and the Chinese empire could thus encompass distinct peoples.[4] Beneath an integrating elite culture, however, lay a variegated set of popular cultures, including linguistic differences, which gave weight and coherence to local identities. The overarching sense of Chineseness, as an elite construction tied to imperial sovereignty claims, was less significant in the everyday life for most Chinese than these localisms, in particular for those who chose to leave the center of civilization and venture overseas in search of profit.

Premodern Japan was also not united by cultural sameness; it was a society constructed from hierarchical status distinctions.[5] Waves of immigrants from the Asian continent to the Japanese isles from ancient times to the early nineteenth century merged with local communities, in spite of cultural differences.[6] These demographically significant surges of immigration to Japan, which included peoples from China, belie the contemporary notion of Japan as a uniquely ethnically homogeneous country.[7] An estimated 3,000 people per year, or about 1.8 million continental immigrants, entered

---

4. The Chinese concept of civilization also extended to the elites of neighboring polities like Korea and Japan, where Chinese precedents served as the basis for administrative practices. As Charles Holcombe argues, "it may be said that there was both one universal elite East Asian high culture and as many different local popular cultures as there were local communities" (Holcombe, *Genesis of East Asia*, p. 45).

5. Ernest Gellner makes this broader point clear by noting that in agrarian societies, both ruling stratum and the "petty communities of the lay members of society" are marked by cultural differentiation. In such a condition, "almost everything in it militates against the definition of political units in terms of cultural boundaries" (Gellner, *Nations and Nationalism*, pp. 10–11).

6. Guo, *Zainichi kakyō*, p. 23. One early example of Chinese migration to Japan was Fujianese trader Li Chong, who took up residence in the city of Hakata on the island of Kyūshū in 1105. A persistent Chinese presence in the city did not result, however, as his descendants integrated with local society.

7. Seki, *Kodai no kikajin*, p. 7. Historian Seki Akira has speculated that 10–20 percent of contemporary Japanese blood has descended from continental immigrants from the ancient period.

Japan during the six centuries from 300 BCE to 300 CE.[8] Several smaller streams between the fourth and ninth centuries brought scholars, monks, and craftsmen from the continent to Japan, and these people and their descendants comprised some 30 percent of the Japanese aristocracy by the end of that period.[9] Subsequently, Chinese settlements of varying size formed along the Japanese coast in the sixteenth century, but became indistinguishably part of Japanese society over the generations.[10]

Nagasaki became the first persistent, large-scale Chinese settlement in Japan after the ruling Tokugawa clan restricted a bustling China trade to that port city in 1635. By century's end, these Chinese had become a prominent commercial, social, and cultural presence. Some reports put their number at around 10,000 of a total city population of 51,395. This figure fluctuated, however, according to the coming and going of Chinese trade fleets.[11] Nagasaki society welcomed the Chinese, who were known locally as *acha-san*, a term implying respect and familiarity.[12] In contrast to later Japanese impressions of the Chinese as exclusively low-wage laborers, the image of the *acha-san* in Nagasaki wood-block prints was often of a kindly, wealthy merchant disbursing trinkets and candy to Japanese children.[13]

The so-called *acha-san* were Chinese by virtue of their visible difference from Japanese society and trade connections with China. Nevertheless, they did not act as a unified community, even if Japanese terminology deemed them a single group. They were subdivided according to occupation and

---

8. Farris, *Sacred Texts and Buried Treasures*, p. 109.

9. Murayama, *Yamanoue Okura no kenkyū*, p. 310; Seki, *Kodai no kikajin*, p. 580. The New Record of Surnames (*Shinsen shōjiroku*) of 815 AD determined that 324 of the aristocratic clans around the Japanese capital originated on the Asian continent, including ancient China and Korea. Of these, around half had Chinese heritage.

10. Jansen, *China in the Tokugawa World*, pp. 7–8.

11. Guo, *Zainichi kakyō*, pp. 21, 34; Berger, *Overseas Chinese in Seventeenth Century Nagasaki*, p. 26. Jansen has placed the Chinese population figure at a more sober "4,888 people, when the junk fleet was in" (Jansen, *China in the Tokugawa World*, p. 29). After 1688, Chinese merchants were forbidden from settling permanently, and thus the average stay was less than six months at a time.

12. Vasishth, "A Model Minority," p. 118; Higuchi, "Nagasaki hanga no kigen," p. 79; *Nihon kokugo daijiten* (Tokyo: Shōgakukan, 2000) s.v. "Acha." *Acha-san* came from *a-chun*, a distant phonetic derivative of the Japanese word for Chinese people, *Chūgokujin*.

13. For numerous examples, see Higuchi, *Nagasaki ukiyoe*, pp. 241–69.

native place.[14] Like premodern communities of Chinese sojourners in Southeast Asia, separate linguistic groups handled different trade goods and cohered around separate religious institutions; their temples housed altars to their local gods and functioned as both community centers and the focus of native-place sentiment.[15] By the end of the seventeenth century, Nagasaki was home to four such Chinese temples, serving the Sanjiang—the "three Jiang" provinces of Jiangsu, Jiangxi, and Zhejiang—Southern Fujian, Northern Fujian, and Cantonese trading groups.[16]

Distinctions between Chinese and Japanese, in the modern, permanent sense, applied only minimally. Two occupational groups in particular lived in an intermediate world between China and Japan: official interpreters and monks. These men, often with Japanese surnames but representing Chinese dialect groups, brokered economic, religious, and intellectual exchanges with Japanese counterparts.[17] Social intercourse with Japanese that developed from these arrangements yielded large numbers of people who intermarried.[18] One example was the first official interpreter appointed in 1604, Feng Liu, who reportedly married a Japanese woman and settled in Nagasaki. Another example was Coxinga (Kokusen'ya, or Zheng Chenggong, 1624–62), the half-Japanese, half-Chinese son of a Ming loyalist and a Japanese woman. His attempt to retake China from the Qing was immortalized in the 1715 Japanese puppet play *Kokusen'ya kassen* (Battles of Coxinga), but he is celebrated as a cultural hero in both China and Japan. It was also possible for Chinese to become Japanese subjects. A Japanese government edict of 1688 in fact promoted integration by decreeing that Chinese who were not merchant sojourners must renounce their loyalty to the Qing or Ming and settle permanently, or else leave the country.[19] In this way,

---

14. Berger, *Overseas Chinese in Seventeenth Century Nagasaki*, p. 104. In the seventeenth century, there were nine primary Chinese groups defined by three occupational statuses (merchant, interpreter, monk) and three native place affiliations (Jiangsu, Jiangxi, and Zhejiang; Southern Fujian; Northern Fujian). The Cantonese were a late arrival to Nagasaki and comprised a smaller trading group.

15. G. Wang, *Chinese Overseas*, p. 57.

16. Uchida, *Nihon kakyō shakai no kenkyū*, pp. 54, 58, 62, 65.

17. Berger, *Overseas Chinese in Seventeenth Century Nagasaki*, p. 136.

18. Guo, *Zainichi kakyō*, p. 28; Xu, "Ryūnichi kakyō sōkai no seiritsu ni tsuite," p. 332.

19. Berger, *Overseas Chinese in Seventeenth Century Nagasaki*, p. 26.

some Chinese in Nagasaki transferred their allegiance to Japan and melted into local society, finding a place in Tokugawa Japan's system of organized differences.[20]

Chinese in the Treaty Port of Yokohama

This social order would undergo radical revision in the nineteenth century as a result of a modified political order: the rise of a global system of nation-states and the intrusion of aggressive Western imperialism into East Asia. These developments eventually forced both China and Japan to conduct their world affairs according to Western norms, which is to say, diplomacy between nominally equal nation-states, and mercantile affairs according to principles of free trade. This spelled an end to the nearly two-millennia-old Sino-centric imperial order in East Asia, a system of diplomacy that was predicated on China's role as fountainhead of civilization. Under conditions of imperialist expansion and nation-building, East Asia concurrently experienced increased global exchange and contact, and clarification of national boundaries, social and territorial.[21]

One concrete manifestation of these opposing forces was the creation of treaty ports in East Asia. The Qing dynasty's catastrophic defeat at the hands of the British in the first Opium War (1839–42) forced it to sign the 1842 Treaty of Nanjing and the 1843 Supplementary Treaty of the Bogue, which opened five treaty ports to international trade, granted British

---

20. Japan's social structure during the Tokugawa period was described by the metaphor of four classes: samurai, farmer, craftsman, and merchant (*shi nō kō shō*). These were hereditary categories derived from Chinese Confucianist political philosophy, and from 1600 helped stabilize society after several centuries of fragmentation and warfare. This formulation, however, did not exhaust the complexity of early-modern Japanese society, which historian Tessa Morris-Suzuki has described as an "infinite set of social gradations defined in terms of ideas of social function, order, propriety, and political submission" (Morris-Suzuki, *Re-inventing Japan*, pp. 82–83).

21. Duara, *Sovereignty and Authenticity*, pp. 17–19. Nationalism and imperialism were linked goals in nineteenth-century European countries. As Prasenjit Duara argues, nationalism served as a "functional support" for imperial projects and overseas expansion, which in turn strengthened the state-building project at home. The role of nationalism in contesting imperialism would not become salient until new assumptions about the universality of nationhood would take hold around the time of the First World War.

subjects unilateral extraterritoriality, and limited Qing powers to set import tariffs. Americans and French secured these same rights through treaties in 1844. Then in 1853, Commodore Matthew Perry led a squadron of American gunboats to Japan and coerced similar concessions from its rulers in 1854. Three treaty ports in Japan, including Yokohama, opened to trade with the Western powers in 1859, with concomitant provisions of extraterritoriality and restrictions on the amount of duties the Japanese government could levy on foreign trade.[22]

Chinese entered Yokohama under this treaty port system, accompanying foreign traders of various nationalities. They built homes and businesses in the so-called Foreign Settlement, a canal-encircled district set apart physically as well as legally from the interior of Japan. Living and working among Western mercantile houses, Chinese compradores and merchants reaped great profits as middlemen in transactions between Japanese and Westerners.

Harold S. Williams's 1958 work *Tales of the Foreign Settlements in Japan* illustrates the prevalence of Chinese in the commercial life of the foreign settlement in its early years.

> In those days when you entered a merchant's office or a foreign bank or knocked at the door of a foreign residence, the person who enquired your business was a Chinaman. The cooks invariably were Chinese and generally the house servants also. The butler, footman and cook at the British Legation were Chinese. When you exchanged your money at the bank or at the exchange shop or purchased a railway ticket, it was a Chinaman who attended to you.[23]

These treaties transformed Yokohama from a sleepy fishing village into a hub of international trade and transportation. More foreign trade was handled at Yokohama than at all the other Japanese treaty ports combined; practically all of Japan's foreign visitors entered via Yokohama, and most of its

---

22. Initially, the other treaty ports in Japan were Nagasaki and Hakodate. From 1868 to 1869, Japan also opened Kobe, Osaka, Tokyo, and Niigata.

23. Williams, *Tales of the Foreign Settlements in Japan*, p. 128. Williams's observations were originally printed as articles in the *Mainichi* newspaper from 1953 to 1957. Williams declared them "historically accurate in every detail," though he rarely cited specific sources. They are best treated as expressions of popular memory.

silk exports passed through its warehouses.[24] The city also gradually developed a diverse cultural world of its own. Baseball and horse racing were first introduced to Japan in Yokohama, and Japan's first bakery, ice-cream shop, and brewery opened there. Western sailors and drifters mingled with Japanese hostesses and ruffians in Yokohama's seedy grog shops on a stretch of Honmura Road called Blood Street.[25] Japanese of more genteel social standing also made use of Yokohama's cosmopolitan consumer culture; novelist Tanizaki Jun'ichirō (1886–1965) was known to have frequented its Western bookstores, and visitors from Tokyo and beyond came to eat at Yokohama's Chinese restaurants.

These restaurants were the product of a Chinatown that coalesced during the 1880s; in this decade, Yokohama's Chinese population became self-sustaining, and numerous community institutions, such as a temple, graveyard, and social clubs, were established.[26] As noted in the introduction, through 1911 the city had the largest concentration of Chinese in Japan. Yokohama was home to 69.2 percent of all Chinese in Japan in 1880, and 54.6 percent in 1890.[27] In this era, Cantonese were primarily involved in import-export, currency exchange, Chinese traditional crafts, or restaurants. A smaller number were from the Sanjiang provinces, near the Chinese treaty port of Shanghai, and derived their skills from the Western presence there; they worked as tailors, barbers, or even piano makers.[28]

---

24. U.S. Bureau of Navigation, *U.S. Navy Ports of the World*, p. 12.

25. This nefarious nocturnal world was memorably referenced by Rudyard Kipling's 1893 poem "The Rhyme of the Three Sealers": "AWAY by the lands of the Japanee, where the paper lanterns glow, and the crews of all the shipping drink, in the house of Blood Street Joe" (Kipling, "The Rhyme of the Three Sealers," p. 258).

26. Ye, "Chūgoku daidō gakkō-shi," p. 558. The rising number of children is a key indicator of this transition from a bachelor society to a self-sustaining community. In 1887, there were some 629 children among 1,730 adults, which increased to 998 children among 2,360 adults in 1891.

27. Yamashita, "Yokohama Chūkagai zairyū Chūgokujin," p. 37; Guo, *Zainichi kakyō*, pp. 47–48; Itō Izumi, "Yokohama kakyō shakai no keisei," p. 5. The Nagasaki Chinese community withered during these decades because of its distance from Japan's major population centers and the opening of more convenient ports for trade; Yokohama's commercial importance derived from its proximity to the Japanese capital of Tokyo.

28. Yamashita, "Yokohama Chūkagai zairyū Chūgokujin," p. 44.

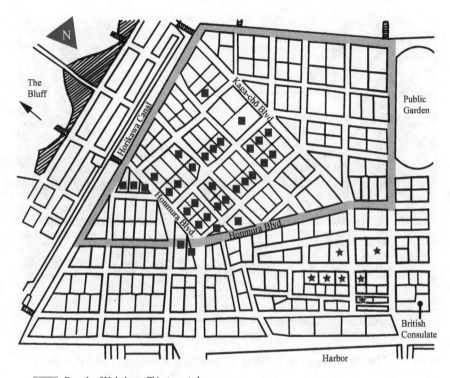

Bounds of Yokohama Chinatown today
Chinese business and residence in cluster A
Chinese business and residence in cluster B

MAP 1. Two clusters of Chinese settlement, ca. 1890: Nankinmachi (A), and the Old Settlement (B). Yokohama Stadium now stands at the former site of the Public Gardens. Created from data in Tatewaki Kazuo, ed., *Japan Directory*, vol. 12 (1890). The map is adapted from YKS, *Kaikō kara shinsai made*, p. 12.

The Japanese called this Chinatown "Nankinmachi" (Nanjing town; Map 1A). At the time, Nankin was a common Japanese synecdoche for China, and at times applied to various things of foreign origin.[29] The district had many other names. Western observers simply called it "China

---

29. Nankin often carried unpleasant overtones. For example, *nankinmushi* meant bedbugs. Residents renamed the district Chūkagai (Zhonghuajie) in the early 1950s, a development described in chap. 5.

FIG. 1.1A. The Old Settlement, ca. 1894. Courtesy of Yokohama kaikō shiryōkan.

Town," whereas Japanese government documents described it as Shinkoku-jin kyoryūchi (Qing settlement). Cantonese residents would call it Tongyan'gai (Tang people's streets), following their use of "Tang people" as a general term for overseas Chinese. This district was a tightly packed grid of two-story brick buildings hung with balconies and decorated with elaborate Chinese-language signage. Roughly circumscribed by the warehouses along Horikawa Canal, Kaga-chō Boulevard, and Honmura Boulevard, it would become a permanent, architecturally distinct feature of Yokohama. Its most distinctive feature was the orientation of its streets, which were tilted relative to the surrounding city but oriented toward the cardinal directions of north, south, east, and west. Quite plausibly, *fengshui* beliefs led Chinese arrivals to select properties here for that very reason.[30]

---

30. Itō Izumi, "Yokohama kaikō to Chūkagai," pp. 24–25. In a sense, then, it was not Chinatown that was tilted, but the surrounding city. Itō Izumi of the Yoko-hama Archives of History clarifies that the Chinese *did not build* the district in

FIG. 1.1B. Chinatown, ca. 1910. Courtesy of Yokohama kaikō shiryōkan.

Although the city had burned to the ground twice over the previous one hundred years, both the alignment of Chinatown's streets and its physical bounds would remain relatively consistent through each rebuilding and redevelopment.

Another zone of concentrated Chinese habitation was in the so-called Old Settlement (Map 1B), beside the customhouse and wharf, which boasted majestic stone Western-style buildings. English-language signage displayed on these streets indicates that these Chinese businesses served a Euro-American clientele and hints at the English-language ability of their owners (fig. 1.1A). Little trace of this former Chinese habitation remains today. Despite the presence of these culturally hybrid Chinese, it was the area known as Nankinmachi that would become permanently associated

---

accordance to *fengshui*, but rather selected these particular blocks. To expand the foreign settlement, the bakufu filled in paddy land whose canal boundaries happened to align with the cardinal directions.

with Chinese characteristics in the minds of Western and Japanese observers, and hence, Chinatown (fig. 1.1B).[31]

Architecturally, socially, and culturally, Chinatown was a city within a city. It was the site of the institutions that gave shape to a Chinese community: the consulate general, the Chinese Guild (Zhonghua huiguan), the Guandi Temple (Guandi miao), a Chinese theater, and a multitude of Chinese restaurants.[32] Celebrated for its exoticism, the district drew crowds of tourists from Tokyo and further afield. In that regard, it gradually became an integral component of a Yokohama local identity. In the encounter between Yokohama locals and Tokyo outsiders, "Nankinmachi" served as a shibboleth separating self and other. As one Yokohama resident explained, it was a common, though forgivable, mistake to misread the characters used to write Nankinmachi (南京町) as "Minamikyō machi" (southern capital town). On the other hand, Yokohama people never called it Shinajingai (Chinaman town) as Tokyo-based reporters—in their ignorance—often did.[33] Voicing the name Nankinmachi implied familiarity and intimacy with the district, as well as an acknowledgment of its status as one of Yokohama's defining local features or specialties (*meibutsu*). It was thus accepted as a distinctive feature of Yokohama City, despite the non-Japanese status of many of its residents.

The city displayed a vibrant cosmopolitanism, but it was stitched together by national distinctions created by the rise of the worldwide system of nation-states and citizenship as an instrument of social closure.[34] Individuals gained their rights of residence and economic activity from their exclusive relationship with a sovereign state. In the treaty ports, early Chinese immigrants were registered under the legal status of their Western employers; after the signing of the Sino-Japanese Amity Treaty in 1871, they

---

31. Otobe, "Yokohama kyoryūchi ni okeru Chūgokujin," p. 88.

32. The Guandi Temple still stands in contemporary Yokohama Chinatown and serves to venerate the deified historical figure Guan Yu, a general during the Three Kingdoms Period (220–80 CE). His worship is particularly common among Cantonese.

33. Kayama, "Nankinmachi o egaku," p. 17.

34. Doak, *History of Nationalism in Modern Japan*, pp. 10–11; Brubaker, *Citizenship and Nationhood in France and Germany*, pp. 21–23. Following Kevin Doak, I use the term "nation" to denote the "collective subject of cultural and political identity," whether defined by civic values or ethnicity, in distinction to the state structure. My use of the adjectival "national" follows this specific definition.

were legally defined as Qing subjects, but acquired the same privileges in Japan as nationals of Western countries.[35] In contrast, the Nagasaki community of the Tokugawa years had not relied in any way on protection or recognition from Ming or Qing dynasties, or any other government for that matter. This nineteenth-century transformation in the relationship between states and peoples changed the significance of migration by making nationality the determining axis of inclusion and exclusion. Where nationality would be informed by ethnic criteria, as in China and Japan, the status of foreignness would be difficult for an immigrant to shed, a central factor in the permanence of Yokohama's Chinese enclave.

The adoption of the nation-state as the model of state sovereignty was not a simple or quick process. For Japan, its juridical rudiments came first; social consciousness and behavior based on the nation-state appeared slowly over many decades.[36] For China, the process largely occurred in the opposite order, with social movements espousing national consciousness forcing political changes from the Qing government.[37] The Sino-Japanese War of 1894–95, in which Japan was victorious, boosted the development of modern nationalism in both China and Japan. The same might be said for ethnic consciousness among Yokohama's resident Chinese. Until this point, there was no self-aware and unified community of Qing subjects; individual

---

35. The one significant difference between Japan's relationship with the Qing empire and the Western powers lay in the reciprocality of the rights enjoyed by Chinese in Japan and Japanese citizens in Chinese treaty ports.

36. Gluck, *Japan's Modern Myths*, pp. 112–13; Morris-Suzuki, *Re-inventing Japan*, p. 167; Doak, *History of Nationalism in Modern Japan*, pp. 219–20. This process began with the Meiji Restoration of 1868 and subsequent political unification and modernization. Meiji leaders abolished hereditary status distinctions within Japanese society and incorporated peripheral lands and their residents as Japanese citizens. From the 1870s, civilian actors, journalists, intellectuals, and local elites then responded to the Western challenge and took up the mission of building a unified sentiment of being Japanese. By the 1890s, a literate population had begun to understand their membership in the Japanese ethnic nation (*minzoku*) through books like Nitobe Inazō's *Bushidō* (Way of the Warrior), journals like *Nihonjin* (The Japanese), and newspapers like *Nippon* (Japan).

37. In the decades between the Opium War and 1894, the Qing dynasty favored more superficial efforts at modernization, sponsoring the implementation of Western technology, but resisting calls to alter the underlying political system.

Chinese enjoyed the same rights as any other foreigner in the treaty port and were economically organized according to dialect group.[38]

The Declining Image of the Chinese

Armed conflict between Japan and the Qing empire inaugurated a celebration of patriotic sentiment in Japan that deepened the hold of the nation on the popular psyche. Japan's victory raised feelings of Japanese pride and a denigration of their hapless Chinese opponents. Naturally, Japanese society held multiple, overlapping images of the Chinese, but they were consistent in generalizing them as a collective subject. When these images began impinging negatively on the lives of Chinese, they, too, began thinking of themselves as one people.

Before the war, Japanese society exhibited a conflicted veneration of Chinese culture. Donald Keene notes that "the various Chinese emissaries who resided in Japan prior to the Sino-Japanese War were entertained with a cordiality not apparent in the more lavish entertainments provided for European or American dignitaries."[39] This cordiality was but one stratum of Sino-Japanese interaction; Noriko Kamachi argues on the contrary that Japanese popular sentiment toward Chinese in the early Meiji period was complex, and spanned "amity, envy, resentment, and contempt."[40] In Yokohama, however, the opportunity for face-to-face contact between Chinese and Japanese appears to have generated social intimacy and friendships between the two peoples. Keene argues that contemporary sources indicate that "the Chinese pedlars in Yokohama were 'extremely well-liked.'"[41] Another memoir confirms this assessment:

> Chinese traveling salesmen with their hair in queues [the long braids that Chinese men wore to signify submission to the Qing dynasty] would come by hefting trunks almost as tall as themselves and speaking in broken

---

38. Glazer, "The Universalisation of Ethnicity," p. 8. These Chinese did not constitute an ethnic group according to the modern sociological definition. Nathan Glazer asserts that an ethnic group is "a social group which consciously shares some aspects of a common culture and is defined primarily by descent," implying the importance of self-awareness in its constitution.

39. Keene, "Sino-Japanese War of 1894–95," p. 125.

40. Kamachi, "The Chinese in Meiji Japan," p. 62. The Meiji period, defined as the reign of the Meiji emperor, lasted from 1868 to 1912.

41. Keene, "Sino-Japanese War of 1894–95," p. 126.

Japanese, which was quite charming. They came by to sell silk fabric mostly, and the Japanese were quite familiar with them, calling them *acha-san, acha-san*. It was only after the start of the war that antagonistic feelings, feelings of contempt swelled among the Japanese. This was in no way the natural feelings of Japanese people.[42]

The terminology used by Japanese observers provides a rough index of their attitudes toward the Chinese. A range of terms was used, from the neutral political designation Qing subject (Shinkokujin) and the ethnonyms Tang people (Tōjin) and Nanjing people (Nankinjin) to the derogatory Chinamen (Shinajin). The continued use of the term *acha-san* signified that residual feelings of good persisted among the common people.

In addition to social presence, intermarriage and romantic unions between Chinese and Japanese brought a certain porousness to the boundary between Chinese and Japanese in Yokohama. Japanese law did not forbid intermarriage with Chinese as certain states in the United States did during the Chinese exclusion era.[43] On the contrary, marriages were common between Chinese and Japanese, a consequence of the small number of unmarried women and overabundance of men in the Yokohama Chinese community—in 1893 there were 2,415 Chinese men compared to 910 women.[44] Japanese women who married Chinese men essentially joined the Chinese community because Japanese law until 1950 stipulated that Japanese wives to foreign men would take the nationality of their husband.[45]

Yokohama-born Chinese revolutionary Feng Ziyou (1882–1958) recalled the prevalence of this gendered pattern of interethnic fraternization and the manner in which they evolved into legal unions: "When workers and merchants from our country reside in Japan, regardless of whether or not they bring a wife with them, most will cohabitate with a Japanese wife. . . . Especially in Yokohama Chinatown, it is customary for Chinese men to start by paying the Japanese women a few yen a month, over time growing closer and more intimate, especially after the birth of a child, and end up

---

42. Arahata, "Meiji sanjūnendai no Yokohama," p. 10.

43. Sohoni, "Unsuitable Suitors," pp. 587–618. Labor and racial issues were, of course, very different in the United States.

44. Kanagawa kenchō, *Kanagawa-ken tōkeisho*, p. 78.

45. C. Lee, "Legal Status of Koreans in Japan," pp. 151–52. Before 1950, a Japanese woman would lose her Japanese nationality when marrying a foreign national because she would be removed from her family's registry (*koseki*).

marrying her."[46] The editors at the English-language *Japan Weekly Mail* also remarked upon this phenomenon, noting that in comparison to the transient Chinese communities in the United States or Australia, in Yokohama the "Chinaman . . . usually ends by marrying a Japanese wife and settling here permanently."[47] Finally, Japanese sources confirm that some Japanese women accompanied their Chinese husbands when they returned to China, and others were buried in the Yokohama Chinese cemetery according to Chinese ritual.[48]

Briefer unions also contributed to the Chinese community if children were born. For instance, a September 1893 article in the Yokohama newspaper *Mainichi shinbun* describes the spread of Japanese-Chinese couples. The article claims that there were some 1,300 Japanese in the Shinajingai, only one-tenth of them male; the majority of the Japanese women were concubines of the Chinese (*nankinmeka*), and the children of such relationships were registered as Chinese.[49]

Relationships between Chinese men and Japanese women should not be read as a simple index of social closeness or integration or as being free from social stigma. The economic dimension to many of these relationships is difficult to ignore. Japanese journalist Kanome Shōzō (1882–1923) despicts one particularly dreary case in a column that ran in the *Tokyo asahi shinbun* in 1916. He describes meeting a woman named Itō Osei living in one of the back alleys of Chinatown. She was raised by a stepmother who was a *nankinmeka,* and Osei did not know whether she was Japanese or of mixed blood. Osei herself had become a *nankinmeka* to an affluent Chinese man forty-five years her senior. This liaison she considered entirely normal for the Japanese

---

46. Feng Ziyou, *Geming yishi,* 1:166.

47. "The Chinese in Japan," *JWM,* June 24, 1899, pp. 613–14. This pattern of intermarriage and permanent settlement is also characteristic of Chinese communities in Southeast Asia.

48. Sun, *Huaqiao zhuangkuang,* pp. 26, 38; Yokohama-shi, *Yokohama-shishi,* 3:903. Citizenship documentation after the 1923 quake described in chap. 3 confirms that Japanese women who married Chinese men became Chinese nationals.

49. "Yokohama kyoryūchi Shinajin machi no Nihonjin," *Mainichi shinbun,* Sept. 22, 1893, p. 5. These numbers are somewhat outlandish; for comparison, the population of Qing subjects in 1893 was 1,862 men, 511 women, and 952 children. However, because the author uses the term "Shinajingai" rather than "Nankinmachi," he may not have been a Yokohama native nor acquainted with the actual circumstances.

girls in the district, and such unions were arranged by secretive brokers. After Osei gave birth to a daughter, she and her stepmother exploited the joyous event to inveigle gifts and loans from the old man, before ultimately abandoning him when he fell sick.[50] Osei, Kanome remarks, did not seem particularly sad about her fate, though it is obvious that Kanome did.

These liaisons that slid ambiguously between prostitution, concubinage, and marriage were characteristic of Japanese rural-urban migration in this era; they were not specific to Chinese men. Many women in the impoverished hinterland sought a life in the booming entrepôt through liaisons with affluent older men, many of them foreign. The case of Tonooka Sue provides another dramatic example. Sue was born in 1875 in nearby Shizuoka prefecture and came to Yokohama at a young age with her mother. Around 1892 she became the mistress to a Chinese shopkeeper known in the district as Achon. Later she took up with an American seaman serving on the USS *Olympia* named George F. Heeney. After Heeney left during the Spanish-American War, she turned her attention to a Japanese puppet-theater performer.[51] All the while, she operated a saloon and brothel called the Rising Sun Inn within the precincts of Chinatown, that is, until the morning of July 17, 1899, when she was brutally murdered by an American paramour.[52] Not all such liaisons ended in tragedy; as later examples will show, many marriages between Chinese and Japanese led to cohesive families even as they bridged economic, generational, and cultural gaps.

Some scholars, on the other hand, retrospectively see only contempt arising from direct contact between Chinese and Japanese in the city. For instance, Ueda Toshio claims that "most Chinese were unenlightened and base, indulging in both opium and gambling, which raised the ire of foreigners and

---

50. Kanome, *Nankinmachi*, pp. 7–10.

51. "Naigaijin no daisangeki," *Asahi shinbun*, July 18, 1899, morning edition, p. 4; "Naigaijin daisangeki no zokuhō," *Asahi shinbun*, July 19, 1899, morning edition, p. 4; "Gaijin sannin goroshi zokudan," *Yorozu chōhō*, July 21, 1899, p. 3. Colorful rumors suggested that Tonooka and a group of six or seven (Japanese) wives of resident Chinese had vied for Kiyoka's affections, with Tonooka emerging the victor of the amorous contest.

52. "Zakkyo tōjitsu kyoryūchi no danchinji," *Yokohama bōeki shinbun*, July 18, 1899, p. 2; Mirā no shikei shikkō," *Asahi shinbun*, Jan. 17, 1900, p. 5. The crime occurred a mere five hours after extraterritoriality expired for Americans. The perpetrator, Robert Miller, would be the first American to be tried and executed by the Meiji justice system.

Japanese alike."[53] This observation that most Chinese indulged in opium and gambling is consistent with North American attitudes toward the Chinese in Chinatowns there. However, the implication of criminality is not supported by Japanese police records. From 1872 to 1876, Kanagawa Prefecture observed 688 crimes committed by Chinese and 2,719 committed by Europeans and Americans. Considering that these two groups were roughly equal in population, the Chinese crime rate amounted to one-quarter that of the Western population.[54]

This gap between subjective perception and objective record may itself be the product of transformed attitudes in the aftermath of the Sino-Japanese War. Japanese opinion of and conduct toward Chinese worsened markedly with the outbreak of war, which was accompanied by a campaign in the Japanese media to paint the Qing empire as uncivilized.[55] The result, in Keene's words, was that "prints, songs and war plays had convinced the Japanese that the Chinese were backward, cowardly and even contemptible, unworthy heirs of a once-great tradition."[56]

China was characterized as endemically backward to highlight Japan's aggressive commitment to Western-style progress. In diplomatic and intellectual circles, this denigration had been prevalent since the 1860s and 1870s; Japan's new mass media now spread these sentiments among the wider public. Popular woodblock prints reinforced the message vividly. The Japanese were depicted as stalwart, tall, and noble in mass-produced woodblock prints; in contrast, the Chinese appeared treacherous, cowardly, and

---

53. Ueda, "Nihon ni okeru Chūgokujin no hōritsuteki chii," p. 4.

54. Cassell, *Grounds of Judgment*, p. 96; Yokohama-shi, *Yokohama-shi tōkei sho*, 1:34; Itō Izumi, "Yokohama kakyō shakai no keisei," pp. 5, 22. It is possible that many crimes committed by Chinese were not reported to Japanese authorities and dealt with internally. Pär Cassell's study of extraterritoriality in China and Japan notes that Chinese associations in Nagasaki wielded a degree of legal autonomy in this regard, and a similar situation likely obtained in Yokohama. However, Yokohama city surveys after they were placed under Japanese jurisdiction also indicate that the Chinese population was largely law-abiding, at least in comparison to other foreigners. For example, in 1901, only 16 Qing subjects were arrested, despite the Qing being the largest nationality group. In comparison, 91 English and 111 Americans were arrested that same year.

55. YKS, *Kaikō kara shinsai made*, p. 14; YKS, *Shisei shikō to Yokohama no hitobito*, p. 69; Iwakabe, "Nisshin sensō to kyoryūchi Shinkokujin mondai," p. 68.

56. Keene, "Sino-Japanese War of 1894–95," p. 142.

undignified. In extreme cases, the Chinese were no longer depicted as the kindly *acha-san*, but as "hideous, sub-human creatures, quivering with terror."[57] Negative racial epithets for the Chinese also proliferated during the war, including *chanchan*, *chankoro*, *bōzu*, and *tonbi*. These terms have obscure origins, but were unquestionably derogatory.[58] Japanese intellectuals apparently approved of these portrayals. The literary journal *Waseda bungaku* praised "the hatred of the enemy felt by our people," for "imparting to them a clear consciousness of the nation, an awareness of what it means to be Japanese."[59] The reciprocal effect of the war on the community of Qing subjects in Yokohama's Chinatown was an awareness of the ramifications of being Chinese in a Japanese city.

The War in Yokohama

Military conflict between the two empires impressed upon Yokohama's Chinese residents the precariousness of their lives and livelihoods on enemy soil. By the early summer of 1894, the unmistakable signs of a building conflict between the Qing empire and Japan generated uncertainty in Yokohama. In June, the crisis was already constraining mercantile activity; Chinese traders began demanding immediate payment for their goods and services, while delaying their own.[60] Direct antagonism between Chinese and Japanese also intensified; on June 20, two Japanese sparked a mêlée by calling out *chanchan* at a Chinese man passing on the street. Several other Chinese rushed to join the fight, and one was stabbed in the neck with a knife.[61]

In July, the Qing consulate began advising its subjects to cut back their trading activities in preparation for the severance of diplomatic ties. Foreign

---

57. Ibid., p. 138.
58. Ibid., p. 139; Vasishth, "A Model Minority," p. 122. The etymologies of these terms have not been definitively established, but they appear linked to avaricious and bestial traits. Scholars have variously speculated that *chanchan* derived from the sound of clinking coins, *chankoro* derived from the Chinese word *Zhongguoren* (Chinese person), *bōzu* (monk) and *tonbi* (pig's tail) referred, respectively, to the monk-like shaven pate and queues that all Chinese men were obligated by the Qing government to maintain.
59. Keene, "Sino-Japanese War of 1894–95," p. 154.
60. "Yokohama zairyū Shinajin no dōsei," *Mainichi shinbun*, June 29, 1894, p. 2.
61. "Nihonjin Shinajin o sasu," *Mainichi shinbun*, June 23, 1894, p. 5.

banks responded to the potential economic and social instability by restricting the issuance of bills of exchange for Qing subjects.[62] After the first clashes at sea on July 25, circumstances in Yokohama deteriorated further. Chinese-run businesses by this time were calling for Japanese police protection, and the Ministry of Foreign Affairs (Gaimushō) and the Home Ministry (Naimushō) jointly issued a protection order on July 26 urging prefectural governors to prevent "rash disturbances and rough treatment of Qing subjects."[63] In this context of anxiety and chaos, many in the community prepared to leave for China.

With the formal declaration of war on August 1, 1894, Consul Wang Fengzao (1851–1918) lowered the Qing flag and returned to China, depriving resident Chinese of representation and the recourse to consular courts. The mutual declaration of war severed diplomatic relations and abrogated the Sino-Japanese Amity Treaty of 1871.[64] In its place, trilateral negotiations between the United States, the Qing empire, and Japan determined that the United States would assume wartime consular jurisdiction over Qing noncombatants in Japan, and vice versa.[65] For the Yokohama Chinese, these diplomatic changes effectively ended extraterritoriality and created widespread confusion over their status, rights, and obligations. The institution that assumed the administrative and representative functions of the departed consulate was the Yokohama Chinese Guild. This organization originated in 1873 as a self-governing body of Cantonese merchants, predating the establishment of the Qing consulate in 1878. The Sino-Japanese War forced upon them a much broader representational function.

Meanwhile, sensational rumors kept tensions at a high pitch. Japanese newspapers in Yokohama spread stories of battle preparation by Chinese toughs in the city. The *Mainichi shinbun*, a Yokohama daily, claimed on August 3 that Chinamen (Shinajin) had been buying up Japanese swords to arm themselves; moreover, the paper alleged that Chinamen thugs had been roaming the streets at night looking to pick fights with Japanese, decrying

---

62. "Shinkoku ryōji no yukoku," *Mainichi shinbun*, July 19, 1894, p. 3.

63. "Shinkokujin hogo no kunrei," *Mainichi shinbun*, July 27, 1894, p 2.

64. Ueda, "Nihon ni okeru Chūgokujin no hōritsuteki chii," p. 11. Qing subjects had achieved consular protection through the 1871 Sino-Japanese Amity Treaty and the establishment of a Qing Consulate in 1878.

65. Iwakabe, "Nisshin sensō to kyoryūchi Shinkokujin mondai," pp. 63–64.

them as East Asian devils (*Dongyang gui*).[66] The veracity of this report is impossible to determine, but true or not, Japanese animosity toward the Chinese was readily perceptible to outside observers. In his dispatch of August 6, 1894, U.S. consul general Nicholas W. McIvor (1860–1915) reported that "prejudice and race hatred runs high amongst the [Japanese] lower classes against the Chinese."[67]

With the end of extraterritoriality and consular protection for Qing subjects, the Japanese government hastily issued a set of provisions to deal with these enemy subjects. Imperial Ordinance (Rescript) 137 of August 4 and Home Ministry Directive 605 of August 11 obligated Chinese to register with the Japanese authorities, placed them under Japanese legal jurisdiction, and gave the Home Ministry the power to restrict their entry into Japan. These measures were framed as efforts to defuse tensions within Yokohama and to protect the life and property of Qing subjects.[68] However, the new legal framework was perceived by Chinese as much less favorable than the previous system, prompting Chinese of all classes to return to China in large numbers.[69] Population statistics indicate that between 1893 and 1894 the population of Qing Chinese in Yokohama dropped by two-thirds, from 3,325 to 1,173.[70]

This exodus was not in any meaningful way stanched by the promises of protection contained in Imperial Ordinance 137, invitations to accept registration contained in Directive 605, or by the Ministry of Foreign Affairs and Home Ministry's protection order of July 26. Western business owners also sought to persuade Chinese to stay, evidently concerned over disruptions to their commercial activities. The most influential members of this community convened a meeting on August 9 to discuss the status of their Chinese employees. Though they acknowledged that "fears among the Chinese are generally strong," they resolved almost unanimously to "advise [their

---

66. Yet, this particular article does temper these rumors with praise for Qing officials: "Despite the tumult, when you meet their officials, they are calm and extremely polite; their expressions of friendship are unexpected" ("Shinajin nihontō o kau," *Mainichi shinbun*, Aug. 3, 1894, p. 1).

67. Dispatch from Nicholas W. McIvor to Department of State, Aug. 6, 1894, No. 47, DDK, vol. 20, RG 59, NACP. The context of McIvor's comments emphasizes, however, that Japanese officials are "unusually broad-minded and efficient men," in contrast to members of the lower class.

68. Paine, *Sino-Japanese War of 1894–1895*, pp. 209–16.

69. "The Imperial Ordinance of the 4th," *JWM*, Aug. 11, 1894, pp. 161–62.

70. Iwakabe, "Nisshin sensō to kyoryūchi Shinkokujin mondai," p. 68.

Chinese employees] to accept the terms and to register accordingly."[71] Their first measure toward this end was to correct certain misconceptions among Chinese residents, such as the belief that registration would make them liable for Japanese military service and subject to additional taxes.[72] The Western business community, however, was no more successful than the Japanese government in stemming the departure of Qing subjects.

The exodus was the result of several interlocking causes. One factor was rising prejudice toward Chinese by ordinary Japanese. Another factor was the economic disruption of the city's core commercial activities, causing difficulties for Chinese merchants. Finally, the disadvantages in legal status, real or perceived, under the new regulatory regime gave rise to anxiety among the Chinese and spurred commercial rivalry and score settling by the Japanese. These underlying social and economic conditions were not ameliorated by Japanese government policy, and there is reason to believe that certain organs of the government, particularly the Home Ministry, preferred this outcome for the advantages it bestowed Japanese in their dealings with the Chinese.

Moreover, Japanese government protection seems to have mattered little in the face of swelling Japanese national pride and contempt for the Chinese. Even after the promulgation of Ordinance 137, persecution of Chinese in the Yokohama settlement continued. Although the Japanese vernacular presses denied any direct harassment of the Chinese, a November 10 *Yorozu chōhō* article noted that Chinese in Yokohama were so scared of Japanese children—who had taken to acting out the Sino-Japanese War in their play—that the Chinese walked "as swiftly as bicycles" to avoid confronting them.[73] In the collective memory of the Yokohama Chinese, Japanese children pelted them with rocks. This assertion gains credence if considered alongside anecdotes of similar stone-throwing incidents against Europeans and Americans later in the decade.[74] Calls to protect Qing subjects carried

---

71. "The Chinese Residents in Japan: Public Meeting in Yokohama," *JWM*, Aug. 11, 1894, pp. 174–75.

72. Dispatch from McIvor to Department of State, Aug. 13, 1894, no. 50, DDK, vol. 20, RG 59, NACP.

73. "Zairyū Shinajin Nihon no kodomo o osoreru," *Yorozu chōhō*, Nov. 10, 1894, p. 3.

74. *JWM*, Nov. 17, 1894, p. 558; "Students and Foreigners," *JWM*, July 8, 1899, p. 34; Feng Ruiyu, "Yokohama Daidō gakkō to Feng Jingru."

in Japanese newspapers ironically reinforce the impression that violent confrontations in the streets of Yokohama actually took place or were a tangible possibility.[75] This anti-Chinese atmosphere was also confirmed, inadvertently, by Meiji-era legal scholar Ariga Nagao, who boasted that the Chinese "need only suffer the insults of society but there are few who suffered loss of property or bodily harm."[76]

The arts also played a role in inciting popular antagonism toward the Chinese. When Kawakami Otojirō's (1864–1911) theater troupe premiered their rendition of *Nisshin sensō* (Sino-Japanese War) in Tokyo on August 31, it was greeted with a violent fervor.[77] The *Japan Weekly Mail* reported that its opening performance was met with an illuminating mishap:

> As one of the vanquished "Chinese" was flying along the *hanamichi* (a stage passage leading through the audience pit) . . . a man sprang from one of the boxes in the pit, seized the supposed [Chinese] and proceeded to administer a sound drubbing, crying that this was a real Chinaman and not a made-up actor. . . . The actor . . . was pleased rather than indignant with the manner in which he had been mauled, attributing the attack to his perfect make-up and thorough imitation of the *chanchan-bozu*.[78]

This form of violent audience participation recurred a few days later, when some hotheaded men again leapt on stage to aid beleaguered Japanese troops caught in a dramatized Qing ambush.[79]

---

75. The *Japan Weekly Mail* noted that "the manner in which the Japanese journals have welcomed the recent Imperial Ordinance relating to the status of the Chinese residents, and the pains they take to advise their countrymen to treat the Chinese with kindness and generosity must be considered as an expression of the sentiments entertained by the educated classes in this country" ("The Spirit of the Vernacular Press during the Week," *JWM*, Aug. 11, 1894, p. 150).

76. Ariga Nagao quoted in Iwakabe, "Nisshin sensō to kyoryūchi Shinkokujin mondai," p. 68. In this passage, Nagao is arguing for the essential humanitarian character of the protections provided by Ordinance 137.

77. Keene, "Sino-Japanese War of 1894–95," p. 142. Kawakami was a founding member of the new school (Shinpa) theater movement, a form of theater linked to the populist and patriotic Liberal Party (Jiyūtō).

78. "Rampant Patriotism," *JWM*, Sept. 1, 1894, p. 252; "An Appreciative Audience," *JWM*, Sept. 15, 1894, p. 310. In this excerpt, the author compounds the slurs *chanchan* and *bōzu*. The play was so popular in Tokyo that two theaters in Yokohama staged copycat versions.

79. "Once Enough," *Japan Weekly Mail*, Sept. 8, 1894, p. 283.

In October when Kawakami's troupe brought the production to Yokohama, it generated a similarly riotous exuberance; three or four attendees
were injured and hospitalized at each performance.[80] Government pronouncements not to mistreat the Chinese were evidently drowned out by a
chorus of anti-Chinese sentiment in the popular media, which clarified the
ethnic boundary between Chinese and Japanese and bestowed upon it palpable and lasting consequences. This atmosphere of maltreatment did not
evaporate after the war. Kawahara Misako, an educator who dedicated
many years to teaching girls in Shanghai and Inner Mongolia, noted that
during her stay in Yokohama from 1900 to 1902, Chinese residents were
unreceptive to offers of help from her and other Japanese; she attributed this
sourness to the condescending treatment they continued to suffer in the
years after the Sino-Japanese War.[81]

In addition to the social climate, the economic climate induced many to
close their shops and return to China. The war enabled Japanese merchants
to seize market share and key concessions from their absent or intimi-
dated rivals. By November 1894, Japanese merchants had gained significant
ground against their Chinese rivals in Korea. A movement by Japanese merchants also sought to transform Japan's military triumph into an economic
victory. Led by the Yokohama and Tokyo General Goods' Guilds, the movement launched a boycott of Chinese stores—which then spread to Japanese
sugar merchants—and called for the repeal of various fees customarily
charged by Chinese middlemen for transactions between Japanese and
Western traders.[82] In both industries, Chinese enterprises and shops eventually caved, and Japanese merchants successfully abolished several fees and
reduced commissions, weakening the economic niche occupied by Chinese
merchants.[83] Chinese merchants were not able to mount a unified response;
they would not mobilize to defend their collective economic interests until

---

80. YKS, *Shisei shikō to Yokohama no hitobito*, p. 68.

81. Kawahara, *Karachin ōhi to watashi*, pp. 107–9.

82. "Japan's Commerce with China and Korea during the War," *JWM*, Nov. 3,
1894, p. 515; "Boycotting Chinese Merchants," *JWM*, May 11, 1895, p. 523. Known
as the "movement to restore commercial rights," this campaign aimed to cancel the
"Nankin commission," "viewing fee," and "measuring/weighing fee" that were
customarily paid to Chinese merchants. Over the years, Japanese merchants had
increasingly considered these fees arbitrary, unjust, and unnecessary.

83. "The Successful Boycott of the Japanese Sugar Dealers," *JWM*, May 18,
1895, p. 551; YKS, *Kaikō kara shinsai made*, p. 30.

1899, when they established the Yokohama Chinese Chamber of Commerce (Hengbin huashang huiyisuo).

Just as the war forged Japanese unity, it produced new conditions that forced Chinese to imagine themselves as one group. Reports in June and July 1894 mention that in contrast to the pell-mell response by the merchant class, working-class Chinese were initially indifferent to the impending war.[84] This attitude immediately changed with the promulgation of the new legal framework to govern Qing subjects and the obligation to register with Kanagawa Prefecture. The regulations also prohibited certain economic activities, such as the production and selling of tobacco and liquor, and, more ominously, placed the Qing under the Japanese legal system.[85]

The end of extraterritoriality was particularly threatening to the Chinese working class. Qing subjects had previously been spared Japan's prohibitions on gambling and opium use, and observers fully expected a clash with Japanese law enforcement. To head off the impending crisis, McIvor met with members of the Qing consular staff on August 2 and worked out an extreme policy to deal with "disorderly characters" who were likely to run afoul of Japanese laws. They jointly decided to list and deport gamblers, opium traffickers and users, and those who simply lacked "upstanding occupations." Those who could not afford a ticket were given one free of charge by the Chinese Guild, but would thereafter be barred from reentering Yokohama.[86] In the end, Japanese police escorted some 500 "disorderly characters," as well as 222 voluntary returnees, to the S.S. *Oceanic* to be transported to Shanghai on August 4.[87]

Naturally, this did not eliminate all crime among the Chinese or preclude legal disputes; Japanese jurisdiction was soon put to the test. As early as September 1, a Qing subject was tried and sentenced by the Yokohama District Court for opium smuggling.[88] One early civil case was adjudicated on September 10, when Japanese rice merchant Kaneko Nuizo brought suit against a Chinese tailor named Ah Shing for the unpaid sum of ten yen,

---

84. "Yokohama zairyū Shinajin no dōsei," *Mainichi shinbun*.

85. Iwakabe, "Nisshin sensō to kyoryūchi Shinkokujin mondai," p. 72; Yokohama-shi, *Yokohama-shi shi*, 3:909–11.

86. YKS, *Kaikō kara shinsai made*, p. 14.

87. Dispatch from McIvor to Department of State, Aug. 6, 1894, no. 47, DDK, vol. 20, RG 59, NACP.

88. "Opium Capture at the Hatoba," *JWM*, Sept. 1, 1894, p. 245.

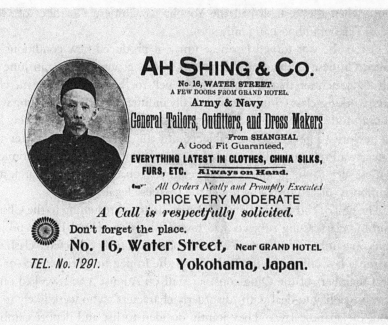

FIG. 1.2. A 1907 advertisement for Ah Shing's tailor shop. Courtesy of Yokohama kaikō shiryōkan.

forty-eight sen, for rice purchased in 1891 (fig. 1.2). The plaintiff's lawyer admitted that "there was no pass book, as both were on friendly terms and such a thing was thought unnecessary." In addition, the statute of limitations constrained legal action to within one year of the date of the last payment. But Kaneko had not brought the suit to Chinese consular courts and contended that the statute of limitations should be restarted from the date that jurisdiction was transferred to Japan. The judge ruled against Kaneko, reasoning that the removal of extraterritoriality in no way altered the timeline.[89] Although the court showed no anti-Chinese bias in this ruling, Kaneko's suit suggests that some Japanese considered it high time to settle scores with Chinese residents.

The war thus brought a social, economic, and political situation that compelled Qing subjects, high and low, to confront a shared crisis. They

---

89. "In the Yokohama-ku Saibansho," *JWM*, Oct. 13, 1894, p. 431.

came to rely on the Chinese Guild, which was metamorphosing from a Cantonese merchant guild with a narrow sphere of activity into an association claiming to speak for a singular Chinese community.[90] They in fact oversaw and funded the forced repatriation of working-class Chinese, and were tasked with promoting registration under Imperial Ordinance 137 for those who remained. After the reestablishment of the Qing consulate general after the end of the war, the Chinese Guild continued in its expanded role. From this time, the Chinese Guild took a more active leadership role, going from simply issuing business and immigration permits and conducting population censuses, to participating in international boycott movements and political protests. In this way, the Chinese Guild would facilitate the construction of a Chinese public consciousness.[91]

The Ethnic-National Optic

The changes wrought by the war exercised a lasting impact on Yokohama society; wartime maltreatment from society and official suspicion sharpened social distinctions between Chinese and Japanese residents. But, Chinese national identity did not simply spring fully formed from the imagination at this juncture. For Yokohama Chinese, identification with China coexisted with the manifold forms of association linked to their native place: local culture, dialect, hometown, and lineage. The war merely changed the relative priorities of these identifications.[92] Prior to the war, Chinese in Yokohama displayed scant attention to the Qing regime or investment in its

---

90. Uchida, *Nihon kakyō shakai no kenkyū*, p. 251.

91. YKS, *Kaikō kara shinsai made*, pp. 13, 43–44; Uchida, *Nihon kakyō shakai no kenkyū*, pp. 251–52. This unity was naturally built on top of existing province- and dialect-based affiliations. It is not coincidental that province-specific associations arose at the very juncture when the Chinese Guild adopted this superordinate role. A Cantonese same-province association was founded in 1898, and the Sanjiang Chinese established a Sanjiang guild (*gongsuo*) in 1900. These institutions maintained social and economic linkages between the Yokohama community and hometowns in the mainland, remitting money, coordinating business ventures, and relaying information. These were the very functions that the Chinese Guild had provided until the mid-1890s for a Cantonese constituency.

92. The multiplicity of identity does not imply that all identifications are equally important. As anthropologist Sonia Ryang argues, "identity consists of layers of qualities that the individual, as an interpreting agent, evaluates hierarchically" (Ryang, *North Koreans in Japan*, p. 166).

influence over Korea. However, with the outbreak of hostilities, Chinese merchant elites suffered economic consequences, and with the loss of extra-territoriality, the working classes confronted a direct threat to their welfare and security. In short, the war imbued their position as Qing subjects with greater social significance.

Changes in the diplomatic order also led to the permanent demarcation of Chinese and Japanese communities. The outcome of the war confirmed Japan as a member of the civilized nations vis-à-vis the Qing empire, help-ing Japan renegotiate its unequal treaties with the Western powers.[93] Al-though the Tripartite Intervention of Germany, France, and Russia in 1895 forced Japan to give up some territorial gains and aroused in Japan a con-sciousness of the West's brute application of power politics, Japan now stood as one with these powers in pursuing concessions in China.[94] The wider political situation elevated the essentialized differences between Chinese and Japanese. This chapter concludes with four examples that illustrate how the war reshaped social life in Yokohama in complex ways. They show first, how the lives of individual Chinese in Yokohama defied simple categoriza-tion in terms of culture, language, and ethnicity; and second, how the war aggravated the ascriptive tendencies that created those very categories.

One case of a Yokohama Chinese with competing attachments to Yoko-hama and China was Bao Tang (1854–1905), mentioned in the introduction. He was an inveterate gambler, and having no particular training, worked at various odd jobs, including foreman, painter, and clerk. In short, he was of working class and had dubious habits, the typical Shinajin of later Japanese imagination. He was thus a likely candidate for repatriation as a "disorderly character" in August 1894. But he was not deported, as demonstrated by his registration document under Ordinance 137, which indicated that he was employed by the German trading firm A. Meier.[95] By that time he was mar-

---

93. Nish, *Japanese Foreign Policy*, p. 49.

94. Japan and the Qing empire signed the Treaty of Shimonoseki on Apr. 17, 1895, and the Sino-Japanese Commercial Pact on July 21, 1896; these treaties re-stored diplomatic and economic ties between the two countries under conditions strongly in Japan's favor. In addition to territorial gains and an indemnity equal to three times Japan's prewar national budget, Japan won most-favored-nation status and unilateral extraterritoriality for Japanese citizens in China.

95. Itō Tatsujirō, *Yokohama bōeki shōkei*, p. 110; Sugawara, *Nihon no kakyō*, pp. 16–17.

ried to Mizorogi Masu. Bao's roots in Yokohama apparently convinced him to remain despite the deteriorating situation.

Bao and Mizorogi lived in a world that was culturally mixed and multiply affiliated. In later years, Bao would leave his mark on both Chinese nationalist movements and Yokohama cultural identity; he was both a supporter of Chinese revolutionary Sun Yatsen (1866–1925) and the originator of the famed Yokohama steamed dumpling known as *shūmai*. Mizorogi was one of many Japanese women who crossed the ethnic boundary to live their lives as Chinese, losing her Japanese nationality in the process, and learning Cantonese well enough to live and work among the Chinese of Chinatown. Their marriage was not without its conflicts: the couple was known for loud arguments in the street when Bao came home at dawn after a night of gambling. But together they raised nine children and built a thriving restaurant business.[96]

Another member of the culturally hybrid Yokohama society was Feng Jingru (1844–1913), who ran a prosperous printing, book-binding, and Western stationery shop. Integrated, socially and sartorially, into the Euro-American community, Feng lived among other educated and affluent Qing subjects in the Old Settlement (Map 1B). The September 29, 1894, edition of the *Japan Weekly Mail* described him as a striking figure in his bowler hat and an old-fashioned European suit. Feng was, however, more extreme in this regard than most of his contemporaries because he even took British nationality. His rather unorthodox move was motivated by his inability to return to the Qing empire because of the crimes of his father, a rebel who was executed during the Taiping Rebellion (1850–1864). His ties to England were not, however, incidental. He spoke fluent English, often went by the name F. Kingsell, and named his shop Kingsell & Co.[97] Like Ah Shing the tailor, Kingsell did much of his business with European and American residents, further demonstrating the web of social and economic relations that permeated the city. Nevertheless, Feng and Bao were far from indifferent to China's political situation, despite strong ties to Yokohama's Japanese and Western communities. Indeed, the two men would later join opposing political factions in a struggle over Chinatown's educational institutions.[98]

---

96. Sugawara, *Nihon no kakyō*, pp. 16–18.
97. Feng Ruiyu, "Yokohama Daidō gakkō to Feng Jingru," p. 35.
98. This episode will be covered in chap. 2.

Nevertheless, the issue of national loyalty in wartime made ethnic distinctions paramount and imposed an ethnic-national optic on this mixed community. The mass media played a central role by rendering hybrid lives into oppositional statuses, either Qing or Japanese. One striking example arose from paranoia over foreign espionage. Various Japanese newspapers reported that Japanese police had arrested a suspected Qing spy on September 10. Though there was a discrepancy in the location of the arrest between papers—the *Tokyo nichinichi* reported that it was in Futtsu, Chiba Prefecture, whereas both the *Nippon* and *Mainichi* claimed it was across the bay at Kannonzaki, Kanagawa Prefecture—it is probable that they are describing the same individual. All other details accord in describing a suspicious, culturally ambiguous individual who at first glance appeared to be Japanese, spoke fluent Japanese, was a long-term resident, and was apprehended with a Japanese individual.[99] Both the *Mainichi* and the *Nippon* took this opportunity to warn their readers of a great espionage plot involving Shinajin dressed to look like Japanese.[100]

After the Tokyo Metropolitan Police questioned the men, however, neither turned out to be spies. The so-called Shinajin was revealed to be twenty-three-year-old Li Shengmei, the Nagasaki-born son of a Fujianese man and a Japanese woman. The *Tokyo nichinichi shinbun* remarked that his background was almost identical to Sino-Japanese hero Coxinga. Li was moreover a troubled youth; he had returned to Fujian with his father around 1892, but was banished from his home for being dissolute and undisciplined. Returning to Japan in February 1894, he stayed with an elder cousin in Tokyo's Tsukiji settlement until that cousin departed for China at the start of the war. Left to fend for himself and without enough money to make the trip to his natal home in Nagasaki, he somehow failed to register with the Japanese government by the deadline set by Imperial Ordinance 137. He then chopped off his queue, donned a blue-and-white cotton kimono, and tried to pass as Japanese. When Japanese police apprehended him, he was accompanying his employer, a medical doctor named Fukushima. After thorough questioning, the police cleared both of them of the

---

99. "Kanchō Shinkokujin hobaku," *Mainichi shinbun*, Sept. 11, 1894, p. 5.

100. "Kanchō no daikeikaku," *Nippon*, Sept. 12, 1894, p. 2; "Kanchō no daikeikaku," *Mainichi shinbun*, Sept. 12, 1894, p. 2.

charge of espionage, though Li may have faced punishment for failing to register.[101]

Even with these facts known, the *Nippon* scurrilously concluded that "mixed children from a foreign parent would be traitors like this."[102] In late nineteenth-century Japan, it seems, even Coxinga would have been considered suspicious for his mixed heritage. Despite the lack of evidence, rumors of Chinese espionage persisted and promoted a sharper sensitivity of cultural purity. In October, rumors emerged that a female spy, allegedly a mistress of Qing statesman Li Hongzhang (1823–1901), had been detected and apprehended on account of her strange accent. The editors of the *Japan Weekly Mail* were probably correct in attributing this and other stories to a war-obsessed imagination: "The story seems to be one of the many canards that are now winging their way through the credulous columns of the Tokyo press."[103]

This paranoia was but an extreme version of new norms of perceiving matters through national categories, a tendency that would persist through the succeeding century. A further example comes from a lengthy article in the *Mainichi shinbun* about an unnamed Qing subject and his Japanese friend. The article narrates a conversation between these representatives of the two belligerent parties on the war, repatriation, and personal safety. In the end, the Japanese man convinces his Chinese friend to remain in Japan, for "Japanese society will never harm peaceful Qing subjects like you." It is impossible to confirm the veracity of the conversation, and it is possible that both individuals were ideal types imagined by the writer. To readers, this was precisely the role they served.[104]

---

101. "Kanchō giwaku no Shinkokujin shūbaku," *TNNS*, Sept. 12, 1894, p. 3; "Ri Seibi no shobun," *TNNS*, Sept. 13, 1894, p. 2.

102. "Shinkoku kanchō yatsu no mimoto," *Nippon*, Sept. 12, 1894, p. 2.

103. "A Female Spy," *Japan Weekly Mail*, Oct. 13, 1894, p. 411; Chu, "China's Attitudes toward Japan," p. 89. There had been talk in the Qing court about using Japanese-speaking Chinese as spies during the conflict, but there is no evidence of any actually deployed to Japan.

104. "Tokyo senmon gakkō Yokohama kōyūkai ni okeru Ōkuma-haku no enzetsu," *YBS*, Mar. 21, 1899, pp. 2–3. It is also possible that the article was intended to stem the tide of Qing repatriation, assuming they read Japanese newspapers. This supposition is plausible, considering Japanese statesman Ōkuma Shigenobu's (1838–1922) 1899 observation that most Chinese merchants in Yokohama were fluent in Japanese.

Nevertheless, this article depicts the unnamed Qing national in a way that highlighted his deep ties to Yokohama. He was "first or second among the Qing residents of Yokohama in property, a stock holder of the Hong Kong Shanghai Bank, a twenty-year resident of Japan, married to a Japanese woman, and blessed with one child." This description in fact applied to many of the affluent, acculturated Chinese men in the treaty port. The article nonetheless attempts to draw conclusions regarding the Qing perspective on Japan and the war. When asked whether he would prefer a Japanese victory or a Qing victory, "he did not respond, but it seems he bears no ill feelings toward a Japanese victory. We should see in this the thoughts of the Qing toward the unsettled circumstances of their own country, and their lack of hostility toward Japan."[105]

The optimism is striking, as is the blatant attempt to see in the two men a direct reflection of relations between Japan and the Qing empire. The ambivalence displayed by the Chinese, which the journalist interprets as lack of hostility toward Japan, may also suggest his ties to his Japanese friend and their shared membership in Yokohama society. His social identities as neighbor, friend, husband, business partner, shareholder, and so on, were not visible through this ethnic-national optic. Before the war, differences were perceived according to cultural and linguistic boundaries, which were in themselves rather porous; thereafter, ethnic and national affiliations became superordinate and mutually exclusive. To bring the discussion back to the streets of Chinatown, as Japanese and Chinese took to denigrating each other as *chanchan* or *Dongyang gui*, individuals found it harder to see, much less express, their multiple identifications.

Conclusion

The war of 1894–95 resulted in a mutual awareness of national and ethnic identities among Chinese and Japanese residents of Yokohama. For the Japanese, the collective identity that mattered most was national, and hence, a political entity; for the Chinese, it was a defensive sense of ethnic unity based around their legal status as Qing subjects. The imperative to differentiate between friend and foe served to obscure other collective identities.

These ethnic distinctions were generated through confrontation and interaction, and three dimensions stand out: first, new derogatory depictions

---

105. "Nisshinjin no taiwa," *Mainichi shinbun*, Sept. 12, 1894, p. 1.

of the Chinese as Shinajin or *chanchan* by Japanese, substantiated by violent confrontation on the streets of Yokohama, transposed national conflict onto the mixed local community. Second, Japanese state efforts to regulate and control the Chinese population during the conditions of war created a specially restricted legal category for the Chinese, setting them apart from other treaty nationals.[106] Third, the deteriorating position of Chinese merchants in their economic rivalry with Japanese and Western competitors fueled a sense of crisis and a demand for organizational solidarity. On the one hand, these three forms of confrontation drove two-thirds of the Qing residents of Yokohama to return to China. On the other hand, those who remained found their well-being and social status more directly tied to their Qing citizenship than before.

Ethnic and national distinctions did not erase or prevent acculturation and varied social transactions. Friendships, intermarriage, and economic transactions between Chinese and Japanese continued and confirmed their participation in a shared local community. The rise of ethnic unity might best be understood as a change in perception and priority. Experiences during the Sino-Japanese War forced individuals to see their lives and environment in ethnic terms and to place this collective identity above all others. However, this development was as yet a passive demarcation of the Chinese, a classification and ascription by others, and experienced as an ethnic boundary rather than ethnic self-awareness. Joint Chinese responses were weak and limited to the actions of the Chinese Guild. Moreover, little evidence supports the existence of an "ethnic nucleus," or the cultural content, symbols, and leadership that define an ethnic group.[107] It would take the arrival of expatriate leaders, themselves galvanized by the Qing defeat in the Sino-Japanese War, to mold the Yokohama Chinese into active Chinese citizens. This process in subsequent years would forge a political consciousness from their inchoate awareness of ethnic unity.

---

106. Iwakabe, "Nisshin sensō to kyoryūchi Shinkokujin mondai," p. 74.
107. Sollors, foreword to *Theories of Ethnicity*, pp. xxii–xxv.

CHAPTER TWO

Expatriate Nationalists and the Politics of Mixed Residence, 1895–1911

The 1894–95 war between the Qing empire and Japan forged a degree of ethnic solidarity among Yokohama's Chinese, but it did not yield a sense of modern ethnicity, much less nationhood. The nation, the idea of a politically sovereign people, was as yet too abstract, as was the concept of a single, unified homeland. In the late nineteenth century, overseas Chinese may have recognized their origin from the Great Qing (Da Qing), but their sense of pan-Chinese identity was primarily cultural, not political.[1] Yokohama Chinese did not join the Qing armies in their fight against the Japanese, and they did not organize aid for the Qing war effort. It simply was not their war.

In the fall of 1911, however, their attitudes toward China indicated an entirely transformed relationship with the homeland. The revolution that would shatter the Qing empire broke out on October 10, 1911. Overseas Chinese around the world had already participated with great vigor in the revolutionary movement, and when the Shanghai revolutionary government called for volunteers from the Chinese diaspora, the Yokohama Chinese responded enthusiastically. Twenty-four youths between the ages of twenty and thirty, wearing white armbands and revolutionary insignia, formed Yokohama's first dare-to-die squad (*gansidui*). On December 6, 1911, they were feted by speeches at the Chinese Guild, before marching

---

1. Kuhn, *Chinese among Others*, p. 248.

amid exploding firecrackers to a waiting steamer bound for Shanghai. In total, more than sixty Yokohama youths would sail to Shanghai, destined to join the revolutionary armies.[2]

The jubilant patriotism and spirit of self-sacrifice inspired by the republican revolution were made possible by changes in the institutions and discourses of self among the Yokohama Chinese. These transformations were catalyzed by the intervention of expatriate activists who entered Yokohama and compelled the resident Chinese to think and to act as Chinese citizens. The Chinese expatriates established schools and published newspapers and journals, the classic instruments of nation building. They attempted to define a Chinese ethnic nucleus distilled from an elite culture that had formerly applied to only the upper fraction of society.[3] In so doing, they convinced many, but not all, in the local community that the ethnic nation was the collective identity that mattered most. Increased political participation, as historian Pamela Kyle Crossley argues, would necessitate greater cultural homogenization, the price paid for membership in a future Chinese republic.[4]

This overall historical trend was not unique to Yokohama. The 1890s and early 1900s were years when overseas Chinese around the world were progressively called upon to help remake China into a modern state. These efforts were undertaken by activists of various stripes, who sought both to nurture concern for homeland and to mobilize the financial and technical resources of the overseas Chinese. The role of these external agents was crucial; historian Wang Gungwu has argued that even in the large communities of overseas Chinese in Southeast Asia, discrimination in a foreign land did not lead to a "passionate self-discovery" of themselves as Chinese. Only after 1900 did Nationalist leaders emerge, following visits by reformers and revolutionaries such as Kang Youwei (1858–1927), Liang Qichao

---

2. "Chūka kaikan ni sensō o inoru," *YBS*, Nov. 7, 1911, p. 7; Ogasawara, *Sonbun o sasaeta Yokohama kakyō*, pp. 93–95.

3. This work was analogous to concurrent Japanese efforts at cultural consolidation that have been described by Chris Burgess as "samuraisation," wherein "characteristics such as loyalty, perseverance, and diligence said to be held by a small (but elite) segment of the population—the samurai—were gradually extended through propaganda, education, and regulation to cover the whole population" (Burgess, "The 'Illusion' of Homogeneous Japan and National Character").

4. Crossley, "Nationality and Difference in China," p. 141.

(1873–1929), and Sun Yatsen.[5] These leaders then led a cultural resiniciza-tion of overseas communities, which introduced a sense of unified Chinese-ness that mitigated province-of-origin attachments as well as clarified boundaries with non-Chinese.

Many of these processes were already under way in Yokohama, particu-larly since the Sino-Japanese War of 1894–95. The local environment of Yokohama also played a role in the rising ethnic consciousness of its Chi-nese residents. Japanese leaders with pan-Asianist concerns were eager to join the Chinese expatriates in Yokohama to aid their nation-building en-deavors; on another level, social friction with a largely antagonistic Japanese public also facilitated the fashioning of Chinese ethnic self-awareness.

The comprehensiveness of this mobilization, however, should not be overstated. As Prasenjit Duara argues, Chinese nation-building efforts faced great obstacles in overseas communities that were both locally acculturated and largely indifferent toward China.[6] The expatriate activists who inter-vened in the social organization of the Yokohama Chinese likewise faced subethnic divisions and competing attachments that bedeviled their efforts to elevate the nation as a terminal community. In Yokohama, the diversity and division among Chinese was made more acute by the split among the expatriates themselves, specifically the competing agendas of Kang Youwei and his disciple Liang Qichao on the one hand, and Sun Yatsen on the other. The two factions drew local supporters from different constituencies, de-fined by existing divisions of economic class, province of origin, and reli-gion. These distinctions did not melt away under the influence of the expa-triate activists; they would continue to structure life among the Yokohama Chinese over the decades to come.[7]

This situation led to a gap between the nationalist ideologies of the politi-cal activists who entered Yokohama during these years and the localized

---

5. G. Wang, "Limits of Nanyang Chinese Nationalism," pp. 143, 145.

6. Duara, "Transnationalism and the Predicament of Sovereignty," p. 1044; G. Wang, "Limits of Nanyang Chinese Nationalism," pp. 147–50. Wang Gungwu's research also bears out this conclusion, finding that apart from activists inflamed by homeland issues, many Chinese were assimilated into local elites or invested in their local community organizations.

7. This pattern held true for Southeast Asia as well; Philip Kuhn describes the new institutions tied to the Chinese state as "umbrella organizations" that presided over "federations of particularistic regional or dialect groups" (Kuhn, *Chinese among Others*, p. 248).

concerns of the Chinese who resided there. Over time the new publications, schools, and social organizations founded by these activists fostered greater participation in the political issues of their homeland. But not all Chinese were thus empowered. The discourse of nation disseminated in Yoko-hama enabled an elite group to claim the authority to speak for a nation and to represent their own interests as those of the collective. This chapter examines this process of political mobilization, its social consequences, and its limits.

Nationalists and Pan-Asianists in Yokohama

The Sino-Japanese War of 1894–95 was indirectly responsible for the politi-cal mobilization of Yokohama's Chinese because Japan's crushing defeat of the Qing empire also emboldened China's revolutionaries and reformers. In November 1895, Sun Yatsen was forced to flee to Japan when Qing authori-ties uncovered his planned uprising in Guangzhou. In Yokohama, the En-glishman Feng Jingru sheltered Sun and his ally Chen Shaobai (1869–1934) on the second floor of his printing and binding shop, Kingsell & Co.[8] From this base, Sun and Chen launched the Yokohama branch of his revolution-ary organization, the Revive China Society (Xing zhong hui), on Novem-ber 20, 1895. Although Qing government agents shut down the organiza-tion a mere ten months later, it introduced many of Yokohama's most influential Chinese to political activism, including Feng Jingru, his younger brother Feng Zishan, an eminent Chinese Christian named Zhao Mingle, restaurateur Bao Tang, and Sun's translator and bodyguard Wen Bingchen (1866–1955).[9]

Meanwhile, in the summer of 1898, Kang Youwei (1858–1927) and his disciples Liang Qichao (1873–1929) and Tan Sitong (1865–98) led the Hund-red Days Reform, a series of reforms under the authority of the Guangxu Emperor (1871–1908). When the Empress Dowager placed the Guangxu Emperor under house arrest and snuffed out the reforms in September, Kang and Liang fled to Japan.[10] Kang Youwei and Liang Qichao transposed

---

8. Feng Ruiyu, "Yokohama Daidō gakkō to Feng Jingru."

9. Ogasawara, *Sonbun o sasaeta Yokohama kakyō*, pp. 22, 42–43. Sun temporarily stayed at Wen's home in 1898 for protection against Qing agents.

10. Miyazaki, *My Thirty-Three Years' Dream*, p. 151; Spence, *Gate of Heavenly Peace*, pp. 48–54. Tan Sitong remained behind and was executed.

their political activism to Yokohama, where they and their constitutional reform movement siphoned away support from Sun's revolutionaries. In this way, three of China's most influential intellectual and political leaders arrived in Yokohama in the years following the Sino-Japanese War, where they applied their political ideas directly to the population of resident Chinese.[11]

Their choice of destination had as much to do with the presence of Chinese supporters as it did with protection offered by well-connected Japanese allies. Despite the recent war between the two countries, a diverse group of Japanese activists, adventurers, and politicians was willing to help Chinese reformers and revolutionaries either remake or undo the Qing government. Three of the most important of these figures were former education and future prime minister Inukai Tsuyoshi (1855–1932), former foreign and prime minister Ōkuma Shigenobu (1838–1922), and the independent activist Miyazaki Tōten (1870–1922). Inukai and Ōkuma were instrumental in allowing Kang and Liang to escape China in 1898, while Miyazaki played a significant role in building Japanese support for Sun Yatsen. These Japanese supporters believed that only an alliance between Japan and a revived China would be able to resist Western domination over Asia.[12] Their pan-Asianism was based on the idea of a common yellow race and ran counter to the mainstream of Japanese ethnicity (*minzoku*) discourses in these years, which elevated the Japanese as an ethnicity above the Chinese.[13]

Ideas of a shared civilizational foundation, primarily understood as the Confucian philosophical tradition, also informed the alliance between Kang and Liang and their most influential Japanese supporters Inukai and Ōkuma.[14] Inukai believed that China and Japan should form an alliance based on this common Confucian heritage, and that Japan had the ability

---

11. Spence, *Gate of Heavenly Peace*, pp. 38, 45. Both factions had long advocated the mobilization of the financial support and technical skills of overseas Chinese to drive their movements. Sun Yatsen had in fact started the first branch of his revolutionary society in Hawaii in 1894.

12. Jansen, *Japanese and Sun Yat-sen*, p. 213.

13. Doak, *History of Nationalism in Modern Japan*, p. 222. Kevin Doak cites the 1897 publication of Kimura Takatarō's article "The Japanese Are a Superior *Minzoku*" as a representative example of this Japanese chauvinism.

14. Najita, "Inukai Tsuyoshi," p. 495. Tetsuo Najita describes Inukai as "at once a genuine Sinophile and a nationalist," and his mediation activities among the Chinese of Yokohama were consistent with both motivations.

and obligation to lead China toward modern nationhood. Ōkuma shared a similar vision of Japan's role in Asia, but with a relatively greater emphasis on Japanese guidance.[15] The discourse of a common race and civilization aside, the common currency in the alliance between Chinese and Japanese elites was the concept of nationhood. As they considered the nation-state the universal form of political legitimacy, they sought to build a modern Chinese nation-state to serve as a Japanese ally, beginning with the Yokohama Chinese.

While exiled in Yokohama, Kang Youwei and Liang Qichao implemented a program spanning publishing and education to create active Chinese citizens (*guomin*).[16] Affluent, educated Cantonese residents responded earnestly to this mission. They were overawed by Kang's and Liang's scholarly credentials and status as former advisers to the Guangxu Emperor; they welcomed these luminaries from the homeland with support and financial contributions. This support came, however, at Sun Yatsen's expense.

By 1899, Feng Jingru and Feng Zishan had transferred their allegiance to Kang and Liang and would prove highly valuable to them. The Feng brothers owned separate printing presses and published several political journals that helped establish Yokohama and neighboring Tokyo as two of the most important bases for Chinese political journalism in the late Qing period.[17] The first of these journals was Liang's *Qingyi bao* (Journal of pure critique), a fortnightly periodical that began on December 23, 1898, and boasted a

---

15. Lebra-Chapman, *Ōkuma Shigenobu*, pp. 143–44. Ōkuma's pan-Asianism was analogous to the American Monroe Doctrine, and comprised both idealistic goals to repay Japan's "cultural debt" to China and pragmatic imperatives to lead industry and commerce in Asia. In 1915 Ōkuma would preside over Japan's infamous Twenty-one Demands to China.

16. Zarrow, "Citizenship in China and the West," pp. 16–17.

17. Dikötter, *Discourse of Race in Modern China*, pp. 107–8; Harrell, "Meiji 'New Woman' and China," p. 124. Frank Dikötter notes that scores of influential journals were published in Japan during this era, which resulted from a flood of Chinese seeking education in Japan. Ten thousand Chinese were enrolled in Japanese schools by 1906. Though their numbers declined after 1911, in this era, "young boys just entering their teens, men as old as in their seventies, and women tottering with bound feet all joined the rush to the east [Japan]" (Y. Lu, *Re-Understanding Japan*, p. 17).

distribution of four thousand copies.[18] Liang's introduction to the first issue stated its nationalist and pan-Asianist mission, calling for unity among the citizens of China, and solidarity among all members of the yellow race to build Asian self-rule. Reflecting gratitude toward his benefactors, Liang intended the journal to "link the spirits of the two countries China and Japan, and unite us in friendly feelings," and to "expound on Eastern learning to preserve the essence of Asia."[19] This statement was consistent with Kang and Liang's political manifesto of January 1898, which cited the Japanese Meiji Restoration as a model for reforming the Qing dynasty.[20]

Sun Yatsen's revolutionary movement differed ideologically from that of the constitutional reformers. Sun was interested in mobilizing Han Chinese ethnic (*minzu*) sentiment to attack the legitimacy of China's Manchu rulers, whereas Liang emphasized the mediating role of the state in creating citizens. The latter sought to modernize the Qing dynasty by making the Manchu Guangxu Emperor a constitutional monarch; the former sought to erect a Chinese nation-state representing the Han ethnicity in its place. Yokohama and Tokyo publications representing these opposing ideologies traded editorial barbs for nearly ten years.[21] Despite the initial hopes of Japanese supporters like Miyazaki Tōten and Inukai Tsuyoshi, Kang's and Sun's respective factions failed to find common ground while in Japan.[22]

Education was another key site of contention. Liang Qichao appropriated a school that had been established by Sun's faction, renamed it, and inflected its educational curriculum with his political program. Sun Yatsen's supporter Chen Shaobai had founded this school in October 1897 with the

---

18. Ogata, "Kakyō no shinbun"; Yokohama-shi chūō toshokan kaikan kinenshi henshū iinkai, *Yokohama no hon to bunka*, pp. 470–71; *BX*, p. 68; "Benguan gedi daipai chu," *Qingyi bao*, 1:259–60. This journal reached all significant Chinese-speaking communities around the Pacific from Singapore to San Francisco. It was not, however, the first periodical published by Chinese in Japan, which was *Dongya bao* (East Asia Journal) that ran from June to October of 1898.

19. "Hengbin qingyi bao xuli," *Qingyi bao*, 1:3–5.

20. De Bary and Lufrano, *Sources of Chinese Tradition*, p. 269.

21. Yokohama-shi chūō toshokan kaikan kinenshi henshū iinkai, *Yokohama no hon to bunka*, p. 471. Liang Qichao and Feng Zishan began publication of the journal *Xinmin congbao* (New people's miscellany) in 1902 and waged a protracted editorial debate with Sun Yatsen's *Minbao* (People's journal) until around 1907.

22. Spence, *Gate of Heavenly Peace*, p. 55; Miyazaki, *My Thirty-three Years' Dream*, p. 163.

name Zhongxi xuexiao (School of Chinese and Western learning) and had delegated its operation to the Yokohama Chinese Guild.[23] When these sponsors requested teachers from Liang Qichao, who was then in Shanghai, Liang sent a contingent of Kang Youwei's disciples and students, including the new principal-to-be Xu Qin (1873–1945). Shortly after their arrival, they usurped the educational mission of the school and renamed it Datong xuexiao (School of great harmony). Kang's influence was obvious to all observers because the school now shared the same name as his Shanghai publishing and translation enterprise, the Datong shuju.[24] The school officially opened under its new name on March 9, 1898, with over one hundred pupils.[25]

The curriculum of the Datong xuexiao aimed to foster a consciousness that was global, egalitarian, patriotic, and Confucianist—new ideals for a modern Chinese subjectivity. The brick, two-story school building itself was constructed in Western style, "clean enough for a Dutchman's dinner table," as noted by the English-language *Kobe Weekly Chronicle* in 1898. Especially impressive to this journalist was the gender equality displayed in the school, which served to furnish the institution with a modern and civilized patina:

> Of the 140, some thirty perhaps are girls, and these in the matter of costume are true daughters of Eve every one of them. (Of course we are speaking of Eve after she got civilized and took to wearing clothes and studying the fashion journals.) Neat alone would scarcely do justice to their appearance, for it is more than that. Neat and stylish might cover the situation. Although they occupy the three front desks in a body, they otherwise are treated exactly the same as the boys; there is no foot-binding for them, either physically or mentally . . . And so it will most likely come to pass that in ten or fifteen years from now we shall be having a Woman's Rights movement in China.[26]

---

23. Chen Shaobai, *Xingzhonghui geming shiyao*, p. 44; Ye, "Chūgoku daidō gakkō-shi," p. 625; Sugawara, *Nihon no kakyō*, p. 39. The original name of the school implied a curriculum of Chinese and Western learning, though it also taught the Japanese language.

24. *BX*, p. 45; Zhang Xuejing, "Datong xuexiao lueshi," pp. 3–7; Prasenjit Duara, "Transnationalism and the Predicament of Sovereignty," p. 1035; "Shinkokujin ni kansuru hōkoku," 1899, DRMFA, ref. B03050064000, JACAR. The term *datong* denoted a universalist utopia in Kang Youwei's thought, which he conceived as the ultimate aim of any nation-building project.

25. "Summary of News," *JWM*, Mar. 12, 1898, p. 253; *BX*, p. 45.

26. "The Chinese School in Yokohama," *Kobe Weekly Chronicle*, Oct. 15, 1898, pp. 306–7; Ye, "Chūgoku daidō gakkō-shi," pp. 514, 518.

FIG. 2.1. Datong xuexiao classroom in 1898. *Source*: "Yokohama ni okeru Shina gakkō," *Tokyo nichinichi shinbun*, June 15, 1898, p. 39.

Moreover, its classrooms were well appointed; a drawing in the *Tōkyō nichinichi shinbun* from 1898 showed a mixed-sex class taught by a mustachioed teacher in suit and waistcoat before a blackboard, globe, and portrait of Confucius (fig. 2.1). The modern facilities, the globe, coeducation, the portrait of Confucius, and the Western dress of the teacher were all integral parts of the lesson and as important to the socialization of the students as the content of the lectures.[27] The connection between Kang and the school's Confucian curriculum was further established by a couplet by Kang

---

27. Bourdieu, "Systems of Education and Systems of Thought," p. 198. These were all innovative features of the curriculum and were expected to contribute to pupils' learning.

Youwei, placed beside the image of Confucius at the front of each class-room, and the use of Kang's and Liang's writings as teaching materials.[28]

These curricular elements derived as much from Kang Youwei's progressive interpretation of the Confucian classics as Japanese models of modern education.[29] Since the 1890 promulgation of the Imperial Rescript on Education, Japanese educational agendas shifted ideologically toward the inculcation of moral, patriotic, and Confucian virtues. In Japanese schools, this rescript was hung at the front of every classroom and sacralized by daily veneration. At the Datong xuexiao, students were similarly compelled to bow before the image of Confucius and Kang's couplet.

Direct appeals for patriotism were also an important component of the school's educational mission. Feng Ziyou (1882–1958), Feng Jingru's son, was a member of the first entering class in 1898 and recalled that newly arrived principal Xu Qin fervently harangued students to rescue their country, meaning China, from calamity. Students recited the following verse daily: "When the country is imperiled, what do we plan to do? Our desires are difficult to accomplish, our exploits are unsuccessful. Be silent and think of this; can we not be ashamed? Encourage the children, exhort with great effort!"[30]

The Datong xuexiao may even be considered a precursor to the first public school system in China, which the Qing court established from 1902 to 1903. Although the two were not administratively linked, both were inspired by the Japanese model and arrived at strikingly similar curricular aims. A 1906 Qing decree itemized the goals of the new empirewide school system: "to inculcate loyalty to the Emperor, reverence for Confucius, and to promote the public spirit, the military spirit, and the realistic spirit."[31] The primary difference between the Qing schools and the Datong xuexiao,

---

28. "Yokohama ni okeru Shina gakkō," *TNNS*, June 15, 1898, 39; Ye, "Chūgoku daidō gakkō-shi," p. 514; *BX*, p. 58. From 1899 to 1902, the school used Liang's account of the failed Hundred Days Reform, *Wuxu zhengbian ji* (An account of the 1898 reform), as a textbook.

29. Spence, *Gate of Heavenly Peace*, p. 33; Duara, "Transnationalism and the Predicament of Sovereignty," p. 1047. Kang's iconoclastic use of Confucianism allowed him to appeal to monarchism but still promote reform.

30. Feng Ziyou, *Geming yishi*, 1:51.

31. Lai, "Teaching Chinese Americans to Be Chinese," p. 196; Harrell, "The Meiji 'New Woman' and China," p. 124; Tsang, *Nationalism in School Education in China*, p. 40.

as well as Japanese primary schools, was the treatment of female education.
Separate schools for girls were not established in China until 1907, and coeducation was never a part of Qing policy.[32]

Given the importance of the school, Sun's faction was not content to allow Kang Youwei's backers free rein; they launched an effort to wrest back
control in the fall of 1898, criticizing Kang as a fugitive traitor. In response, Principal Xu Qin hung a sign at the school declaring Sun Yatsen
unwelcome on the grounds. A meeting called in January 1899 to resolve a
dispute over the election of school trustees even ended in a brawl.[33] During the meeting, Wen Bingchen fiercely denounced Sun's opponents. Singling out Feng Zishan, Wen roared, "What's an Englishman doing here!
Get out right now!" apparently mistaking Zishan for his older brother.[34]
In the ensuing shouting match, Wen was joined by a number of hotheaded
youths, including Bao Tang, who started a mêlée that ended all produc-
tive discussion for the evening. After this meeting, the school was trapped
in a deadlock, unable to continue operation without directors at the helm.[35]
However, Inukai Tsuyoshi had been following the situation closely and
offered to mediate between the two factions and to provide financial support for the school.[36] In gratitude, the Chinese Guild offered Inukai the
post of honorary principal. He accepted, and thus he and his political ally
Ōkuma Shigenobu stepped into the fray of Chinatown's ideological
struggles.[37]

---

32. Lai, "Teaching Chinese Americans to Be Chinese," p. 196; Purcell, *Problems
of Chinese Education*, pp. 67–68; Tsang, *Nationalism in School Education in China*, pp.
39–40. The Ministry of Education of the new ROC established coeducational
schools in 1912.

33. *BX*, p. 46. Kang's faction within the Chinese Guild had argued that suffrage should only be extended to members of the mercantile class, and this
position was vigorously opposed by Sun's primarily working- and middle-class
supporters.

34. Ogasawara, *Sonbun o sasaeta Yokohama kakyō*, pp. 88–89. Feng Zishan had not
taken British nationality.

35. Zhang Shu, *Hengbin zhonghua xueyuan*, p. 35. The forty-five trustees of the
Chinese Guild appointed a slate of directors entirely from Kang's faction, from
principal on down. Yet continuing conflict drove several officials of the school to
tender their resignations over the next month.

36. *BX*, p. 46.

37. "Datong xuexiao kaixiaoji," *Qingyi bao*, 2:591–94; Feng Ruiyu, "Yokohama
Daidō gakkō to Feng Jingru." Inukai's contact with Chinese activists in

FIG. 2.2. Inukai Tsuyoshi (speaking), and Ōkuma Shigenobu (seated, middle) at the Datong xuexiao. *Source*: Lin Huiru, ed., *Xiaoxue xinduben*, vol. 1 (1903).

Ceremonies and speeches at the school reveal that Inukai and other Japanese allies regarded themselves as champions of pan-Asian ideals. Inukai and Ōkuma attended the March 18, 1899, opening ceremony of the Datong xuexiao and led the assembled dignitaries to bow three times before the image of Confucius before entering the schoolhouse. Next, Inukai and Ōkuma gave speeches on the shared civilizational roots of the Qing and Japanese empires, and the hope that Japan could serve as a nation-building model (fig. 2.2). In his speech, Inukai stressed his veneration of Confucius and commitment to modernization, declaring that "from my office as principal, I will take the methods of world civilization and apply it to the

---

Yokohama was likely facilitated by Miyazaki Tōten and Feng Jingru; Miyazaki was by then well acquainted with Sun Yatsen and Chen Shaobai and had hoped for a rapprochement between the two Chinese factions. Feng Jingru had supported both Kang Youwei and Sun and also enjoyed regular contact with Inukai and Ōkuma.

teachings of Confucius." The event concluded with a boisterous affirmation of solidarity between the Qing and Japanese empires:

> The Japanese seated in the hall stood up and gave a rousing cheer of "Long live his Excellency the Emperor of the Qing Empire!" . . . Then the Chinese stood and cheered "Long live his Excellency the Emperor of the Great Japanese Empire!" and all joined in with the cheer. Next, the Japanese stood again and called out "Long live the Datong xuexiao!" and all responded. Finally, the Chinese stood and cheered "Long live Count Ōkuma! Long live Mr. Inukai!"[38]

Many other, less famous Japanese also became involved with the school. Kawahara Misako, a Japanese teacher mentioned in chapter 1, taught from 1900 to 1902.[39] More than thirty Japanese teachers worked at the school between 1898 and 1909, comprising at most 27 percent (3/11) of the faculty. They taught physical education, military training, Japanese language, and music.[40] The involvement of eminent Japanese individuals at the Datong xuexiao indicates that they considered it an integral part of a wider pan-Asian movement.

Schools, Factions, and Subethnic Divisions

In histories of Yokohama Chinatown, the Datong xuexiao is often cited as the founding moment of a *huaqiao* community in Yokohama.[41] As described in the introduction, the term *huaqiao*, meaning diasporic Chinese, was a normative ideal of patriotic attachment to the motherland, that is to say, the way overseas Chinese should feel about China.[42] Indeed, the school's emphasis on homeland politics and the involvement of three of the most important political and intellectual leaders of modern China left a deep imprint on its historical legacy. Present-day Yokohama has two Chinese schools, both of which claim to be lineal descendants of the Datong xuexiao.[43]

---

38. "Daidō gakkō kaikō shiki," *YBS*, Mar. 19, 1899, p. 2; "Datong xuexiao kaixiaoji," *Qingyi bao.*

39. Kawahara, *Karachin ōhi to watashi*, pp. 107–9.

40. *BX*, p. 55. Liu Wuji, *Su Man-shu*, p. 21.

41. Zhu Jingxian, *Huaqiao jiaoyu*, pp. 148–49; Zhou, "Riben huaqiao jiaoyu lüekuang," p. 180.

42. G. Wang, *Chinese Overseas*, pp. 46–47; Ye, "Chūgoku daidō gakkō-shi," p. 536. The term was deployed in the 1890s by the Qing government, reformers, and revolutionaries alike to mobilize Chinese living overseas.

43. The establishment of these two schools will be discussed in chap. 5.

However, in the 1890s the concept of *huaqiao* was as yet an unrealized ideal, not a description of the actual consciousness of Yokohama's Chinese residents. Contrary to the historical narratives that place the Datong xue-xiao at the center of a movement to unify the community at the end of the nineteenth century, the school was a highly divisive issue that led to the establishment of competing educational institutions. Conflicts over the school were more than simply a battle between Sun Yatsen and Liang Qichao. The Chinese of Yokohama were not passively shaped by expatriate agendas; although subjected to competing ideologies, individual Chinese in Yokohama tended to view the factions in their own terms.

Members of Kang and Liang's faction in the local community were educated and affluent, such as Feng Jingru and the trustees of the Chinese Guild, and almost exclusively Cantonese.[44] Thus a strong undercurrent of partisanship was behind their claims of national representation. Because of the Confucian scholasticism at the center of Kang and Liang's political movement, they bore more in common with educated Japanese than with many of the Chinese craftsmen, cooks, and laborers in Chinatown. These working-class Chinese, including Bao Tang, were more receptive to Sun's faction. Japanese government reports claimed that working-class and unemployed Chinese were swayed to join Sun's faction not by his revolutionary ethos, but by the fear that their voices would be excluded by the elite members of the Chinese Guild.[45]

These marginalized Chinese would seek to establish their own schools. In 1908, Sun's supporters established an educational wing of their Revolutionary Alliance (Tongmeng hui) in Yokohama, which evolved into a school known as the Hengbin huaqiao xuexiao (Yokohama school for diasporic Chinese).[46] This school was the most significant rival to the Datong xuexiao because it contested its legitimacy on its own terms, that is, as a representative

---

44. Yoshinao, *Inukai Bokudō den*, 2:727.

45. Vasishth, "Model Minority," p. 120; "Shinkokujin ni kansuru hōkoku." Japanese observers labeled these lower-class supporters ruffians (*gorotsuki*). The term probably referred to Chinese laborers and servants who always comprised the majority of the Chinatown population. According to population statistics from 1869, only 36 out of 1,002 Chinese were merchants or compradores. The remainder were laborers, craftsmen, women, and children.

46. *BX*, p. 71. This school was perhaps the earliest institution in the city to employ the term *huaqiao*.

of the Chinese nation. In spite of its connection with the revolutionary movement, the Huaqiao xuexiao was defined as much by class background as by ideology. In addition to the children of Revolutionary Alliance members and later Chinese Nationalist Party (Guomindang; GMD) members, the school enrolled many children of working-class families. These Chinese had been largely excluded from attending the Datong xuexiao and had periodically expressed their ire through violence. The Huaqiao xuexiao catered specifically to their needs by offering reduced tuition rates.[47]

Hence, an overlapping ideological and class-based rivalry unfolded between the Datong xuexiao and the Huaqiao xuexiao during these years, extending to the students themselves, who, it is said, often exchanged harsh words or blows when they met on the street.[48] In more congenial moments, this rivalry played out on the baseball diamond where the schools fielded competing teams in Yokohama and national baseball tourneys.[49]

Huang Lixiang (1912–99) was a second-generation Yokohama Chinese who personally experienced this interschool rivalry. His father was no affluent merchant, banker, or printer, but rather a ship painter who worked in Hong Kong before hopping a French vessel for Yokohama in 1893 at the age of eighteen. He continued in that trade for a time and married a Japanese woman from Tsujidō, a nearby coastal village. Together they opened two Chinese restaurants and raised Lixiang and his five siblings in a bilingual household. They managed to send the children to the Huaqiao xuexiao. Huang Lixiang remembers relations between students of the two schools as cold, but not necessarily belligerent: "When we would pass each other on the street, we wouldn't acknowledge each other. We wouldn't fight, but we wouldn't speak either. We might become friends after graduation, but not while we attended those schools. . . . The Huaqiao xuexiao was on Sun Yat-sen's side and full of poor kids, right? There were lots of rich kids at the Datong xuexiao, and they were full of themselves."[50]

Chinese Christians also objected to the management of the Datong xuexiao. These Chinese were primarily members of the Yokohama Union Church,

---

47. Liu Wuji, *Su Man-shu*, p. 21; *BX*, p. 68. In an incident far larger than the January 1899 brawl at the Chinese Guild, a mob of working-class Chinese broke into the Datong xuexiao grounds in 1902 and wrecked the property.

48. *BX*, pp. 71–74.

49. This aspect of life in Yokohama is explored more fully in chap. 3.

50. CKK and YKS, *Yokohama kakyō no kioku*, pp. 18–19, 23.

which had established a mission in the Chinatown area in the 1880s.[51] Many originally sided with Sun because he was a baptized Christian, and they specifically rejected Confucianism—the tradition intended to unify all Chinese—as a pagan ritual. Feng Ziyou's memoir attests to the conflicts this attitude generated: "There was a Christian student named Zhao Zibin who was expelled by a teacher [from Shanghai] named Chen Yin'nong for refusing to bow [before the image of Confucius]. For this, the school earned a great deal of antipathy from the Christian students."[52] This paralleled the experience of Japanese Christians such as Uchimura Kanzō (1861–1930) who in 1891 famously refused to bow before a portrait of the Japanese emperor and was forced to retire from Tokyo First Higher School (Ichikō).[53]

The most prominent Chinese Christian in Yokohama and their de facto leader was Zhao Mingle, an affluent Cantonese dealer in ceramics and textiles.[54] He briefly served as treasurer for the Yokohama branch of Sun's Revive China Society, but subsequently broke with its expatriate leaders.[55] In 1899, Zhao Mingle and other Chinese Christians joined a Qing consulate initiative to establish a separate school, named the Zhonghua xuetang (Chinese academy).[56]

The school soon ran into financial difficulties and was rescued in late 1903 by another marginalized group, the Sanjiang Chinese. These Chinese were linguistically distinct from the Cantonese majority of Chinatown, and their school rectified the long-standing absence of educational opportunities in their preferred Ningbo dialect.[57] Mismanagement led to the school's closure in 1905, but Sanjiang Chinese established a more successful school

---

51. "The Study of the Yokohama Union Church," Yokohama Union Church, accessed Dec. 5, 2007, http://www.yokohamaunionchurch.org/history2.html.

52. Feng Ziyou, *Geming yishi*, 1:51; Ye, "Chūgoku daidō gakkō-shi," p. 625; Spence, *Gate of Heavenly Peace*, p. 44.

53. Christians, at least since the early eighteenth-century Catholic-Chinese Rites controversy, considered the worship of Confucius a form of idolatry. Uchimura Kanzō's refusal to bow before the portrait of the Meiji Emperor and Imperial Rescript on Education was based on similar grounds.

54. Ide, *Nihon shōkō eigyō roku*, p. 270. Zhao Zibin may in fact have been related to Zhao Mingle, but there is no textual proof.

55. Ogasawara, *Sonbun o sasaeta Yokohama kakyō*, p. 42.

56. *BX*, p. 69.

57. "Hengbin zhi Sanjiang jiyouhui," *Zhejiang chao* 7 (1903), pp. 6–7; "Zhu Lize xuexiao yu zhonghua xuetang," *Zhejiang chao* 10 (1903), p. 11. The Ningbo dialect

called the Zhonghua xuexiao (Chinese school) in 1913. This latter school enjoyed greater longevity and enrolled more than one hundred students at a time.[58]

Finally, in 1916 Chinese members of the Anglican Church relocated the Zhicheng xuexiao (Will and way school) from Tokyo's Tsukiji district to Yokohama. This relatively small school educated about fifty boys and was located at the former address of Feng Jingru's Kingsell & Co. at block fifty-three of the Old Settlement. It was thus situated within the cluster of Chinese settlement most culturally integrated into Yokohama's Western community. Not coincidentally, its curriculum emphasized Christianity and English, rather than Chinese language.[59]

Contestation over education in Chinatown reflected wider debates among scholars, activists, and politicians over community representation, but individuals in Yokohama were also greatly motivated by class, native place, or religious affiliations. The expatriates and the local Chinese residents saw instrumental benefits in colluding with one another, but their motives were not identical. Moreover, this collusion was asymmetrical. Expatriate intellectuals had the ability to narrate and record the struggle in terms of homeland issues, yielding the latter-day impression of a smoothly developing community of *huaqiao* in Yokohama.

The 1899 Debate over Mixed Residence

Through education and publishing, expatriate activists brought agendas of reform or revolution to the Chinese of Yokohama. However, the sphere of their activities also encompassed social and political matters in the local community. For instance, in 1898 the constitutional reformers inaugurated annual commemorations of Confucius' birthday; this new tradition incorporated parades and gymnastics by students from the Datong xuexiao and was publicized by Liang Qichao around the Pacific via his *Qingyi bao*.[60] This

---

was a compromise for the Sanjiang Chinese; this group was diverse, but shared many of the same ritual observances, and their dialects were related.

58. Zhang Xuejing, "Datong xuexiao lueshi"; *BX*, p. 63.

59. Church Missionary Society, *Mission to Chinese Students*; Yokohama shi-yakusho, *Shishi kō, kyōiku hen*, p. 280; *BX*, p. 75; YKS, *Kaikō kara shinsai made*, p. 48. Kingsell & Co. was destroyed in a fire around 1901.

60. Feng Ziyou, *Geming yishi*, 1:52; "Hengbin di si ci chong si Kongzi shengdan ji," *Qingyi bao*, 11:5969–70.

event was an overt attempt to link Yokohama Chinese with a wider imagined community of compatriots.

A more directly political application of expatriate leadership took place in the summer of 1899 when diplomatic developments between Japan and the world called into question the legal status of Chinese residents in Japan. Beginning with the July 1894 Anglo-Japanese Treaty of Commerce and Navigation, Japan successively renegotiated its unequal treaties with the Western powers, the juridical foundations of the treaty ports. Revised treaties were scheduled to go into effect on July 17, 1899, and would end the forty-year history of the Foreign Settlement, terminate extraterritoriality, and remove restrictions on residence for Western nationals.[61] While Japan beyond the treaty ports prepared for an era of mixed residence, or direct contact with foreigners, the Chinese were in limbo. The new treaties did not define any change in their status. Ever since the Sino-Japanese War, their rights had not been tied to the treaties with the Western powers, and there was thus no legal necessity to lift restrictions on Chinese residence or commercial activities at this time. However, Japan had persuasive diplomatic and moral reasons to revise their treatment of Chinese in concert with the new treaties. Connections between sympathetic Japanese leaders and the constitutional reform faction would prove crucial when Chinese in Japan petitioned the Japanese government for these rights.

To Japanese, the revised treaties were the culmination of their government's primary foreign-policy initiative of the late nineteenth century, that is, to rectify a blight on national pride, sovereignty, and economic autonomy.[62] These impending changes, however, also unleashed powerful anxieties about Japan's position in the world and relationship to China. On one side, China served as a metonym for the unenlightened Asia that Japan should cast off to join the civilized West.[63] On the other, China was part of

---

61. Kanagawa-ken keisatsu-shi hensan iinkai, *Kanagawa-ken keisatsu shi*, p. 556. Whereas treaties with most of the Western powers went into effect on July 17, 1899, there was a minor discrepancy with France and Australia, whose treaties went into effect on August 4.

62. As early as the time of the Iwakura Mission (1871–73), Japanese political leaders unsuccessfully attempted to renegotiate the unequal terms of the treaties, which granted extraterritoriality to treaty nationals in Japan and limited Japan's ability to set tariffs.

63. See Fukuzawa, "On De-Asianization," pp. 129–33.

a pro-Asia cause that would legitimize Japan's quest for national power in competition with the West.[64] In the midst of public ruminations about Japan's relationship to the West, ideological fractures were generated in Japan around the question of whether Chinese would be "left in the pot" after treaty nationals had been granted the right of mixed residence in the interior.

The Japanese government did not issue its policy on Chinese residence and immigration until July 10, a week prior to enforcement of the new treaties. By that time, public controversy on the subject had simmered through spring and early summer. The controversy began at the top, where the Japanese Ministry of Foreign Affairs and Home Ministry occupied opposite positions on the issue. According to an unnamed bureaucrat, the Ministry of Foreign Affairs feared that singling out the Chinese for exclusion would gravely damage Japan's diplomatic and commercial interests. The Home Ministry opposition apparently derived, on the other hand, from the fear that Chinese would encroach on Japanese labor and small business, damage Japanese customs, and spread disease. This view also drew upon a residual resistance toward granting mixed residence for any foreigner, much less the Chinese.[65]

National and Yokohama newspapers were equal participants with the government ministries in inflecting these points of contention. The *Jiji shinpō*, a newspaper founded by pro-West educator Fukuzawa Yukichi (1835–1901), stood as the strongest advocate among the Japanese press for enacting restrictions on residence for Chinese. In one striking editorial, the paper articulated the position that equality with the West and China were mutually exclusive conditions: "It has taken years of struggle to achieve a status of equality with the civilized countries of the West . . . because they have formerly seen us as the same as the Chinese, or worse, even below the Chinese." Citing the reasons why the United States and Australia have also excluded the Chinese, the editorial explained that those same reasons also apply in Japan: "Civilized laws are made to govern civilized people, and the Chinese have not yet attained that level."[66]

---

64. Oguma, *Genealogy of "Japanese" Self-Images*, pp. 78–79.

65. "Chinese and Mixed Residence," *JWM*, July 1, 1899, p. 4; "Shinajin zakkyo mondai: kyoseki ronsha no okubyō (1)," *Mainichi shinbun*, June 27, 1899, p. 1; "Shinajin zakkyo mondai: seifunai no shin jōiron," *Nippon*, June 25, 1899, p. 1.

66. "Shinajin no zakkyo mondai," *Jiji shinpō*, June 13, 1899, p. 2.

This obsequious pro-West view was contested by advocates of Asian solidarity. The *Mainichi shinbun* declared in response that Japan ought not be complicit with the racist discrimination against Asians demonstrated by countries such as the United States: "You will see that if Japanese try to enter America *en masse* as the Chinese laborers did, they will be slandered in the same way as the Chinese."[67] The *Nippon*, a nationalist paper that advocated a mission for Japan to lead Eastern civilization, also exemplified this stance.[68] In June, it ran editorials arguing that exclusion of the Chinese would damage Japan's own status: "The exclusion of Chinese is a policy initiated by the United States and Australia, an Anglo-Saxon policy that is ideologically founded on exclusion of Asians, the exclusion of the so-called yellow race, which includes us Japanese."[69] Such popular affirmations of Sino-Japanese affinity echoed statements made by Inukai, Ōkuma, and other Japanese leaders involved with the Yokohama Chinatown community, men whose Asianism was part and parcel of their nationalist commitments.

The debate also invoked the issues of hygiene and labor competition, suggesting the manner in which the Japanese public viewed the Chinese among them. Since the Sino-Japanese War, Chinese were increasingly seen by the Japanese as lower-class workers, predisposed toward vice and squalor, rather than mercantile rivals. The debate solidified this image of the Chinese, now predominantly known derogatorily as Shinajin rather than the more formal term Shinkokujin. This characterization was based on ascribed qualities that included economic habits—"the Shinajin are industrious, thrifty, and seeking profit from menial trades"—as well as character and conduct—"avaricious and mean, foul and unclean" and prone toward opium addiction. Chinese had thus been recast as economically and socially threatening immigrant laborers, a portrayal that replaced their earlier image as persevering, profit-seeking merchants.[70] A letter from a reader to the newspaper *Yokohama bōeki shinpō* illustrates the pervasiveness of this view among average Japanese: "Regarding the issue of Shinajin mixed residence in Japan's interior, I have one request. I want them to create a law strictly

---

67. "Shinajin zakkyo mondai: futatabi (2)," *Mainichi shinbun*, July 3, 1899, p. 1.
68. "Kokusaiteki dōgi," *Nippon*, Mar. 23, 1899, p. 1.
69. "Shinajin zakkyo mondai: seifunai no shin jōiron," *Nippon*, June 25, page 1.
70. Ibid.; Yokohama-shi, *Yokohama shishi*, 3:905–6; Toyama, *Chūzan zonkō*, p. 405.

proscribing the inherent filthiness of the Shinajin. Everything else, I don't mind."[71]

On a more abstract level, the import of the term "Shinajin" appears to have been a deliberate denial of their status as Qing subjects, implying that the Chinese were ungoverned, anarchic immigrants. A polemical essay printed in the *Yokohama bōeki shinpō* in early July of 1899 renders this point explicit: "We should not consider diplomatic relations with Shina [China] the same as with Euro-American countries because Shina does not have the qualifications to be considered a complete country. . . . They are evidently already a destroyed country; their people are no longer Qing subjects, but are Shinajin, a race [*shu*] who move from place to place."[72]

Seeing a grave danger to their social and economic rights, Cantonese elites in Yokohama spearheaded a movement to petition the Japanese government for the same rights that were to be granted Westerners. These Chinese elites in Yokohama drew together Chinese representatives from the other treaty ports of Hakodate, Kobe, and Nagasaki to send a petition, signed by 143 prominent members of the business community, minus the British national Feng Jingru, to Japan's Ministry of Foreign Affairs appealing for the right to mixed residence.[73] The communiqué that accompanied the petition was written by none other than Liang Qichao, and the movement was empowered by the nationalist rhetoric, political connections, and organizational wherewithal of the constitutional reformers in their midst.

This petition helped unify certain Chinese in Yokohama even as it connected them with homeland political movements. Most of the pro-Kang managers of the Datong xuexiao were signatories of the petition, and Liang Qichao's *Qingyi bao* served as the chief vehicle of its publicization.[74] Two of the Christian opponents of the Datong xuexiao, including Zhao Mingle, were also among the petition's supporters, suggesting that the petition movement smoothed over some of the differences among upper-class Cantonese residents. Still, Sanjiang and Fujian Chinese, as well as Sun Yatsen's lower-class supporters, were not involved. As far as can be documented, all

---

71. "Hengen shū," *YBS*, July 5, 1899, p. 3.

72. "Shinajin no naichi zakkyo ni tsuite (2)," *YBS*, July 6, 1899, p. 1.

73. "Naichi zakkyo ni taisuru Shinajin no chinjō," *Mainichi shinbun*, July 1, 1899, p. 2; "Shinkokujin ni kansuru hōkoku." As a British national, F. Kingsell did not sign the peitition, but his younger brother Feng Zishan did.

74. "Ji Zhongguoren qingqiu neidi zaju shi," *Qingyi bao*, 3:1269–86.

of the signatories of the petition were of Cantonese origin. Even Chen Dexin, the Fujian-born manager of Yokohama's largest Chinese-run trading firm Shunhezhan, was absent from the list. Moreover, the movement, like the establishment of the Datong xuexiao, proceeded without official support or acknowledgment from the Qing government.[75]

Despite the partisan composition of the petitioners, Liang's communiqué was presented to the Japanese media and politicians as representative of the Chinese view. On June 29, Liang met with several Japanese government officials, including Ōkuma and Inukai, and officially presented the petition to Foreign Minister Aoki Shūzō (1844–1914). This occasion became another opportunity for Japanese and Chinese political allies to assert a pan-Asian alliance and challenge Western dominance over Asia. In these meetings, they emphasized the commonalities between Chinese and Japanese as people of the same continent, same race, and same script (*dōshū dōshu dōbun*), and thus appealed to a pan-Asianist political platform.[76]

The petition also forcefully intervened in discourses on Chinese characteristics, as it refuted, point by point, the Japanese impression of the Chinese as filthy Shinajin laborers. The petitioners presented themselves as politically conscious Qing subjects and countered assumptions about the class composition of the Chinese by bringing attention to the Chinese business community. Liang argued that if the Chinese were to be excluded, their feelings of good will would evaporate and Japan could end up losing the per annum 80–100-million-yen business carried by Chinese traders.

The petition did not advocate for working-class Chinese, and in fact paid scant attention to their rights and dignity. Instead, the petitioners argued that there would be little social disruption from Chinese migrant laborers because few would risk traveling to a foreign country for a miniscule wage differential. Moreover, coming close to acknowledging the potential criminality of this group, they argued that the Japanese police would be entirely capable of dealing with infractions from the small number of Chinese laborers. Finally, Liang concluded the appeal with a statement that "his country would not entertain any umbrage against Japan if she thought it

---

75. YKS, *Kaikō kara shinsai made*, p. 39; "Ji Zhongguoren qingqiu neidi zaju shi," *Qingyi bao*.

76. YKS, *Kaikō kara shinsai made*, p. 31; "Chinese and Mixed Residence," *JWM*; "Ji Zhongguoren qingqiu neidi zaju shi," *Qingyi bao*.

expedient to impose some restriction upon the immigration of the labouring classes."[77]

In the end, these elite Cantonese petitioners were rewarded with their wished-for rights of mixed residence in the interior of Japan. An extraordinary session of the Japanese cabinet on July 10, 1899, resolved that after August 4 migrant laborers would be restricted to the former treaty-port foreign settlements, whereas merchants and industrialists (*shōkōgyōsha*) would be allowed residence on the same basis as Europeans and Americans.[78] The details regarding the enforcement of this policy were specified on July 27, with the promulgation of Imperial Rescript 352, and Home Ministry Directive 42 on July 28.[79]

The Yokohama press heralded this compromise between positions advocated by the two ministries as pragmatic, nondiscriminatory, and a victory of Asian brotherhood over Anglo-Saxon racism. They lauded the Japanese government's solution as superior to the Chinese exclusion policies of the United States and rejected arguments made by papers like the *Jiji shinpō* that Japan would be better off following Western example.[80] Despite these positive appraisals of the legislation's wording, it in fact constituted a legal system intended to halt any significant immigration from China. This goal was explicitly stated in Home Ministry Directive 728 of the same year, which claimed that these "measures have preemptively prevented problems of Qing migrant labor."[81]

Nevertheless, the petitioning elites of Yokohama Chinatown construed no insult to the dignity of the Chinese or the yellow race through these legislative acts. At the opening ceremony of the Chinese Chamber of Commerce on August 4, 1899, its president, Lü Yingbin, praised Japan's

---

77. "Chinese and Mixed Residence," *JWM.*

78. "Shinajin zakkyo mondai no ketsuryō," *YBS,* July 12, 1899, p. 2.

79. Rescript 352 declared that "laborers without special permission from government authorities would not be permitted to live or work outside of the Foreign Settlement [*kyoryūchi*] or the zone of mixed residence [*zakkyochi*]" (YKS, *Kaikō kara shinsai made,* p. 31). Directive 42 defined laborers as those engaged in farming, fishing, mining, forestry, construction, manufacturing, transport, stevedoring, and others, though it allowed an exemption for those engaged in domestic employment such as cooks or servants.

80. "Chokurei 352: Shinajin zakkyo seigen," *Mainichi shinbun,* July 31, 1899, p. 1.

81. Guo, *Zainichi kakyō,* p. 40.

benevolence for this neighborly act of friendship.[82] Chinese business own-ers established this body to coordinate their mercantile activities to compete with Western firms in a battle for markets in Japan's interior. Although it was founded on practical imperatives for the local community, it was, like the petition, tightly connected with the nation-building agendas of Kang Youwei and Liang Qichao.[83] The chamber's bylaws indicate a suit-ably tutelary component to its operations: article 5 stated that "all mem-bers must put patriotism first" but also that "all members will associate with honorable Japanese to link both countries substantively together in friendship."[84]

This body thus expressed the rhetoric of its expatriate sponsors and en-dorsed cooperation with Japanese; it raised political awareness among Chi-nese merchants just as the Datong xuexiao did for their children. In ensuing years, the chamber, and the Chinese Guild in which it was housed, would demonstrate this political consciousness; in 1905, they coordinated local Chinese merchants to reproduce a transnational movement to boycott American goods in response to the maltreatment of Chinese in America.[85]

---

82. "Ji Hengbin Huashang huiyisuo kaihui shi," *Qingyi bao*, 4:1539–42; "Zailiu Qingguoren zhi zhaodaihui," *Qingyi bao*, 5:2443–50. Half a year later, on Feb. 21, 1900, 105 Chinese merchants held a celebratory dinner in honor of the Japanese authorities for the passage of Rescript 352. With Ōkuma, Inukai, Foreign Minister Aoki Shūzō, and Yokohama Mayor Umeda Yoshinobu in attendance, the Chinese merchants gave a cheer of "Long live the Japanese Emperor and the Japanese peo-ple!" and invoked the friendship between people of the same race and the same script.

83. "Zairyū Shinkokujin no shōgyō kaigisho secchi," *YBS*, July 29, 1899, p. 2; "Correspondence: Chinese Chamber of Commerce," *JWM*, Aug. 12, 1899, p. 160. The organ's connection with Kang and Liang is suggested by the participation of the same elite individuals in the Chinese Chamber of Commerce as in the Datong xuexiao and the Chinese Guild, and the additional fact that all three were located together at Yamashita-chō block 140. There were also suspicions among Yokohama Chinese that its directors were biased toward Kang Youwei's faction.

84. "Ji Hengbin Huashang huiyisuo kaihui shi," *Qingyi bao*.

85. "The Chinese Boycott in Yokohama," *JWM*, Aug. 19, 1905, p. 197; Gerth, *China Made*, pp. 127–29. In 1905, protests by Chinese in America generated an en-ergetic boycott movement around the Pacific, led by native-place associations, chambers of commerce, reformers, and revolutionary activists. This movement operated independently of the Qing government, which issued a decree at the end of August 1905 to suppress the boycott. Despite its negligible economic impact, the

They promoted a unity of national purpose, but were at this stage far from militant toward Japan. Chinese residents in Yokohama did not participate in another transnational boycott movement against Japanese products in the spring of 1908. Merchants in Guangzhou and Hong Kong sent impassioned representatives to Yokohama as well as Kobe, but those trading communities remained quiescent. They presumably felt that the cause was not inflammatory enough to merit their economic sacrifice.[86]

At the advent of mixed residence, the Chinese of Yokohama were coalescing into an ethnic group, with leadership, shared interests, and a discourse of identity. The petition movement was a watershed in this process. It did not, however, involve all Chinese in the port city despite its broad representative claims. More precisely, it tied many of Yokohama's Cantonese elites to the constitutional reform group and their institutions, forming a clique that claimed to speak for the rights of Chinese in general but advocated their own partisan interests.

Cultural Hybridity and the Era of Mixed Residence

Before 1899, a large number of Chinese had in fact already been enjoying "mixed residence" of a sort in Chinatown, intermarrying and conducting business with both Japanese and Westerners. The social reality of late-Meiji Chinatown demonstrated a kind of urban mixing and cultural exchange that defied the national boundaries espoused by Japanese and Chinese elites. The outcome these Chinese elites fought for, freedom to reside and conduct business beyond the treaty ports, would moreover bring ambivalent outcomes for Chinese social cohesion. The new juridical regime also meant a proliferation and intensification of the forces of integration that had theretofore been confined to the foreign settlement.

---

boycott created the organizational foundation for future anti-imperialist boycotts and raised awareness of product nationality.

86. "The Boycott," *Japan Weekly Mail*, Apr. 25, 1908, pp. 430–31. This international incident sprung from the Feb. 5, 1908, Qing seizure of the Japanese vessel *Tatsumaru,* which had been ferrying arms to Chinese antigovernment activists. Nevertheless, because Qing actions contravened international law, Japan coerced from the Qing government an apology and indemnity. Some Chinese considered this an affront to Chinese national dignity, but others felt that the matter was rather minor.

An 1897 article in the *Jiji shinpō* newspaper claimed that each year some two hundred mixed Chinese-Japanese children were born in Chinatown.[87] Feng Ziyou's memoir noted that half of his class at the Datong xuexiao were mixed children (*ainoko*) of Chinese fathers and Japanese mothers. Like Huang Lixiang, most were fluent in Japanese and brought up among Japanese family members.[88] This mix of cultural influences was captured in illustrations used in Datong xuexiao textbooks created by the famed half-Japanese poet, writer, and painter Su Manshu (1884–1918), who himself was a graduate of the school.[89] Principal Lin Huiru compiled these textbooks, entitled *Xiaoxue xinduben* (New readers for elementary school), in 1902 to replace Liang Qichao's writings with a more practical curriculum. Composed according to the most current pedagogical methods, these texts avoided topics and themes "rarely seen and seldom heard" by the students, focusing each lesson instead on "things familiar to their lives" in order to "draw forth their interest."[90]

Lesson 8 of volume 1, "An Upstanding Brother," depicted a sister lecturing her younger brother, both in Japanese garb, at the veranda of a Japanese home (fig. 2.3). Lesson 48 of volume 1, "Letter and Carp," portrayed girls in ruffled dresses with ribbons and a hat, calling to mind the description of Datong xuexiao schoolgirls in the *Kobe Weekly Chronicle* (fig. 2.4).[91] These images reflect a culturally hybrid community and a curriculum that drew from local knowledge as well as a nationalist agenda.

---

87. "Nankinmachi (2)," *Jiji shinpō*, Mar. 21, 1897, p. 10. This number appears to be somewhat inflated, perhaps to incite a sense of scandal among the Japanese readership. These children became Qing subjects when registered as children of Chinese fathers, or Japanese if registered as born out of wedlock, according to the patrilineal citizenship laws of both Japan and the Qing dynasty.

88. Feng Ziyou, *Geming yishi*, 1:166; "The Chinese in Japan," *JWM*, June 24, 1899, pp. 613–14.

89. Liu Wuji, *Su Man-shu*, pp. 7, 15–16; Feng Ziyou, *Geming yishi*, 1:164–70. Su was born of a union between a Japanese woman named O-Sen and a Cantonese merchant employed at a British-owned tea company.

90. Lin Huiru, *Xiaoxue xinduben*; Lincicome, *Imperial Subjects as Glocal Citizens*, p. 85. These educational aims are consonant with the developmental education doctrine (*kaihatsushugi*) that was the vanguard of Japanese pedagogical thinking from the 1870s to the mid-1880s; this localized and child-centric doctrine held that children should learn first about their immediate surroundings and expand their knowledge outward over time.

91. Lin Huiru, *Xiaoxue xinduben*; *BX*, p. 64.

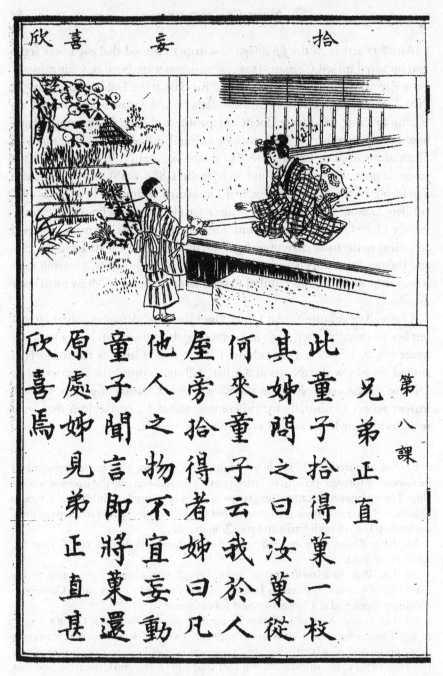

FIG. 2.3. "An Upstanding Brother," book illustration by Su Manshu. *Source*: Lin Huiru, ed., *Xiaoxue xinduben*, vol. 1, lesson 8 (1903).

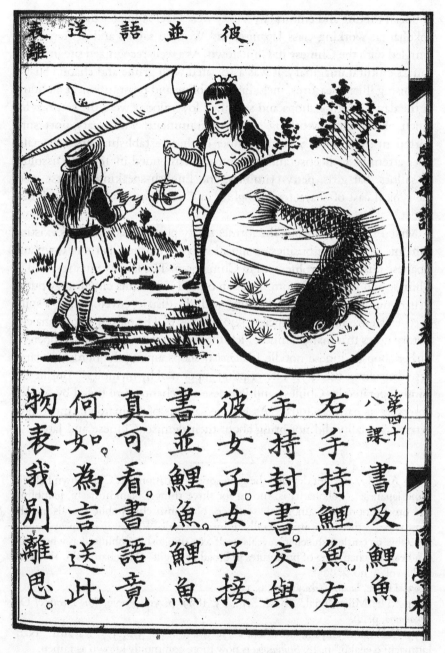

第四十八課　書及鯉魚

右手持鯉魚。左
手持封書。交與
彼女子。女子接
書並鯉魚。鯉魚
真可看。書語竟。
何如。為言送此
物。表我別離思。

FIG. 2.4. "Letter and Carp," book illustration by Su Manshu. *Source*: Lin Huiru, ed., *Xiaoxue xinduben*, vol. 1, lesson 48 (1903).

Social mixing and cultural hybridity were facts of life for the denizens of
Yokohama. Working-class Japanese and Western sailors and drifters often
mingled with the Chinese in Chinatown. As a well-recognized site in Yokohama's cultural imaginary, it was associated with grime and chaotic bustle,
promising illicit pleasures, including gambling and prostitution, at all hours
of the day.[92] Its grog shops and so-called low saloons were the settings for
much of the city's working-class entertainment. The treaty port supported an exceptionally large number of these establishments, especially
after attempts to license and to control them ended in 1874.[93] Dissolute
ex-sailors, bar girls, petty criminals, and English-speaking Chinese were
the typical cast of characters mingling in Chinatown, especially on Blood
Street.[94]

Mixed residence outside the former treaty ports accelerated this existing
dynamic, as Chinese businesses spread into the Japanese parts of town and
Japanese businesses proliferated in Chinatown. The latter influx resulted in
Chinese and Japanese becoming, as an official Yokohama city history put it,
"harmoniously united in friendship," with the district enveloped in "a spirit
of co-existence and co-prosperity [*kyōzon kyōei*]." The official Yokohama city
history notes that many Chinese "left the confines of Chinatown to open up
barber shops, Chinese noodle [*shinasoba*] shops among the bordering Japanese districts of the city," a description supported by memoirs.[95] Businesses
jointly operated by Chinese and Japanese merchants were noted by outside
observers as early as 1903.[96] As for the saloons of Chinatown, the end of
extraterritoriality did not bring about their demise. Chinese and Japanese,

---

92. An 1897 account detailed the grotesque fascination that Chinatown held for
some Japanese: "Yokohama is known for three things: Nankinmachi, gambling,
and prostitution. And among these three, Nankinmachi's public morals are the
most vile. . . . the stores are generally filthy and crude. What at first appears to be a
vegetable or cuttle-fish seller, reveals itself as a thuggish gambling den where you
can hear the chattering of prostitutes in broad day light" (Yokohama-shi, *Yokohama
shishi*, vol. 3, no. 2: 905).

93. Hoare, *Japan's Treaty Ports*, p. 117.

94. "The Miller Trial," *JWM*, Sept. 23, 1899, p. 318; Poole, *The Death of Old
Yokohama*, p. 20.

95. Yokohama shiyakusho, *Shishi kō, fūzoku hen*, pp. 572, 577; Kayama, "Nankinmachi o egaku," p. 18. *Shinasoba* is now more commonly known as ramen.

96. Uchida, *Nihon kakyō shakai no kenkyū*, p. 221; Yokohama shinpōsha, *Yokohama hanjō ki*, p. 130.

rather than Western-owned, businesses rose in prominence among them from the early 1900s.[97]

Chinatown's dangerous allure did not evaporate, but rather became a fixed trope in descriptions of the enclave. The district was described by a Japanese writer in 1903 as "thronged, boisterous, chaotic, dark, and unclean," evoking mystery and danger. "Within its narrow confines, we can barely guess at what dangers lurk, what diseases fester, what sorts of villains roam, what conspiracies are plotted."[98] Nevertheless, the text does not linger on this cautionary message, but proceeds to describe the pleasures of Chinese food and drink. Chinatown had become one of Yokohama's famous sites (*meisho*), just as Chinese cuisine had become one of Yokohama's local specialties, drawing large numbers of diners from neighboring Tokyo.[99]

The role of Yokohama's Chinese cuisine in the district merits special consideration because of its contribution to the city's cultural identity. Chapter 3 deals with its wider influence on Japanese culture. But pertinent to the current chapter, many Yokohama Chinese restaurants actively turned toward attracting Japanese customers in the era of mixed residence. Chinese food, known as Nanjing cuisine (*nankin ryōri*) to Meiji-era Japanese, was already considered an integral part of Yokohama culture by the late 1880s. But in the decade from 1900 to 1910 many restaurants became known by the Japanese pronunciation of their name.[100] A Japanese description of Chinatown in 1903 noted, with apparent disappointment, the adulteration of Chinese signs for the benefit of Japanese consumers.[101]

Another culinary manifestation of mixed residence that left a particularly long legacy was the birth of the Yokohama *shūmai*, an open-topped steamed

---

97. Tatewaki, *Japan Directory*, 32:105, 39:581–87.

98. Yokohama shinpōsha, *Yokohama hanjō ki*, p. 129.

99. Ye, "Chūgoku daidō gakkō-shi," pp. 509–510; Hiramatsu, "Yokohama meibutsu," p. 20; Yokohama shinpōsha, *Yokohama hanjō ki*, p. 135; Muraoka, "Yukikau benpatsu sugata," p. 64. The demand for Chinese food and drink among Yokohama residents was also demonstrated by the presence of counterfeit Chinese liquor produced in the Japanese part of town.

100. YKS, *Kaikō kara shinsai made*, p. 24. One prominent example from the Anglo-American *Japan Direction* was the Chinese restaurant Pingzhenlou. In 1904 the restaurant was indicated as "Ping Chang & Co." in the *Japan Directory*, but from 1910 its listing changed to "Hei Chin Row," a romanized version of the Japanese pronunciation of its name.

101. Yokohama shinpōsha, *Yokohama hanjō ki*, p. 138.

dumpling derived from Cantonese cuisine. Bao Tang, one of the instigators of the brawl at the Chinese Guild during the Datong xuexiao dispute earlier in the year, moved with his Japanese wife Mizorogi Masu into the neighboring district of Isezaki-chō after the inauguration of the new legal regime.[102] Leaving behind battles over community representation, he and his wife founded Hakugatei (Chinese: Boyating) in late 1899, the first restaurant in Japan to make and serve *shūmai*. By 1902, Hakugatei was already known as one of Yokohama's most prosperous Chinese restaurants, and in 1903 it was prominent enough to merit mention alongside the most famous of such establishments, Enpōrō (Yuanfanglou) and Heichinrō (Pingzhenlou).[103] Situated outside Chinatown, Hakugatei's *shūmai* was clearly aimed at Japanese consumers, and over time, indelibly transformed Yokohama's culinary culture. So in food as in pleasure, Chinese and Japanese joined forces in Yokohama society, blurring some of the cultural boundaries between themselves.

This intensified border crossing and mutual acculturation between Chinese and Japanese contributed to a distinctive local culture that was already heavily influenced by European and American cultures. Though not verbally articulated, this local culture implicitly contested the idea of nations as bounded cultural and social units by virtue of its coproduction by individuals of many nationalities.

Conclusion

From the Sino-Japanese War of 1894–95 through the early 1900s, the Chinese of Yokohama began to see themselves by degrees as a single ethnic nation, unified by shared interests and difference from the Japanese. This process was determined by the imperatives of patriotism and self-defense during wartime, and later actively expedited by expatriates who introduced homeland politics to the Yokohama Chinese. Solidarities between Chinese

---

102. Isezaki-chō was known as Yokohama's busiest entertainment and shopping district in the late-Meiji period. As it was described in 1903, "Isezaki-cho's hustle and bustle is truly the greatest in Japan, exceeding far and away even Tokyo's Asakusa, Osaka's Sen'nichimae, or Kyoto's Kyōgoku" (Yokohama shinpōsha, *Yokohama hanjō ki*, p. 103).

103. Ide, *Nihon shōkō eigyō roku*, p. 251; Sugawara, *Nihon no kakyō*, p. 18. Bao and Mizorogi apparently operated a restaurant prior to 1899 as well, though not much is known about it.

and Japanese leaders with pan-Asianist visions also promoted this nation consciousness because their political agendas dovetailed in the face of Western imperialism. Yet confrontational voices also aided in the process; Japanese efforts to paint the Shinajin as unhygienic, anarchic, and prone to criminality spurred elite Cantonese residents of Yokohama to reject this characterization by offering a self-representation as Shinkokujin in its place.

Chinese ethnic consciousness in Yokohama was therefore on display by the early years of the twentieth century, anchored by an ethnic nucleus of Confucian tradition, ideas of shared descent, and expatriate leadership. These leaders moreover sought to turn this Chinese ethnic identity into nationhood by promoting the ideal of a politically active citizenry, a concept they saw implemented with great effectiveness by Japanese leaders. In these early years, however, this sense of nation was in no way predetermined. It was still a contested aspiration, divided between competing ideas of the Chinese nation as either *guomin* or *minzu*, and undermined by numerous sub- and non-national forms of identity. The version of Chinese identity proffered by these elites did not exhaust the possible configurations of nationhood that could arise from the nascent ethnic Chinese identity. In the terminology used by Etienne Balibar, it was not the only "ideal nation" that could germinate from a "fictive" Chinese ethnicity.[104] As seen by the persistent divisions in Chinese education in Yokohama, these competitors were not so easily suppressed.

Over time, however, ideas of Chinese patriotism conveyed in education and publishing intensified community cohesion and political linkages with the homeland. But the two political factions did not benefit equally. Sun Yatsen's deployment of *minzu* came to dominate understandings of the Chinese people after around 1905, legitimated by anti-Manchu revolutionary activism.[105] At the same time, Kang and Liang's competing constitutional-reform movement declined in the face of pointed attacks on their support of the Manchus by younger and more radical activists, and the Qing dynasty's own reform efforts that undercut their agenda.[106] In the fall of 1911, the revolution that Sun had been yearning for finally arrived as anti-Manchu

---

104. Balibar, "Nation Form," pp. 140–41.
105. Karl, *Staging the World*, pp. 3, 118.
106. Spence, *Gate of Heavenly Peace*, pp. 104–11. With the death of the Guangxu Emperor in 1908, and his replacement by the boy-emperor Puyi, the feasibility of a constitutional monarchy receded even further.

uprisings spread across China. This revolutionary fervor also touched the Chinese in Yokohama. By November, Japanese journalists observed numerous political meetings and celebrations in support of the revolution; they also noted the fact that many Chinese men had cut off their queues.[107]

Thus we return to the dare-to-die squads introduced at the start of the chapter. In early December, Wen Bingchen helped organize the first team to join the fight against the Qing dynasty.[108] Twenty-four youths left on December 6, and another twenty on December 7, including Zheng Zhuo of the Datong xuexiao's Yellow Dragon baseball team. A third squad of volunteers departed on December 11.[109] The imprint of the enclave's new patriotic education was unmistakable. Yokohama had become home to a community of politically conscious and patriotic Chinese citizens who contributed to the establishment of the Republic of China (ROC).

This consciousness did not yet extend to all individuals of Chinese descent. Expatriate elites claimed to represent a community, but masked the political, partisan nature of their role in it. New discourses of Chinese identity also granted local elites a legitimizing ideology of national representation that reinforced local socioeconomic hierarchies. Equally significant were the forms of social and economic integration with the host community of Yokohama, which intensified after 1899 as Chinese increasingly contributed to Yokohama's local culture. This Yokohama culture, with diverse origins and influences, would become a resource for later articulations of an inclusive local identity.

But for the moment, it is enough to conclude that processes of integration and differentiation between Chinese and Japanese were operating simultaneously in turn-of-the-century Yokohama. Nationhood was now a part of this mixed community's conceptual vocabulary, even if it was not yet established as social reality. These were thus transitional years for the Chinese in Yokohama, with contradictory forces establishing the institutional, economic, ideological bases for the future elaboration of their national and local

---

107. "Chūka kaikan ni sensō o inoru," *YBS*; "Shiretsu naru Nankin gaitō no kakumei netsu," *YBS*, Nov. 10, 1911, p. 7; "Zaihama kakumeitō no hana," *YBS*, Nov. 14, 1911, p. 7.

108. Ogasawara, *Sonbun o sasaeta Yokohama kakyō*, pp. 93–95.

109. "Kesshitai nijūyon mei Shanhai ni mukai kairan," *YBS*, Dec. 7, 1911, p. 7; "Dainiji kesshitai Shanhai e zokuhassu," *YBS*, Dec. 8, 1911, p. 7; "Daisan kesshitai yuku," *YBS*, Dec. 11, 1911, p. 3.

identities. Diasporic nationalists had so far undertaken Chinese nation building in Yokohama without state support. Their mission would be pursued with much greater invasiveness and effectiveness after the establishment of the ROC in 1912, a regime that would become intensely concerned with the status, education, and regulation of its overseas citizens. The application of this state power on Chinese life in Yokohama will be the subject of the next chapter.

CHAPTER THREE

Cooperation, Conflict, and Modern Life in an International Port, 1912–32

By the 1910s, Yokohama Chinatown had become a mythologized and integral part of the Yokohama cityscape. The district's mysterious atmosphere was enthusiastically lauded by writers with a taste for the exotic. Japanese journalist Kanome Shōzō's 1916 essays on the district, published together in 1924 as *Nankinmachi*, describes the district as invidious and inscrutable, a "fathomless darkness . . . One step into this town and your first impression will be akin to that of a traveler thrown into a wholly different world." Visitors, Kanome asserts, are assaulted by an inexpressible unease, for "no one knows what secrets lurk, what unimaginable things occur."[1] These tropes were already well codified, and negative though they sounded, they also presented Chinatown sites and sights as not-to-be-missed tourist attractions for Japanese visitors. Foremost was the "arresting sight" of the Guandi Temple, where Japanese visitors from the countryside crowded to gawk at the splendid calligraphy and at the foot-bound Chinese women worshipping there.[2] Chinese were members of the Yokohama community, but their foreignness added to Yokohama's distinctiveness within Japan.

---

1. Kanome, *Nankinmachi*, p. 1; L. Pan, *Sons of the Yellow Emperor*, p. 305. This characterization is not far from the sinister film depictions of New York's Chinatown, which nonetheless imbued the district with a dangerous, thrilling allure. But today's visitors to Yokohama Chinatown receive starkly different impressions.

2. Kanome, *Nankinmachi*, pp. 17–18. The calligraphy on display was credited to the Guangxu Emperor (1871–1908) and Qing statesman Li Hongzhang (1823–1901).

This chapter examines the complex processes by which Yokohama Chinese became *huaqiao* even as they integrated into Yokohama society. The years 1912–32 saw the establishment and consolidation of the Republic of China (ROC), and the subsequent linking of overseas Chinese communities to the new state. By the end of these two decades, the Chinese state—spurred in part by conflicts with Japan—would develop both the justifications and institutional means to control their overseas citizens. This process was also experienced by Chinese worldwide. After the 1911 Chinese revolution, institutions at home and abroad that were based in subnational affiliations, such as guild halls (*huiguan*) and native-place associations (*tongxianghui*), flourished in new roles promoting nationalism and modernization.[3] Nationalists successfully stitched these groups into a nested hierarchy under the emergent nation. National identity, heretofore the rhetoric of selected elites in Yokohama Chinatown, gradually became more deeply embedded in social life. Chinese now integrated into Yokohama society more explicitly as representatives of the Chinese nation.

This overall process was not unique to Chinese nationalism. By the end of the nineteenth century, Japanese were also arriving at a consensus that ethnic groups should be sovereign political units. In the hands of Japanese ethnologists such as Yanagita Kunio (1875–1962), Japan's local cultures and histories were similarly recast as foundations of a national culture.[4] And in the aftermath of the First World War, discourses of ethnic nationalism became extremely influential worldwide.[5]

Across the same time frame, ethnic-national identity acquired a much stronger legal and institutional basis.[6] The imperative to regulate overseas Chinese played a role in the creation of *jus sanguinis* nationality laws in both

---

3. Kuhn, *Chinese among Others*, p. 30; Goodman, "New Culture, Old Habits," pp. 77, 80.

4. Kimura, "Kyōdoshi, chihōshi, chiikishi kenkyū," pp. 12–15.

5. Doak, *History of Nationalism in Modern Japan*, p. 10.

6. Kuhn, *Chinese among Others*, p. 249. Clarification regarding the use of the term "ethnicity," rather than "race," is necessary. Philip Kuhn argues that Chinese overseas nationalism in the early twentieth century portrayed the Chinese "nation" as "a 'race' in danger of being extinguished in a social-Darwinian battle for survival." The concept of race (Chinese: *zhong*; Japanese: *shu*), however, was used by Chinese and Japanese pan-Asianists to include both Chinese and Japanese peoples. In the Japanese context, then, Chinese were understood as an ethnicity within the yellow race.

countries. The Japanese citizenship law of 1899 was strictly patrilineal. Although Japanese officials initially considered opening citizenship to those of foreign ancestry born in Japan, citizenship was deliberately restricted to bloodline in order to exclude Chinese immigrants and their descendants. Naturalization provisions were so onerous that only 303 people naturalized from April 1899 to June 1950.[7] The debate over mixed residence for the Chinese thus exerted an influence on the form of social closure instituted in Japan.

Similarly, the Chinese citizenship law of 1909 was *jus sanguinis* and informed by an understanding of the Chinese as an ethnic community. Coming less than three years before the collapse of the Qing regime, the law was a belated attempt to establish internationally recognized guidelines for Chinese citizenship. It decreed that naturalization to foreign citizenship would not be granted without a discharge from the Qing government, suggesting that the law was also intended to prevent the large-scale naturalization of overseas Chinese and the attenuation of their political attachment to the homeland.[8] In this way, both Chinese and Japanese citizenship laws were responses to overseas Chinese settlement.

With the creation of the ROC in 1912, the new Chinese state attempted to intervene more deeply into the affairs of its overseas nationals through its diplomatic offices. There were limits, however, to the influence the state could exert among the acculturated and socially integrated members of the Yokohama Chinatown community. Native place, dialect, and class differences continued to divide this community. Political schisms among the leadership of Republican China made it especially difficult for national institutions to bridge such subnational differences. In particular, the young government split over the political rivalry between revolutionary ideologue Sun Yatsen and the first president, military leader Yuan Shikai (1859–1916).[9] In 1913, Sun and his Nationalist Party (GMD) launched their Second Revolution

---

7. Guo, *Zainichi kakyō*, p. 75; Morris-Suzuki, *Re-inventing Japan*, pp. 189–90. Although post–World War II Japanese citizenship law is still *jus sanguinis*, its naturalization procedures have become more streamlined and permissive. In 1994 alone, 11,146 people naturalized as Japanese citizens. Citizenship in postwar Japan will be discussed in chap. 5 and the conclusion.

8. Tsai, "The Chinese Nationality Law," pp. 407–8. This law was inherited by the ROC after the collapse of the Qing in 1912.

9. Yuan was commander of the Beiyang Army, the most powerful military force in China.

against Yuan's regime. When Yuan crushed the insurrection, Sun fled China and began another stint as an expatriate in Japan and elsewhere. This ouster of China's most prominent revolutionary organizer brought a crisis of political legitimacy for the ROC, which culminated in disunity and warlord rule by the end of the decade.

Schools continued to serve as markers of community disunion, and the number of Chinese-run schools in Yokohama proliferated, rather than consolidated, in the years after 1911. The two largest schools in Yokohama's Chinatown, the Datong xuexiao and the Hengbin huaqiao xuexiao, conducted classes in Cantonese, but were divided by political allegiance and economic status. After 1912, the Datong xuexiao became linked to the Chinese Progressive Party (Zhonghua jinbu dang), an outgrowth of Kang Youwei's defunct constitutional reform movement and, more recently, Yuan Shikai's support base.[10] On the other hand, the Huaqiao xuexiao, founded by Sun Yatsen's Revolutionary Alliance (Tongmeng hui), continued on as a wing of the GMD, supported by working- and middle-class Chinese.[11] The differing sources of political legitimacy displayed at the two schools were apparent even to Japanese observers. Whereas a plaque at the Datong xuexiao bore the words of President Yuan Shikai, "Become our new people" (*zuo wo xin min*), the Huaqiao xuexiao displayed Sun Yatsen's slogan, "Cultivate ability for the country" (*wei guo yu cai*).[12]

In one revealing episode, on October 10, 1913, five hundred members of the Chinatown elite gathered at the Chinese Guild to celebrate the second anniversary of the founding of the ROC. Principal Liu Lianfu of the Datong xuexiao delivered a speech in Cantonese, before ceding the floor to Principal Miao Qinfang of the Huaqiao xuexiao. When Miao began his speech, however, students from the Datong xuexiao stood up and drowned him out with calls of "We don't understand Mandarin!" At a loss to stop the shouting match that ensued, the Chinese Guild organizers called an end to the speech and moved on to the next item on the program.[13] This was a petty dispute, to be sure, but one that implied competing visions of an authentic national

---

10. Kanome, *Nankinmachi*, p. 14. In 1916, Wu Tingjia concurrently held the posts of principal at the Datong xuexiao and president at the Yokohama branch of the Chinese Progressive Party.

11. *BX*, pp. 71–74.

12. Kanome, *Nankinmachi*, p. 23.

13. "Minkoku sōritsu shukuga: Shukuga no seki ni mo nanboku shōtotsu," *YBS*, Oct. 11, 1913, p. 1.

culture. The ROC had recently sanctioned Mandarin as its official language, but could not force all overseas Chinese to respect this decision.[14]

Outside observers were at times bemused by this political rivalry. Kanome Shōzō observed two Chinese schoolchildren fighting in the street in 1916. As he described in his newspaper columns, one student cried, "You Yuan Shikai! You thief!" The other retorted that one should not speak ill of the president. Kanome wryly remarked that these children were honest mirrors of adult society around them.[15] For Chinese in Yokohama, national affiliation was clouded by confusion over the legitimate locus of authority.

By the 1920s, however, many of these divisions among Chinese in Yokohama would recede in importance as the GMD brought most of China under unified political control.[16] Burgeoning Sino-Japanese conflict and rivalry also spurred a greater acceptance of Chinese unity and patriotism. These political developments allowed the ROC to pursue more invasive and active interventions into overseas Chinese communities. The experiences of the Yokohama Chinese during the tragic 1923 Kantō earthquake and Japan's invasion of Manchuria in 1931-32 further convinced them that their treatment as foreigners in Japan depended greatly on the active protection of their homeland government.

Chinese Food, Baseball, and the Culture of Modern Japan

The various cultures of Chinatown were part of Yokohama's cosmopolitan tapestry. Kanome noted that young Chinese women who graduated from the coeducational schools in Chinatown "spoke fluent Japanese and wore fashionable half-coats." Like the Japanese "modern girl" of the 1920s, these

---

14. Tsang, *Nationalism in School Education in China*, p. 66. Earlier that same year, the ROC had convened an Association for the Unification of National Pronunciation (Duyin tongyi hui) that authorized Mandarin as the official language.

15. Kanome, *Nankinmachi*, p. 20.

16. Yuan Shikai died in 1916, and in the power vacuum that followed, a host of warlords deployed their armies to seize territories that they then ruled as de facto autonomous states. Meanwhile, Sun Yatsen and his GMD established a base in Guangzhou, in the far south of China. After Sun Yatsen's death in 1925, his protégé Chiang Kaishek (1887-1975) assumed control of the GMD, and in 1926 launched his Northern Expedition to bring the warlords to heel. By the summer of 1928, Chiang Kaishek's armies had seized the city of Beijing and succeeded in uniting much of China's territory under one government.

women were liberated and educated; their "thirst for knowledge had taught them they are equal to men."[17] Affluent Chinese sometimes conducted their weddings in a culturally hybrid fashion, with guests dressed in Chinese and Western formal wear and presided over by a Christian preacher.[18] However, the Yokohama Chinese contributed most prominently to the culture of modern Japan through Chinese food and baseball. In a memoir written in the late 1930s, Yokohama-born journalist and local historian Kayama Kazan (1877–1944) recalled the Chinatown of his youth as a place awash in the smell of garlic and cooking pork. Like other Yokohama-ites, Kayama would often go to Chinatown for meals. In an anecdote that combined two quint-essentially Yokohama leisure activities, he recalled going to eat *shūmai* after a baseball game and setting a record of forty-eight *shūmai* in one sitting. Kayama declared that for the plebeian masses, these pork dumplings "reigned supreme"; around 1910, they only cost one sen each and were so big you couldn't eat them in a single bite, "not like the Japanized versions you see now [in the late 1930s]."[19] Baseball and Chinese food were quotidian elements of Yokohama life before they spread throughout Japan as markers of cultural modernization, and the Yokohama Chinese participated in popularizing both.

CHINESE FOOD AND MULTICULTURAL GASTRONOMY

Food scholar Katarzyna J. Cwiertka points out that the introduction of foreign cuisines, far from adulterating a Japanese national culture, aided in its consolidation. The late nineteenth-century entry of Western cuisine (*yōshoku*) allowed Japanese to construct a homogenized Japanese cuisine (*washoku*) that encompassed Japan's diverse, local foodways.[20] In relational fashion, Chinese cuisine—*shina ryōri* or *chūka ryōri*—also emerged as a genre of knowledge

---

17. Silverberg, "Modern Girl as Militant"; Kanome, *Nankinmachi*, p. 30. The Japanese modern girl, or *moga*, was a media-disseminated depiction of a new generation of women in the 1920s who were fashion-conscious, liberated, and economically independent.

18. Kanome, *Nankinmachi*, pp. 14–15.

19. Kayama, "Nankinmachi o egaku," pp. 17–19. One hundred sen is equal to one yen. Although his memoir is undated, Kayama's reference to a long-term war with China suggests that it was originally written around 1939. The author is also known by his birth name, Michinosuke.

20. Cwiertka, *Modern Japanese Cuisine*, p. 12.

and taste during these decades. Previous imports from China—soy sauce, tofu, miso, chopsticks—were already integrated into Japan's culinary culture, but this newly defined conception of Chinese food was marked and maintained as foreign.[21] The categorization of foreign and domestic foods simultaneously produced a coherent Japanese national cuisine, each comprising one leg of what Cwiertka has termed a "Japanese-Western-Chinese tripod."[22]

Japan's multicultural gastronomy helped nurture a modern mass society, with a new consciousness of Japan's place in the world. By the first two decades of the twentieth century, Japanese in larger cities were regularly consuming Chinese and Western cuisine at specialty restaurants. These national consumption practices can be traced to foreign contact in more localized contexts. Japanese elites gained an appreciation for French cooking at banquets held at select venues in Tokyo, and Japanese of somewhat humbler background became acquainted with American and English dishes at treaty port hotels, restaurants, and foreign residences.[23] Likewise for Chinese cuisine, port cities were points of entry. Chinese in Nagasaki during the Tokugawa period introduced elements of their native cuisine, which led to a short-lived boom in a Sino-Japanese hybrid cuisine known as *shippoku ryōri*. Chinese cuisine in Yokohama, already recognized as a feature of the city by the 1880s, had a wider and more lasting impact. Many of the constituent elements of Chinese cuisine in Japan passed first through the hands and kitchens of the Yokohama Chinese. Bao Tang's restaurant Hakugatei in Isezaki-chō, the first restaurant in Japan to serve *shūmai*, introduced some enduring innovations to this Cantonese dumpling. Sometime during the 1910s, Bao Tang's son Bogong devised the shrimp *shūmai* for his predominantly Japanese clientele, which quickly spawned competitors.[24] In later

---

21. Watanabe, "1920-nendai no 'shina ryōri' (1)," pp. 21–22.

22. Cwiertka, *Modern Japanese Cuisine*, p. 139; Cwiertka, "Eating the World," pp. 90–91. According to Cwiertka, these three poles of Japan's culinary culture manifested the legacies of Japan's tradition, "universal" modernity, and Asian empire. Barak Kushner concurs, explaining that "Japanese foodways grew out of both a dialogue within Japan's colonial empire and a discourse bent on separating the concept of national food away from and in distinction to China" (Kushner, "Imperial Cuisines in Taishō Foodways," p. 145).

23. Cwiertka, *Modern Japanese Cuisine*, pp. 15–18, 36–42.

24. Sugawara, *Nihon no kakyō*, p. 24. *Shūmai* are traditionally made from pork, but Bao Bogong began using locally caught shrimp during the early Taishō years.

years *shūmai* of various forms would be served across Japan. Yokohama Chinese also helped spread the appeal of *shinasoba*, the wheat noodles served in soup that would later be known as ramen. In 1910, Ozaki Kan'ichi, a former official at the Yokohama customs house, hired thirteen Cantonese cooks from Yokohama and opened a restaurant in Tokyo. This establishment, Rairaiken, was perhaps the first Japanese-owned restaurant to serve *shinasoba*.[25]

The 1910s then were a watershed for Chinese cuisine in Japan, as Chinese eateries, often managed by Japanese but employing Chinese staff, began proliferating in most major cities.[26] By 1923, there were more than one thousand cheap Chinese eateries in Tokyo, where the most popular foods were *shinasoba*, *shūmai*, fried rice, and fried noodles.[27] As Kayama's memoir suggests, Japanese tastes for Chinese food spread first among the lower classes who were attracted by its low cost. In the 1920s, Huang Lixiang ran a restaurant in Yokohama called Qizhen, and confirmed that the most popular dishes at the time were *shūmai* and *shinasoba*, costing two and ten sen respectively.[28] In comparison, noodles at Japanese restaurants typically ranged from ten to forty sen. Western cuisine items were considerably more expensive. At the Tokyo Mitsukoshi department store in 1925, ice cream alone cost fifteen sen and a sandwich thirty sen.[29] Many Chinese residents in Yokohama responded to the popularity of Chinese noodles by opening noodle shops, particularly after the 1923 earthquake destroyed the city's banks and port facilities and left few viable business options. Huang recalls that, as the city rebuilt, even the Shanghainese tailors and barbers gave up their trades and opened *shinasoba* shops.[30]

---

25. Cwiertka, *Modern Japanese Cuisine*, p. 144. Kushner, *Social and Culinary History of Ramen*, pp. 156–58. However, competing stories about the introduction of ramen to Japan variously point to restaurants in the cities of Sapporo and Kitakata.

26. Kushner, "Imperial Cuisines in Taishō Foodways," pp. 146, 155. Before the 1910s, Japanese outside of Yokohama apparently held Chinese restaurants in low esteem. As quoted by Kushner, Kodama Kagai (1874–1943) wrote in 1911 how "sad and decrepit" these establishments were and decried the way the "stench of pig fat" clung to them.

27. Cwiertka, "Eating the World," pp. 103–4.

28. CKK and YKS, *Yokohama kakyō no kioku*, p. 20.

29. Cwiertka, *Modern Japanese Cuisine*, pp. 52–53.

30. CKK and YKS, *Yokohama kakyō no kioku*, p. 24.

Several other factors furthered the incorporation and naturalization of Chinese cuisine in Japan. Chinese food became important to military menus, an urbanized workforce, and the popular imagination of Japan's empire. Military planners made efforts to spread knowledge of nutrition and provide healthy meals to children and recruits, and promoted foreign cuisine along the way. Western items like cutlet, stew, and rice curry were useful to these planners, because such foods were an economical way to fulfill the military's high-calorie requirements. From 1923, the army also introduced Chinese dishes for their similarly high meat and fat content, and because they used ingredients like soy sauce and rice that were familiar to recruits. By the start of the Second Sino-Japanese War in 1937, curries, croquettes, and Chinese stir-fries were among Japanese soldiers' favorite dishes.[31] Economic and social trends also laid the foundations for the incorporation of Chinese foods; urbanization and industrialization led to greater demand for cheap and calorie-rich foods in Japan's cities. The rising number of labor migrants from China also helped introduce those foods to the Japanese working masses at inexpensive restaurants and food stalls.[32] Finally, these trends merged with a growing interest in Asia as the site of Japan's imperial expansion in the 1920s and 1930s. To Japanese of the time, as Cwiertka argues, "Chinese food and drink translated colonialism into a concrete experience."[33]

Cookbooks and recipes also aided the spread and naturalization of Chinese cooking. From the 1920s, cookbooks for Chinese cuisine proliferated rapidly in Japan.[34] Nakamura Toshiko's 1927 Chinese cookbook, *Katei de dekiru oishii shina ryōri* (Delicious Chinese food you can prepare at home), opened with a declaration that the book is a response to the rising popularity of Chinese food over Western food and the accompanying interest in preparing it at home. Nakamura herself believed Chinese cuisine to be the most delicious in the world.[35] These and other works also highlighted the popularity of *shūmai*; Nakamura included recipes for pork, crab, and shrimp

---

31. Cwiertka, *Modern Japanese Cuisine*, pp. 79–84.
32. Kushner, "Imperial Cuisines in Taishō Foodways," pp. 157–58.
33. Cwiertka, "Eating the World," p. 114; Watanabe, "Zasshi 'Eiyō to ryōri,'" p. 21; Kushner, "Imperial Cuisines in Taishō Foodways," p. 159.
34. Cwiertka, "Eating the World," p. 101.
35. Nakamura, *Katei de dekiru shina ryōri*, pp. 1–2.

versions of the dumpling.[36] Pioneering scholar and promoter of Chinese cuisine Yamada Masahei also published a recipe for *shūmai* in the July 1925 issue of *Fujin no tomo* (Woman's friend).[37] Similarly, the March 6, 1928, edition of the national paper *Yomiuri shinbun* carried an article titled "Delicious *Shūmai*, the Way to Make It—and Eat It." As the article noted, *shūmai* had become such a trendy dish that laypeople were trying their hands at making it.

A rare example, for the time, of a Chinese writing about Chinese food for a Japanese audience was Bao Bogong. Bao contributed a set of recipes to the March 1936 issue of the magazine *Eiyō to ryōri* (Nutrition and cooking), which began the previous year as an outgrowth of the Home Nutrition Research Association (Katei shokuyō kenkyū kai).[38] Bao's recipes, in an article titled "Some Good Chinese Dishes for Winter," were meat-oriented, with pork, chicken, and ham playing central roles; they reinforced the notion that Chinese cooking was nutritious in the hearty, caloric sense prized by military planners (see Appendix). Bao did not, however, offer his family recipe for *shūmai*. Readers would have to wait until the December 1936 issue for Yamada Masahei's exceedingly detailed instructions on how to prepare pork and crab versions of it.[39] Given the nature of the journal, it is plausible that Bao participated in the association's classes and worked directly with Yamada. One year before the outbreak of full-scale war between China and

---

36. Ibid., pp. 23–26.

37. Watanabe, "1920-nendai no 'shina ryōri' (1)," p. 23.

38. Bao Bogong, "Fuyu ni oishii shina ryōri," pp. 23–26; Watanabe, "Zasshi 'Eiyō to ryōri'," pp. 11–12, 20; Kagawa, "Sōkan ni atatte," pp. 2–4. The husband and wife team of Kagawa Shōzō and Aya established the association in 1933, which later evolved into the Kagawa Education Institute of Nutrition; they were involved in vitamin research and hoped to educate the public in healthy eating and illness prevention. Kagawa Aya became famous for demonstrating that eating rice with the husk intact, instead of polished white rice, would prevent beriberi. She was also an early promoter of a version of the food groups. Students and former students published the journal *Eiyō to ryōri* to provide print versions of their cooking lessons. Although the journal only had a distribution of several thousand in the 1930s and 1940s, Watanabe Takahiro argues that it had a major impact among cooking instructors and culinary specialists.

39. Watanabe, "Zasshi 'Eiyō to ryōri'," pp. 11–12, 15; Yamada, "Shūmai to shinasoba," pp. 22–25. This article was just one of 371 that Yamada would contribute to the journal over his lifetime.

FIG. 3.1. An advertisement for Hakugatei's *shūmai*, "a Yokohama specialty." Source: *Yokohama maichō shinpō*, November 15, 1927, p. 3.

Japan, the two were actively popularizing Chinese cuisine in kitchens and restaurants around Japan.

Noodles and *shūmai* were working-class favorites that brought Japanese diners to Yokohama Chinatown, and Chinatown chefs were instrumental in bringing these dishes to Japanese diners in other cities. But at the same time, the growing popularity of Chinese cooking around Japan also ignited Yokohama pride in its Chinese restaurants. Yokohama residents zealously maintained the distinctiveness and superiority of their Chinese food, in opposition to the homogenizing imperatives of a national culinary culture. In light of the growing national popularity of *shūmai*, Bao Bogong regularly ran advertisements in Japanese newspapers touting his *shūmai* as a Yokohama specialty (fig. 3.1). The city also showed pride in its high-end Chinese establishments.[40] Two prominent examples were Heichinrō, originally founded in 1885 and potentially the oldest still-operating Chinese restaurant

---

40. These restaurants served banquet-style meals—meaning meals priced according to the number of tables and courses desired rather than individual dishes.

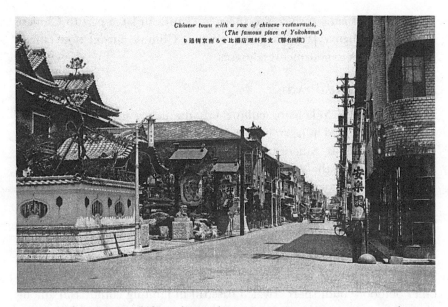

Chinese town with a row of chinese restaurants,
(The famous place of Yokohama)
り通街京南るせ比據店理料那支 〔勝名濱横〕

FIG. 3.2. The Heianrō (left) and Manshinrō (center) restaurants, postcard, 1935. Courtesy of Yokohama kaikō shiryōkan.

in the 1930s, and Manshinrō (Wanxinlou), which opened in 1933.[41] A *Yokohama bōeki shinpō* article from July 23, 1934, presented these two establishments as the old and new faces of Chinatown's Chinese cuisine; they were the "true pride of Yokohama [*hontō no Hama jiman*]" because Chinese restaurants of this caliber could be found in neither Tokyo nor Osaka.

This boast by the *Yokohama bōeki shinpō* suggests the rise of a broader Japanese interest in Chinese banquet fare, which enjoyed a small boom in the 1930s. In those years, a range of high-end Chinese restaurants of this kind opened in Tokyo, often decorated in elaborate chinoiserie style.[42] And in Yokohama, a Japanese man named Numada Yasuzō opened the palatial Heianrō (Ping'anlou) on the edge of Chinatown in 1935. The chefs there were Chinese, naturally enough, but the restaurant was housed in a grand, Japanese-style building (fig. 3.2). These Japanese-run restaurants followed in the footsteps of luxurious establishments that had been operating in

---

41. YKS, *Yokohama Chūkagai 150-nen*, p. 47.
42. Cwiertka, "Eating the World," p. 114.

Yokohama Chinatown since the 1880s.[43] Thanks in large part to Chinese living in Yokohama, Japanese appreciation of Chinese cuisine now ranged from cheap eats to gourmet restaurants.

Another pillar of Yokohama culture was the newly introduced game of baseball, first played in Japan by Americans in the Yokohama foreign settlement. By the 1880s, American games of baseball were supplanting English cricket matches at the Yokohama Athletic Club. Meanwhile, at least from the 1870s, American educators Horace Wilson, F. W. Strange, G. H. Mudgett, and Leroy Janes were busy promoting baseball at Japanese schools.[44] One Japanese school in particular, the First Higher School, contributed greatly to the game's popularity in Japan when their team soundly defeated the Yokohama Athletic Club team in a much-heralded international contest in 1896.[45] By the turn of the twentieth century, as Donald Roden argues, no other outdoor youth sport "rivaled baseball in igniting enthusiasm among players, spectators, and readers of an expanding popular press."[46]

The victories of the First Higher School team contributed greatly to Japan's sense of national dignity because baseball was more than just a game. As an American import during the treaty-port era, it especially inflamed the ardor of working-class Japanese when Japanese teams proved they could defeat their American counterparts. Moreover, as it caught on in Japan, promoters lauded the game for fostering the so-called Japanese virtues of spirit, honor, and courage. These views closely followed those of late nineteenth-century Americans and English, who similarly linked excellence in sport with national greatness and civilizational superiority. Such particularist arguments aside, competitive sport served as a point of contact between societies and, at the very least, showed that the two sides could play the same game and by the same rules.[47]

---

43. CKK and YKS, *Yokohama kakyō no kioku*, p. 66. Yokohama-born Nakaji Kiyoshi (b. 1920) recalled from his youth that Yokohama residents would dine at these restaurants on special occasions.

44. Roden, "Baseball and the Quest for National Dignity," pp. 518–19.

45. Ibid., pp. 521–24; Whiting, *You Gotta Have Wa*, pp. 27–34.

46. Roden, "Baseball and the Quest for National Dignity," p. 513.

47. One should not assume that harmony was a natural outcome of these competitions. Donald Roden, in his study of baseball exchanges between Japan and the

Yokohama Chinese learned the game as well, and participated in city, prefectural, and Japan-wide tournaments through school-affiliated or community teams.[48] Moreover, they also played for national pride, and their involvement was similarly understood to carry international importance. Chinese teams gained prominence in Yokohama from around 1905, when Cantonese teenager Liang Fuchu (1891–1968) founded his first baseball team.[49] In later years, this team would be known as the Chinese Athletics Club (Zhonghua tiyu hui, hereafter CAC), and would sponsor a variety of other athletic activities.[50] On the baseball diamond, the CAC twice won glory for the Chinese community, capturing the Yokohama City pennant in 1922 and 1930. Liang himself would later become known as "the father of Chinese baseball," and his lifelong dedication to the sport was attributable to his upbringing in Yokohama.[51] After he arrived in the city from Xiangshan, Guangdong Province, at age ten, he was deeply marked by baseball's popularity in the city and galvanized by the consistently poor performance of Chinese teams. In a stroke of luck, his team's fortunes were boosted by the visit of a Chinese-American player from Hawaii named Luo An in 1906. Liang convinced him to remain in Yokohama both to coach baseball and to teach English at the Huaqiao xuexiao.[52]

In the first annual Kanagawa Prefecture Baseball Tournament of 1917, Liang's CAC team made an impressive showing. There was no mistaking the team's national affiliation; they took to the field wearing uniforms emblazoned "Chinese" on the front, and the Chinese consul general attended their more important games. But nationality was no impediment to participation. Thousands turned out for their May 11, 1918, game with YMCA, a hotly anticipated "international" match, according to a local paper. There was

---

United States in the late Meiji period, is not sanguine on this point, but notes that these international games "perhaps" created "a shared, bilateral culture of home runs and stolen bases in the clear interest of friendly relations between the two nations" (Roden, "Baseball and the Quest for National Dignity," pp. 519–20, 532).

48. Reaves, *Taking in a Game*, p. 34. In China, Western and Chinese educators spread a similar interest in developing physical fitness in the 1880s, and by 1895 three Chinese schools were fielding baseballs teams.

49. Liu Yi, "Ji xianbei Liang Fuchu," pp. 8–16.

50. "Chūka marason," *YBS*, June 24, 1918, p. 3. The club sponsored events such as an annual foot race, which was inaugurated on the morning of June 23, 1918.

51. Liang Youwen, "Yi xianfu," pp. 22–29; Itō Izumi, "Ryō-ke," p. 52.

52. Liu Yi, "Ji xianbei Liang Fuchu," pp. 8–16.

a smattering of applause and cheers for the Chinese as the lead changed back and forth and the CAC team stole ten bases. In the end, they won the hard-fought game six to five.[53] Their subsequent game with the Shōyū team in June 1918 deeply impressed a Japanese correspondent from the *Yokohama bōeki shinpō*, who declared, "Today, when many teams lack the drive to compete, I find it extremely ironic that the ones who demonstrate the most spirit [*iki*] are Chinese." "Spirit," apparently, was a particularly Japanese virtue on the baseball diamond. The journalist also applauded the "sportsman-like attitude" of the Chinese, though they ultimately lost the game.[54] Liang himself was a model of sportsmanship. He served as one of ten umpires in the fifth annual Kanagawa prefectural tournament in 1922, demonstrating his zeal for promoting the sport and the respect he received from the wider Yokohama community.[55]

Chinese school teams also participated in local tourneys, and both Datong xuexiao and Huaqiao xuexiao fielded formidable teams. During the 1920 National Youth Baseball Tournament, the Huaqiao xuexiao team advanced to the Yokohama City finals in the higher school division (*kōtōka*). There, they fell to Honchō Elementary School by a score of ten to two. The Datong xuexiao team, coached by Liang Fuchu, fared even better in the elementary school division (*jinjōka*). Dramatically and perhaps ironically, they qualified to represent Yokohama City on the national stage by defeating all local opponents. Battling for Chinese and Yokohama pride alike, they nevertheless made a quick exit by losing their first game at the national tourney in Osaka.[56]

Two years later in November 1922, Liang's CAC team finally won the Yokohama City championship (fig. 3.3).[57] By then, they had established themselves as powerhouses in Yokohama. They advanced to the semifinals of the

---

53. "Yosen shiai daiichi nichi," *YBS*, May 11, 1918, p. 5; "Yosen shiai no daiichi nichi," *YBS*, May 12, 1918, p. 5.

54. "Yakyū taikai daini nichi," *YBS*, June 23, 1918, p. 5; "Yakyū taikai daisan nichi," *YBS*, June 30, 1918, p. 5.

55. "Honsha shusai daigo kai kenka yakyū taikai," *YBS*, May 7, 1922, p. 5.

56. Itō Izumi, "Ryō-ke," p. 52. YKS, *Kaikō kara shinsai made*, p. 49; *BX*, p. 72; "Yokohama yosen shiai," *Jiji shinpō*, July 13, 1920, p. 11; "Yokohama kesshō shiai," *Jiji shinpō*, July 16, 1920, p. 11; "Zenkoku yūshōsen hajimaru," *Jiji shinpō*, Aug. 7, 1920, p. 6. Their non-Japanese status did not trouble baseball fans in Osaka, where they were welcomed by cheering crowds.

57. Liang Fuchu, *Bangqiu yundong*, p. 10.

FIG. 3.3. The Chinese Athletics Club after winning the Yokohama City baseball tournament in November 1922. Liang Fuchu is in the back row, on the left. Photograph courtesy of Liang Youyi.

prefectural tournament in 1923, before falling to perennial rival Shōyū.[58] This early summer campaign proved to be the last that Liang shared with his five brothers. Two months later, a massive earthquake struck the city and the world literally came down around them. It would be facile to conclude that these international matches contributed to greater harmony between China and Japan, but they did carry local significance. Chinese participation in these athletic events was an index of how ethnically inclusive and cohesive the Yokohama community could be.

Integrating the Diaspora: The Kantō Earthquake and the Manchurian Incident

The members of this mixed local community, however, lived through an era of deteriorating relations between China and Japan. From the 1910s

---

58. "Chūka no zensen mo munashiku, shōyū katsu," *YBS*, June 25, 1923, p. 5.

through 1920s, China and Japan engaged in an escalating rivalry that would lead to military conflict by the start of the 1930s. The cooperative nation-building project between China and Japan—which had been led by men like Sun Yatsen, Liang Qichao, Ōkuma Shigenobu, and Inukai Tsuyoshi—foundered after Ōkuma delivered the Twenty-one Demands of 1915.[59] Chinese students denounced the Demands, attacked the Japanese cabinet's 1917 decision to extend loans to the Beijing warlord government, and launched a wide-ranging protest movement on May 4, 1919. Chinese exchange students in Japan replicated these homeland movements and repeatedly demonstrated in Tokyo. Rising labor migration from China to Japan also generated grave social tensions.

Chinese labor migration, a bugbear of the Japanese public in the 1890s, was on the rise in the 1910s into the early 1920s. The measures enacted in the summer of 1899 to exclude Chinese workers did not bar Chinese traveling salesmen from entry to Japan because they were classified as merchants.[60] Many, however, changed to construction, factory, and other restricted occupations after entry. Moreover, Japanese labor brokers were permitted to hire migrant laborers to deal with a worker shortage during Japan's World War I economic boom. As a result, the total population of Chinese in Japan rose from 8,529 to 22,427 from 1910 to 1920, swelling with new groups of laborers from Zhejiang and Shandong Provinces.[61]

---

59. Ōkuma, formerly a supporter of the Datong xuexiao, became prime minister for the second time in April 1914. With most of Europe at war, his cabinet saw an opportunity to strengthen Japan's position in China by issuing an ultimatum to Yuan Shikai's government in Beijing, calling for economic rights in Manchuria and Inner Mongolia; joint Sino-Japanese management of strategic coal and iron works; and most humiliating to Chinese sovereignty, the stationing of Japanese police and economic advisers throughout northern China. Yuan's government accepted these conditions, but only after the most egregious clauses were dropped. Japan gained little but the enmity of Chinese society, which rallied nationalist fury around the country in protests and boycotts.

60. Japan's government maintained this loophole because they feared a reciprocal move to limit the entry of Japanese merchants into China.

61. Oda, *Nihon ni zairyū suru Chūgokujin*, pp. 23–27; Niki, *Shinsaika no Chūgokujin gyakusatsu*, p. 135. These two linguistically distinct regions had been deeply affected by political upheaval and produced labor migrants with different specialties. Migrants from Shandong typically sold medicines or fans, or were craftsmen who mended bowls. Those from Zhejiang hawked umbrellas or locally quarried green soapstone prized for seals or sculptures.

After the conclusion of the war, Japan's economy sank into depression, and labor disputes multiplied. In this context, Chinese laborers often became scapegoats for larger economic ills and triggered strong anti-Chinese sentiment. Violent confrontations between Chinese and Japanese laborers in the Tokyo-Yokohama area were not uncommon from 1915 to 1923.[62] Social and economic pressure spurred the Japanese government to respond in a heavy-handed manner, raising the stringency of requirements for entry into Japanese ports and deporting Chinese laborers who had already arrived.[63] Tokyo-based Chinese activists responded to this mistreatment of their conationals by founding the Mutual Aid Association of Chinese in Japan (Qiaori gongji hui) in September 1922. Founded by a young activist named Wang Xitian (1896–1923), this organization sought to defend Chinese laborers from Japanese government policy and antagonism from Japanese society.[64]

Yokohama Chinese did not participate in this organization because, by and large, the new labor migrants did not settle in Chinatown. Despite the rapid rise in total population of Chinese in Japan, the Chinese population of Yokohama City remained flat at around four thousand. Moreover, labor migrants from other parts of China were not the immediate concern of the affluent, acculturated, and predominantly Cantonese community of Yokohama Chinatown. Likewise, diplomatic crises failed to move them to action.[65] For instance, the May 12, 1918, edition of the *Yokohama bōeki shinpō* reported that 180 Chinese had boarded a ship in Yokohama to return to China in protest of the Japanese cabinet's China policy. On that very same page, the newspaper reported the exploits of Liang Fuchu's CAC baseball team against

---

62. Niki, *Shinsai ka no Chūgokujin gyakusatsu*, pp. 136–37; "Nankin ryōri no fukuro tataki," *YBS*, Oct. 1, 1915, p. 1; "Takashima-eki kōnai de nisshi ninpu tatakau," *YBS*, Feb. 15, 1923, p. 5.

63. Ōsato, "Zainichi Chūgokujin rōdōsha, gyōshōnin," p. 213; Niki, *Shinsai ka no Chūgokujin gyakusatsu*, pp. 137–41.

64. Niki, *Shinsai ka no Chūgokujin gyakusatsu*, pp. 137–38; Ōsato, "Zainichi Chūgokujin rōdōsha, gyōshōnin," p. 213; Ōsato, " 'Yokohama bōeki shinpō' o tōshite miru zairyū Chūgokujin," p. 105.

65. "Kageki Shinajin, hanketsu ni fukusu," *YBS*, Feb. 15, 1921, p. 5. There is but one isolated case of a Cantonese-born resident of Yokohama arrested for publishing extremist political views in this era. It took place in February 1921.

their YMCA rivals.[66] Although politically radical Chinese students were in ferment, long-term Chinese residents carried on with their lives in Yokohama, at least for the time being. The Kantō earthquake of 1923 and the Japanese invasion of Manchuria in 1931–32, however, would alter this situation, as well as their relationship with the homeland government.

"THE DEATH OF OLD YOKOHAMA"

Two minutes before noon on September 1, 1923, a magnitude 7.9 quake centered in Sagami Bay shook Yokohama and Tokyo to ruins. The massive convulsions nearly leveled downtown Yokohama, and much of the city was then incinerated by a swiftly moving conflagration. From this destruction came a new era in the history of Yokohama Chinatown. Antagonism toward Chinese residents flared in the quake's aftermath, the culmination of anxieties and antagonisms that had developed in the preceding years. This experience brought home the message that they were not equal members of local society.

The most vivid English-language record of the tragedy was written by Otis Manchester Poole, an American businessman who settled in Yokohama in 1888. He was in his office at Dodwell & Co., Ltd. when the quake struck, and he watched it bring down almost all of Yokohama's Western-style buildings and destroy Chinatown completely.[67] From what Poole could see, there was little left of the district, and little hope for survivors: "Beyond extended a flat waste of brick, tiles and timber, all that was left of densely populated Chinatown. It seemed to have gone down en masse; as far as one could see there was nothing but gaping walls and smothered roads."[68]

A later survey conducted by the Chinese consulate general determined that the disaster killed more than 1,700 out of 5,721, or close to 30 percent of

---

66. "Yosen shiai no daiichi nichi," *YBS*; "Shina gakusei gojūmei kikoku su," *YBS*, May 23, 1918, p. 5. Another group of fifty Chinese students were reported to be leaving from Yokohama, and sixty more from Kobe on May 23. The students were protesting the cabinet of Prime Minister Terauchi Masatake, who had extended loans to the warlord government of Duan Qirui in return for territorial concessions.

67. "Yokohama no daikenchikubutsu hotondo tōkai shitsukusu," *Ōsaka mainichi*, Sept. 2, 1923, evening edition, p. 6.

68. Poole, *Death of Old Yokohama*, p. 37.

Yokohama's Chinese population.[69] In comparison, 4.8 percent of the aggregate Yokohama population was killed in the disaster, indicating Chinatown's disproportionately lethal conditions; its narrow streets were buried under rubble in moments, leaving no escape path from the fires, a situation that mirrored that of poorer sections of Tokyo.[70] Four were killed when the ROC consulate general fell, including Consul General Chang himself. Chaotic and densely populated Blood Street was completely leveled, where block 136 yielded thirty-two Chinese bodies, one of the highest tolls of any single address.[71] The two main Chinese schools also yielded high casualties: at least twenty-three perished at the Datong xuexiao, and more than eighteen died at the Zhonghua xuexiao.[72] One year after his team electrified Chinatown by winning the Yokohama City pennant, Liang Fuchu lost four close family members in the quake: his brothers Cheng'gen, Chengrong, and Chenglin, the core of his CAC baseball team, as well as his son Youtian.[73]

Like most Western company employees, Poole worked in downtown Yokohama but lived up on the Bluff with his family. Escaping the firestorm that arose from innumerable lunchtime stoves among the rubble and fallen timbers, Poole reunited with his family and spent the night on a friend's yacht. The following day, they joined the throngs of American and European refugees on the steamship *Empress of Australia*.[74]

Some affluent Chinese had a similar evacuation experience. Bao Mingchang, the son of Chinese Guild founder and former compradore Bao Kun, emerged unharmed from the rubble of his employer, the Chartered Bank. He then followed the same route Poole had taken back to his family on the Bluff, but discovered that his father had died in the fire along with thirteen other family members and servants. Bao Mingchang eventually

---

69. Sun, *Huaqiao zhuangkuang*, pp. 6–7.

70. Itō Izumi, "Yokohama daishinsai," pp. 3–5. There was a minor discrepancy between Chinese consular records and Japanese records, the latter of which indicated 2,011 deaths out of a population of 4,647.

71. The only blocks with higher body counts were block 82 with 44 bodies, and block 140 with 49. The latter included the tolls from the Chinese Guild and the Datong xuexiao.

72. Sun, *Huaqiao zhuangkuang*, pp. 13–16.

73. Liang Fuchu, *Bangqiu yundong*, p. 10.

74. Poole, *Death of Old Yokohama*, pp. 40, 43–78.

found safety on board the French steamship *André Lebon*, where he reunited with his wife and child.[75]

Poole and Bao's cases were not typical for the Yokohama population at large, nor ordinary Chinese; not everyone had access to the ships and their stocks of food and water. Poole observed the fate of the vast majority of the survivors when he went ashore the following day. On the waterfront near the Grand Hotel, he had to force his way "through knots of waiting refugees, mostly distressed Chinese."[76] The Chinese were particularly disadvantaged in this regard; Western- and Japanese-operated ships primarily aided their own nationals, and Chinese consular representation was disrupted by the consul general's death.[77] In one case, the Japanese postal vessel *Ajiagō* took aboard four hundred Chinese on September 2 and provided provisions, but demanded they disembark the following day. When the Chinese refused to be sent back to the shore, Wen Delin of the Chinese Chamber of Commerce prevented a riot by paying for passage to Kobe for the entire cohort of Chinese refugees.[78]

Liao Jinzhu, the six-year-old daughter of a Cantonese merchant father and a Japanese mother, was one of the huddled Chinese on the shore. When the quake struck, she was at home with her mother and siblings. She heard her mother cry out "Earthquake!" in Japanese, and moments later she and her family dove under a table as their house collapsed around them. Their neighbors came calling for them and managed to dig a path to the back door. Liao's family then joined a mass of terrified Chinese and Japanese survivors scrambling across the roofs of collapsed buildings for the presumed safety of the waterfront. Along the way, she heard the faint whinnying of horses buried in the rubble underfoot, and when they reached the water, she realized that few of their Chinatown neighbors had made it out.[79]

---

75. Yokohama shiyakusho shishi hensangakari, *Yokohama-shi shinsai shi*, 5:662.

76. Poole, *Death of Old Yokohama*, p. 84.

77. In one case, those on board the *Empress of Australia* took no action when two half-naked men approached the ship until they "noted that the two figures were white, not coppery" (Poole, *Death of Old Yokohama*, p. 101).

78. Kanagawa-ken keisatsu shi hensan iinkai, *Kanagawa-ken keisatsu shi*, 1:785; Itō Izumi, "Yokohama daishinsai," p. 6. For gestures such as this, the Kanagawa Prefectural Police praised Wen Delin for providing outside help to the foreign police (*gaiji keisatsu*) to resolve ethnic conflicts between Chinese and Japanese.

79. Yasui, Chen, and Guo, *Hanshin dai shinsai to kakyō*, pp. 221–23.

In an experience that was perhaps typical for these refugees who escaped Chinatown, they scarcely had any food or water for five days. Liao did not recall receiving any food or water handouts from the authorities. They only "bought" some rice from the wreckage of a half-demolished store, where her mother left behind some cash to prove they were not looters. Liao also received a single rice ball from a generous Shanghainese man on September 5. She and her family huddled under a makeshift shelter until they boarded a ship for Kobe on September 6.[80] According to police records, Yokohama City began distribution of water and food rations on that day, and these rations were made available to foreign residents. But some Chinese memoirs dispute this claim, and recall instead that Yokohama City turned away Chinese survivors.[81] In addition, there was a rumor that a Datong xuexiao student was shot for taking food rations. The Japanese government sought to suppress news of such events, but only exacerbated the atmosphere of fear and uncertainty.[82]

Worse than neglect, Chinese survivors also suffered direct threats from Japanese society. Rumors of marauding Koreans and escaped convicts looting and poisoning wells began spreading within hours after the quake.[83] This situation led to a civilian massacre by vigilantes, police, or army units that killed as many as six thousand ethnic Koreans, out of a population of twenty thousand in the Kantō region.[84] For the Chinese refugees on the waterfront, these rumors sparked fears of being mistaken for so-called lawless Koreans (*futei Senjin*) and lynched in the same manner. One memoir recounted that they were told to wear armbands so they would not be mistaken for Koreans.[85] This was a genuine danger for anyone speaking accented Japanese. Three Chinese construction workers in a rural area of Kanagawa Prefecture

---

80. Ibid., pp. 225–27.

81. Itō Izumi, "Yokohama daishinsai," pp. 5–6; Kanagawa-ken keisatsu shi hensan iinkai, *Kanagawa-ken keisatsu shi*, 1:955. The latter document merely asserts that foreigners were eligible for this assistance, and that between September 26 and October 25 some 416 foreigners received rations. It is not clear if any rations were distributed to foreigners before this date, and most had already evacuated to Kobe or elsewhere by then.

82. Itō Izumi, "Yokohama daishinsai," pp. 6–7.

83. Kanagawa-ken keisatsu shi hensan iinkai, *Kanagawa-ken keisatsu shi*, 1:918–19.

84. Ryang, "Tongue That Divided Life and Death."

85. Yasui, Chen, and Guo, *Hanshin dai shinsai to kakyō*, p. 235.

were indeed killed because they were mistaken for Koreans, and a ROC investigation documented a similar incident in Tokyo.[86]

The danger to Chinese lay not only in being mistaken for Korean. Anxieties over Chinese migration and labor competition revealed themselves in attacks against Chinese laborers across Yokohama and Tokyo in the days and weeks after the quake. Some of the vigilantes implicated in attacks on Koreans even used anti-Chinese epithets, boasting to kill "ten or twenty *chanchan bōzu*."[87] An estimated eight hundred Chinese, mainly contracted laborers from Wenzhou in Zhejiang Province, were killed or wounded by Japanese police, military, and vigilante units in Tokyo and Yokohama.[88] In an incident closely paralleling the murders of Japanese socialists and anarchists, Japanese military police apprehended and summarily executed labor activist Wang Xitian.[89] Although the principal targets of the massacre were migrant workers who were socially, economically, and linguistically distinct from the residents of Chinatown, all Chinese became potential targets.[90] On September 2, a doctor named Huang Wendeng was found drowned in Yokohama harbor with his hands and feet bound. On the same day, a Cantonese restaurant worker was murdered and his body bound to an electric

---

86. Kanagawa-ken keisatsu shi hensan iinkai, *Kanagawa-ken keisatsu shi*, 1:861–62; Zhonghua minguo liu-Ri lingshiguan, *Riben zhenzai cansha huaqiao an*. In Tokyo, a Chinese exchange student named Han Chaochu was beaten unconscious by a mob of Japanese vigilante youths because Han, as displayed on his identification papers, is a common Korean surname.

87. Ryang, "Tongue That Divided Life and Death."

88. Niki, *Shinsai ka no Chūgokujin gyakusatsu*, pp. 33–34, 84; Itō Izumi, "Yokohama daishinsai," p. 8. On September 3, in the worst single incident, 174 Chinese migrant workers were rounded up from their dormitories in Ōjima, Tokyo, taken to a clearing, and beaten to death. Within Kanagawa Prefecture, 79 Chinese were killed and 24 injured in similar acts of violence.

89. The most famous of these cases was the Amakasu Incident of September 16, when Japanese police arrested and murdered feminist writer Itō Noe, her lover, anarchist Ōsugi Sakae, and his young nephew.

90. Ōsato, "Zainichi Chūgokujin rōdōsha, gyōshōnin," p. 214; Niki, *Shinsai ka no Chūgokujin gyakusatsu*, pp. 56, 182. Only 4 of the 79 killed in Kanagawa Prefecture were of Cantonese origin, the dominant linguistic group in Chinatown. The overwhelming majority were from Zhejiang, contracted by Japanese bosses to work in towns surrounding Yokohama. In some cases, however, the antipathy toward low-wage Chinese laborers extended toward their Japanese bosses as well; several Japanese foremen were also killed in these attacks.

pole, a manner of lynching consistent with how Japanese vigilantes dealt with their Korean victims.[91]

The experience of the earthquake and its aftermath polarized the survivors along ethnic-national lines. For the Chinese, these events reinforced their sense of vulnerability as a group in Yokohama. The process of reconstruction likewise provided conditions strongly favorable for Chinese unity because Chinese came to rely more heavily on the ROC consulate general and diplomatic representatives. Yokohama's many Chinese schools were rebuilt as a single institution, and its diverse associations and clubs would thereafter cleave to the authority of the GMD and the Chinese state. Individual lives in the community would be reshaped by these augmented ties to the homeland.

The recovery process naturally bound together diverse Chinese constituencies. Networks connecting Yokohama, Kobe, Shanghai, and Hong Kong became crucial for the evacuation of Chinese. Chinese associations at each port coordinated the flow of information and people. The quake also transformed Liang Fuchu from first baseman, coach, and umpire into a leader of a different sort. After losing four of his family members in the quake, Liang evacuated to Kobe, where he marshaled a team of forty Chinese volunteers to return to Yokohama to recover bodies from the rubble. From September to October, they recovered 982 bodies and buried them in the Yokohama Chinese Cemetery.[92]

Meanwhile, a sixty-seven-year-old Zhejiang Chinese named Kong Yunsheng led the surviving Yokohama Chinese community, a striking turn considering that the prequake population was 73 percent Cantonese.[93] Kong had been the principal of the Zhonghua xuexiao for Sanjiang Chinese, and was the only surviving trustee of the Chinese Guild in the city. He petitioned the ROC ambassador to promote consulate officer Sun Shijie to the position of temporary consul general for Yokohama. Then Sun and Kong, representing the consulate general and the Chinese Guild, respectively, dispensed aid to Chinese survivors and reconstructed documentation for their

---

91. Itō Izumi, "Yokohama daishinsai," p. 10; Poole, *Death of Old Yokohama*, p. 91.

92. Sun, *Hengbin da zhenzai*, p. 6; Itō Izumi, "Yokohama daishinsai," p. 23. This team was descriptively titled the "Kobe-Osaka Huaqiao Aid Group, Yokohama-bound Mission for the Recovery of the Bodies of Our Deceased Friends."

93. YKS, *Kaikō kara shinsai made*, p. 16. Prior to the quake, Zhejiang Chinese only made up 14 percent of the Chinese population.

property, bank accounts, and citizenship status. Although the loss of bank books and seals was an economic inconvenience, these organizations recognized that citizenship papers were desperately needed to protect working-class Chinese who might be mistaken for Koreans and come to harm in the Japanese hinterland. Moreover, given the increasing strictness of Japanese immigration officials toward Chinese, returning to Yokohama would be difficult without proof of former residence.[94]

The process of rebuilding educational institutions also enhanced the long-term cohesion of the community. Kang Youwei and former Datong xuexiao principal Xu Qin independently wrote letters to Japanese allies asking for support, and Kong Yunsheng rallied the Sanjiang Chinese to donate funds for a new school. In September 1925, the Japanese government granted a permit for the unification of three pre-quake Chinese schools.[95] Rebuilding was then greatly aided by a grant of 25,000 yen from the Office of Cultural Affairs for China (Taishi bunka jigyō jimukyoku) of the Japanese Ministry of Foreign Affairs.[96] This unified school was named the Yokohama Chinese Public School (Hengbin zhonghua gongli xuexiao) and opened on October 16, 1926. Reflecting the majority of Chinatown's population, the school used Cantonese as the primary language of instruction, and despite Kong Yunsheng's involvement, the school only offered one class a week in Shanghainese.[97] Memoirs of former students, however, mention the absence of earlier corrosive political rivalries.[98]

---

94. Sun, *Huaqiao zhuangkuang*, pp. 4–5, 26, 28. The Chinese Guild used its funds to transport many survivors back to China. The consulate general negotiated funding from Yokohama City and Kanagawa Prefecture to build a wooden structure on the waterfront to house those who remained in the city or returned.

95. YKS, *Kaikō kara shinsai made*, p. 50. Foreigners required permits to operate schools in Japan; in this instance, the Japanese government consolidated existing permits for the three schools.

96. Itō Izumi, "Yokohama daishinsai," p. 30. Acceptance of this money was not uncontroversial, since it derived from the Boxer Indemnity paid by the Qing Empire to Japan in 1901. Whereas other nations had decided to remit this money directly back to the ROC, Japan preferred to follow America's earlier example of employing the money to foster Chinese education. Some Chinese activists criticized the acceptance of this money because it implied complicity with Japanese cultural imperialism.

97. CKK and YKS, *Yokohama kakyō no kioku*, p. 133.

98. BX, pp. 79–80; Itō Izumi, "1920-nendai nakagoro no Yokohama kakyō shakai," p. 6.

NEW INSTITUTIONS FOR A SINO-JAPANESE COMMUNITY

After the 1923 Kantō earthquake, Japanese aesthetes and writers lamented the death of the exotic and nefarious Chinatown of old. Several nostalgic depictions of its prequake heyday appeared in the mid-1920s, including reprints of Kanome Shōzō's newspaper columns.[99] Meanwhile, sporadic clashes and brawls between working-class Chinese and Japanese continued.[100] Nostalgia and hostility were two sides of the same essentialist coin; in concert, they served to reinforce the consciousness of national differences between Chinese and Japanese. In this social context, Chinese were integrating into Yokohama more explicitly as Chinese nationals, a process that was facilitated by a host of new Chinese institutions.

The 1920s were the years that Chiang Kaishek and the GMD were constructing a unified homeland. This new state power led to a proliferation of organizations in Yokohama representing the Chinese and making them national representatives. A Kanagawa Prefecture survey of foreign-run associations in Yokohama in August 1928 listed twenty Chinese entries; fifteen were founded since 1919, with eight from 1919 to 1923, and seven more from 1924 to 1927.[101] These linked the Chinese community with the ROC, above province-of-origin differences. They were also symptomatic of a new phase of governmental involvement in overseas communities. From this time, the ROC consulate general began asserting its will more directly on the

---

99. Kanome's essays on Chinatown from 1916 were republished in 1924 as a record of this lost world. Similar sentiments were carried in a January 26, 1926, article in the newspaper *Yokohama maichō shinpō*, which expressed great sadness over the fact that "we can no longer experience the gaudy colors and strange smells of Chinatown. . . . if [novelist] Tanizaki Junichirō could see it now he would definitely be shedding great tears." The following year, the newspaper serialized a potboiler detective drama called *Shigure kouta* (A ballad of late autumn rain) set in prequake Chinatown.

100. "Nisshijin no tobaku," *Yokohama maichō shinpō*, Aug. 13, 1926, p. 3; "Yamashita-chō no kenka, Shinajin o naguru," *Yokohama maichō shinpō*, Aug. 17, 1926, p. 2; "Shinajin jūsūmei to hōjin gomei no rantō," *Yokohama maichō shinpō*, Dec. 29, 1926, p. 2. Newspapers frequently reported violent incidents between Chinese and Japanese during these years, including a wild brawl at a secret gambling hall, an altercation on a Chinatown thoroughfare, and a scuffle that began in a Chinatown bathhouse and spilled out into the streets.

101. Kanagawa kenchō, *Warera no Kanagawa-ken*, pp. 538–40.

operation of the Chinese Guild, even dictating the details of its bylaws and elections.[102]

New organizations aided in the rebuilding process even as they helped anchor a Chinese identity tied to the homeland. They also demonstrate the way that Chinese and Japanese adopted the language of international relations in the titles and missions of their new organizations.[103] The Sino-Japanese Society (Chūnichi kyōkai), established in 1919, helped negotiate the Japanese government funds for the new Chinese school and counted the Chinese consul general, the Yokohama City mayor, and Kanagawa Prefecture governor as honorary members. Its avowed purpose was to promote Sino-Japanese amity (*Nikka shinzen*) and mutual cultural development (*sōgo no bunka hattatsu*) between Chinese and Japanese residents in Yokohama.[104] In that vein, in April 1924 it sponsored a Buddhist memorial service for Chinese and Japanese earthquake victims. A similar organization was the Sino-Japanese Comrades Association (Chūnichi dōshikai), established in 1929 as a town assembly to promote local mercantile and industrial development for Yokohama's economic recovery.[105] The terminology used in the titles of these organizations was explicitly international, helping naturalize the national categories of Chinese and Japanese even as the organizations brought a mixed community together.

The various new Chinese associations differed in their relative emphases on national and local issues. Consider the similarly titled Federation of Overseas Chinese Associations in Japan (Zhu-Ri huaqiao lianhe hui) and General Assembly of Yokohama Huaqiao Associations (Hengbin huaqiao tuanti zonghui), which nonetheless had very different leadership and goals. The federation was founded in Tokyo in 1924 and was followed by a Yokohama branch in March 1925. Its membership overlapped with the GMD

---

102. Izumi, "1920-nendai nakagoro no Yokohama kakyō shakai," p. 2.

103. Ibid., p. 29; Iriye, *China and Japan in the Global Setting*, pp. 42–47. The 1920s were a time of great activity for Sino-Japanese associations, which, according to Iriye Akira, took place in a global context of cultural internationalism.

104. "Shina kankei dantai oyobi Shinajin dantai," 1927, DRMFA, ref. B02130906400, JACAR; "Daidō gakkō fukkyū ni seifu ga hojo, Chūnichi kyōkai no honsō seikō," *YBS*, Apr. 1, 1925, p. 2. The slogan "Sino-Japanese amity" would adopt a much darker connotation during the Second Sino-Japanese War. See chap. 5.

105. "Chūnichi kyōkai no tsuichōkai," *YBS*, Apr. 12, 1924, p. 2; "Yamashita-chō gaijingai no mezamashī hatten, Chūnichi dōshikai mo soshiki saru," *YBS*, June 24, 1929, p. 5.

and the late Wang Xitian's Mutual Aid Association and sought foremost to elevate involvement in mainland political issues and to promote Mandarin as the national language. They held weekly Mandarin seminars, but made little headway against the well-established use of Cantonese in Yokohama and at the school.[106] The general assembly was established in 1926 and, in contrast to the federation's emphasis on patriotism and equality, represented Yokohama Chinese elites and promoted Sino-Japanese amity. The membership of the general assembly was not composed of individuals per se, but of representatives of existing organizations. Many of these leaders were second-generation Yokohama Chinese, including Bao Bogong of Hakugatei and Bao Mingchang of the Chartered Bank.[107] By then, the Japanese-born Chinese were an influential generational cohort in the community.[108] They had Chinese citizenship and self-identified as Chinese, but were fluent in Japanese, and many were born of Sino-Japanese parentage. Their experiences and interests naturally differed from those of newly arrived Chinese student activists or laborers.[109]

One exceptional organization that included Chinese and Japanese members but avoided national terminology was the Yamashita-chō Self-Governance

---

106. Itō Izumi, "1920-nendai nakagoro no Yokohama kakyō shakai," pp. 3–7; *Yokohama maichō shinbun*, June 13, 1925, p. 2; *Yokohama maichō shinbun*, June 15, 1925, p. 2. The federation argued for support of the Shanghai strikers during the general strike of June 1925. Despite the harm the strike was causing to the economic interests of Yokohama merchants, the federation managed to raise five hundred yen from the local community to send to the strikers.

107. Itō Izumi, "1920-nendai Yokohama kakyō shakai," pp. 12–17. In the mid-1920s, Bao Bogong was the vice president of Liang Fuchu's CAC, which was represented in the general assembly.

108. Yokohama-shi, *Yokohama-shi tōkei sho*, 18:37. The exact population of second-generation Chinese in Yokohama is difficult to ascertain because official records relating to the Chinese population only recorded nationality and province of origin. Place of birth had no bearing on the official classifications of people under *jus sanguinis* citizenship laws. Nevertheless, this cohort must have comprised a significant fraction of the Chinese population. There were 903 Chinese children in Yokohama in 1898, all or most of whom were born locally; if they remained in the city as adults, they would have comprised 23 percent of the Chinese population of 3,887 in 1918. If we assume an equivalent number of children in 1918, also likely to be born locally, the total proportion of those born in Japan could have been as high as 50 percent.

109. Itō Izumi, "1920-nendai Yokohama kakyō shakai," p. 16.

Federation (Yamashita-chō jichi rengōkai), founded in April 1924 by the indefatigable Liang Fuchu and a Japanese associate named Iizumi Kinjirō. This organization claimed to represent the district of Yamashita-chō, which encompasses Chinatown, and aimed to maintain order and public safety, help rebuild Yokohama, and foster self-governance. In that sense, it was similar to neighborhood organizations in most Japanese cities, but strikingly, accepted Chinese members as part of the local self. This organization boasted three hundred members by 1927, and wielded no small social influence. Under Liang Fuchu's leadership, they facilitated joint action on issues relevant to all residents of Yamashita-chō. For instance, in January 1925, Chinese and Japanese gathered at the Chinese-run Friendship Theater (Washin gekijō) to hear Liang speak out against the city's new building codes proposal that would impede reconstruction in the district. This joint effort eventually forced a compromise between residents and Yokohama City.[110]

During the 1920s, a steady solidification of a Chinese identity took place, which was overdetermined by political mobilization and ethnic stereotypes. The various new organizations of the 1920s were the functional units of a mixed local community, but one overlaid by the format of international relations. However, even as Chinese identity came to be accepted as an organizing principle in the community, Yokohama Chinese maintained a strong attachment to local place. Local identities had traditionally been directed toward Chinese province of origin; for the second generation, Yokohama City seems to have acquired increasing importance in this regard.

DIASPORIC CHINESE AND THE MANCHURIAN INCIDENT

At the start of the 1930s, military conflict between China and Japan broke out once more, with deep repercussions for Yokohama's international community. Foremost, Japan's attack on Chinese warlord Zhang Xueliang's forces in Manchuria on September 28, 1931, dissolved the cooperative spirit that Yokohama's Sino-Japanese institutions had enjoyed in the 1920s. The Japanese public reacted ecstatically to news of Japanese victories, spurring

---

110. "Shina kankei dantai oyobi Shinajin dantai"; "Yamashita-chō hatten ni kyōryoku jichi rengōkai setsuritsu hakkai shiki," *YBS*, Apr. 11, 1924, p. 2; Itō Izumi, "1920-nendai nakagoro no Yokohama kakyō shakai," pp. 31–32. The organization's name was subsequently given greater national specificity as the Yamashita-chō Sino-Japanese Federation (Yamashita-chō Nikka rengōkai), but its goals remained the same.

the rapid expansion of newspaper distributions. As in the First Sino-Japanese War (1894–95), the obverse of this war fever was animosity toward Chinese residents in Japan. The Japanese pretext for invasion hinged on charges of Chinese provocation, and many in Japan accepted this claim at face value. They blamed the conflict on Chinese intransigence and anti-Japanese sentiment that threatened Japanese citizens and economic interests on the mainland.[111]

In one example, a twenty-five-year-old Chinese barber in Tokyo named Chao Zhengyu was forced to abandon his business when relations with Japanese society turned icy. After the outbreak of the Manchurian Incident, people in town began spreading threatening rumors about his shop—"don't go to the Shinajin barber shop"—and his Japanese wife—"how can that woman become the wife of a Shinajin!" Children threw stones at their shop, and even their long-standing customers became afraid to enter. On the evening of December 3, 1931, Chao and his wife disappeared from town along with their young children. A Japanese newspaper article claimed that Chao had returned to Shanghai, but he had in fact gone into hiding at his wife's natal home.[112]

This experience of ethnic friction was typical for Chinese living outside Chinatown; many thus sought shelter by moving to the ethnic enclave. Xu Xiulan had been living in Mishima, Shizuoka Prefecture, where her father operated a Chinese restaurant. With the outbreak of war between China and Japan, Japanese customers immediately shunned their restaurant, and Xu's family decided to return to Yokohama Chinatown, where she was born.[113]

Chinatown, however, was by no means insulated from war-related anxieties. Much as in 1894, the Chinatown community reacted with great unease to the outbreak of military conflict between China and Japan.[114]

---

111. "Nikka jitsugyō no tai Shi ketsugi," *Asahi shinbun*, Nov. 17, 1931, p. G3.

112. "Kokoro naki seken ni naku, Shinajin tokoya no shujin tsuma o ribetsushi yukue fumei," *Asahi shinbun*, Dec. 5, 1931, p. 2. After the war, his son opened a Chinese restaurant in Asakusa named Seika (Zhenhua), and now runs a chain of ramen restaurants called Yōshū shōnin in Tokyo and Yokohama.

113. Ceng, "Yukari," p. 7. In 1932 they opened Anji, a restaurant specializing in rice porridge (*zhou*), which she operates to this day.

114. Not all resident Chinese were distressed. Reportedly, baseball games continued, and a teacher from the Chinese school proclaimed to a Japanese reporter that "the students are fine because this sort of thing has happened many times

Deteriorating economic conditions and a generalized fear for their safety led to a large-scale exodus starting in September 1931.[115] In contrast to the situation in 1894 when responsibility fell upon extragovernmental organizations like the Chinese Guild, the ROC consulate general explicitly encouraged the return of Chinese nationals to the motherland, using the slogan "Resist Japan and rescue the nation" (*kangri jiuguo*) and offering free passage by ship.[116] According to Japanese estimates, the Chinese of Yokohama largely answered the call. As the Chinese population of Yokohama dropped from 4,300 to around 1,500, newspapers reported that "the lights had gone out" in Chinatown.[117]

One of those who left was Ling Yintang (b. 1925), whose father owned a rattan furniture company. Ling recalls returning to Hong Kong with his family in 1931, where they stayed for approximately six months until the end of the fighting in Manchuria and Shanghai.[118] Some Chinese separated from their children and Japanese wives, like Chinese cook Liu Weigui, whose family was left in desperate economic straits until he returned.[119]

Like Ling and Liu, most Chinese returned to Yokohama after major combat ended in the spring of 1932. However, at this juncture, baseball hero and community leader Liang Fuchu left Yokohama for good. His resurrected CAC baseball team had taken the Yokohama City pennant one more time in 1930, but rising Japanese nationalism and anti-Chinese sentiment imbued in him an abiding sense of Chinese patriotism.[120] After his departure, he built an esteemed career as a baseball coach and popularizer of the sport in Hong Kong, Taiwan, and China. In the words of his son, Liang

---

before" ("Shizuka na Nankinmachi, fūunkyū mo karera ni wa hibikanu," *YBS*, Sept. 21, 1931, p. 5).

115. "Zairyū no Chūka gakusei zenbu kikoku o ketsugi," *YBS*, Sept. 30, 1931, p. 7; "Shinajin zoku zoku hikiagu," *YBS*, Oct. 22, 1931, p. 7.

116. "Tada de kaereru to kikoku Shinajin sattō," *YBS*, Dec. 6, 1931, p. 7.

117. "'Kōnichi kyūkoku' nanno sono, fukeiki ga kowai Chūgokujin haru kaze kisou, jikyoku o gyaku ni kyoryūmin fueru," *YBS*, Feb. 25, 1932, p. 7. This assertion in a Japanese newspaper may have been an exaggeration. The majority of the district's population was, after all, Japanese.

118. Ceng, "Ou," p. 7.

119. "Yamashita-chō Nankinmachi no sangeki," *YBS*, Mar. 6, 1934, p. 7.

120. *BX*, p. 90. Incidentally, the legacy of this Chinese baseball team persisted even after Liang's departure; the pitcher of the 1930 CAC team, Liu Laizhang, later became the first Chinese national to play in the Japanese professional league.

Youwen, Liang Fuchu was "a patriotic *huaqiao*," who by winning two city championships in Yokohama "won honor for our nation, and gave pride and inspiration to his fellow *huaqiao*."[121] Narrated in this way, Liang's career becomes a paradigmatic tale of nationalist awakening. But such a reading of his life masks his other roles in the city of Yokohama, which dramatized the complexities of national and local identifications and the potential solidarities that Chinese and Japanese could share. His career in Yokohama coincided with and reflected an era of national identities in cooperation, followed by the dissolution of that promise in the early 1930s.

Conclusion

As the ROC extended its authority over the Chinese homeland, it also enacted further measures to control its overseas nationals. The regime reiterated its *jus sanguinis* citizenship law in 1928, and enacted a law in 1929 requiring the registration of all overseas citizens. In April 1932, the ROC reorganized the Overseas Chinese Affairs Committee (Qiaowu weiyuanhui; OCAC).[122] The timing was not coincidental. The new OCAC defined as its mission the dissemination of a sense of national consciousness in response to escalating national crises, specifically the invasion of Manchuria in 1931 and battles between Chinese and Japanese forces in Shanghai in 1932.[123] These goals were promoted through a network of representatives dispatched to overseas Chinese communities.

---

121. Liang Youwen, "Yi xianfu," p. 22.

122. Kuhn, *Chinese among Others*, pp. 266–67; Qiaowu weiyuanhui, *Qiaowu wushinian*, pp. 17, 42. This organization was preceded by a number of similar bodies, including the Overseas Chinese Affairs Bureau (Qiaowuju) of Sun Yatsen's revolutionary government in Guangzhou, established in 1923, and the Overseas Party Affairs Department of the GMD, established in 1928.

123. The ROC defined the ten aims of the OCAC in a 1931 statute: "One, research the conditions for overseas Chinese; two, leadership and management of overseas emigration; three, management of conflicts between overseas Chinese [*qiaomin*]; four, administration of overseas Chinese associations; five, leadership for investment, business operations, and travel; six, support and aid for overseas Chinese; seven, leadership, management, and investigation of overseas Chinese education; eight, leadership for overseas Chinese who wish to return to China for education; nine, financial aid for overseas Chinese education; ten, dissemination of culture" (Qiaowu weiyuanhui, *Qiaowu wushinian*, p. 37).

In the years following the Manchurian Incident, the ROC further tightened its control over overseas Chinese communities. One of its most far-reaching policy initiatives was the assimilation of educational institutions to mainland standards. Autonomously produced and localized textbooks, like those used at the turn of the century by the Datong xuexiao, would no longer be permitted. Texts and curricula were now subject to authorization by the ROC Ministry of Education. On November 26, 1932, the OCAC decreed that all overseas Chinese education would include Mandarin. As early as 1903, various bodies in the homeland had regulated education and promoted the use of Mandarin and the vernacular (*baihua*) written language to culturally unify the domestic population; for the first time, a Chinese central government had the wherewithal to compel overseas schools to comply with these policies.[124] The state had ordained that Mandarin was the national language, and it would no longer be mocked.

The Chinese of Chinatown had become more fully integrated into the Chinese nation through these decades. Political and cultural identity had consolidated against a clear foe, the Japanese, whereas internal linguistic differences were mitigated by the emphasis on Mandarin education. Nevertheless, even as the consolidation of Chinese identity as *huaqiao* subordinated provincial affiliations to the idea of a Chinese nation, many still identified with the local Yokohama community. The leaders of Chinese associations during this time were largely of the acculturated second generation. Moreover, Yokohama Chinese contributed to Yokohama society and culture, as shown by baseball and Chinese cuisine. These examples provide a fitting illustration of the linked processes of integration and differentiation. For Japanese, the codification of Chinese food as a foreign cuisine was no obstacle to its appreciation; rather, its foreignness enabled its integration as an exotic feature of Japanese consumer culture. Likewise, Liang's baseball team was a regular participant in local tourneys, but *as* the Chinese team. For Chinese, baseball and Chinese food helped unify those of different provincial origins into a common culture, in the sense that even Shanghai tailors

---

124. Qiaowu weiyuanhui, *Qiaowu wushinian*, pp. 55–56; Tsang, *Nationalism in School Education in China*, pp. 66–68, 85–87. The Qing dynasty established a system to vet and authorize textbooks in 1903, a policy that was continued by the Republican government. In 1928, the Chinese government ordered a switch to the vernacular written language for all textbooks used in Chinese schools.

were opening restaurants to sell *shinasoba*, originally a product of northwest China, and all were joining to cheer Liang's baseball team.

From the 1910s to the 1930s, the vocabulary available to describe identities was increasingly constrained by nationalist ideologies in both China and Japan. For Yokohama Chinese and their Japanese neighbors, it became difficult to conceive of commonalities and solidarities outside the rubric of Sino-Japanese cooperation. In other words, their integration into Yokohama society was as foreigners, specifically, as *huaqiao*. By the 1930s, deepening conflict between China and Japan would further narrow the latitude available to individuals to act according to their other, nonnational identities. And for the Chinatown community, the greatest tragedies were to yet come. When the skirmishes between Chinese and Japanese troops at the Marco Polo Bridge near Beijing escalated into full-scale fighting in the summer of 1937, many Chinese in Yokohama chose to remain. They judged, incorrectly, that the fighting would end quickly, as it had in 1931–32. And as China and Japan descended into total war, Japan's Ministry of Foreign Affairs and Home Ministry faced the thorny issue of how to deal with an entrenched community of potential enemies in Yokohama. Their solution, as we will see, was to co-opt the discourses of Chinese identity and the very institutions that the ROC employed to produce patriotic national subjects in the first place.

CHAPTER FOUR

Sino-Japanese War, Sino-Japanese Friendship, and the Yokohama-ite Identity, 1933–45

> Most important it is to respect, understand, and honour the Chinese traditions and social customs. Japanese should be true Japanese and Chinese should be true Chinese. Between friends, tolerance and sympathy are most important.
>
> —General Itagaki Seishirō

This message from Japan's Army Minister Itagaki Seishirō was distributed to Japanese soldiers in the China theater in an April 29, 1940, pamphlet that explained that their mission was "to overthrow the régime that is resisting Japan," and set forth the proper behavior for imperial subjects while in China.[1] In the midst of the Sino-Japanese War of 1937–45, a war of annihilation against Chiang Kaishek's Republic of China (ROC), this message of friendship and pluralist respect may seem ironic or incongruous. Nevertheless, this policy was consistent with the way Japan legitimated the war as a struggle for Asian liberation. In the spring of 1938, Japan's Foreign Minister Ugaki Kazushige noted in his diary that "We Japanese always say that 'China for the Chinese' is what we desire, that this is our basic policy."[2] These pronouncements indicate the way that pan-Asianist—as well as ethnic-nationalist—discourses were deployed in the service of imperialist expansion and war.

This chapter examines how these strategic imperatives shaped Japan's wartime treatment of the Chinese in Japan. The Japanese state, through its rhetorical commitment to ethnic-national distinctions under an umbrella of Asian unity, became an active participant in the construction of

---

1. Itagaki, "Japan to Assist, Not Oppress, China," p. 164.
2. Boyle, *China and Japan at War*, p. 148.

Chineseness. The Yokohama Chinese maintained their identities as such through both resistance to and complicity with these imperatives. After the Marco Polo Bridge Incident, a brief skirmish between Chinese and Japanese troops west of Beijing on July 7, 1937, China and Japan descended into full-scale, though undeclared, war. Thus began the conflict which Japan called a holy war (*seisen*) and China named a war of resistance against Japan (*kangri zhanzheng*). The Chinese of Yokohama would have to choose between these two irreconcilable ways of defining the conflict.

Many Chinese chose to leave the city behind. At the start of the war 3,747 Chinese nationals lived in Japan's Kanagawa Prefecture, centered on the port city of Yokohama. Two years later in March 1939, with much of their homeland under Japanese occupation, 2,364 Chinese, some 60 percent, remained.[3] This community was still sizeable, and Japan's Foreign Police (Gaiji Keisatsu) sought to dominate, not disband, its organizations to force their collaboration for domestic and foreign propaganda among other purposes. This situation led to some ironic continuities for the Chinese population of Yokohama when the Japanese government appropriated nation-building institutions created by the ROC in its war against that state.

These maneuvers were connected with developments in the Chinese homeland. As the Japanese army conquered large swaths of Chinese coastal territory, its various wings installed collaborationist regimes. The first of these with aspirations of national representation was the Beijing Provisional Government. It was inaugurated on December 14, 1937, with a roster of former ministers of various warlord regimes.[4] Japan's Home Ministry declared in one of its publications that "the new regime is the voice, the hope of the Chinese people," and began efforts to redirect national legitimacy away from Chiang Kaishek's government.[5] The Beijing regime was then superseded in March 1940 by the Reorganized National Government of China under former Chinese Nationalist Party (GMD) deputy·leader and disciple of Sun Yatsen, Wang Jingwei.[6] Japanese police coerced Chinese institutions in Yokohama to support the collaborationist regimes (fig. 4.1).

---

3. *YSSII*, p. 938.

4. Boyle, *China and Japan at War*, pp. 85–91.

5. Naimushō, "Shin seiken to zairyū kakyō," p. 28.

6. Boyle, *China and Japan at War*, p. 238. Another collaborationist regime had been located in Nanjing, called the Reformed Government of the Republic of China, but it was never considered a national government.

FIG. 4.1. Yokohama Chinese waving Japanese flags and marching in support of Japan's war in Asia. *Source*: "'Warera mo takakai nukan,' zai-Hama kakyō kangeki no gyōshin," *Kanagawa shinbun*, January 13, 1943, p. 2.

According to Japanese propagandists, this cooperative spirit would be the new Chinese patriotism, and Chinese were to be spokesmen for a narrative that Japanese military actions served to liberate, not dominate, China.

For the Yokohama Chinese, their concurrent identifications with both China and Yokohama posed a painful dilemma. Should they stay in Japan, they would almost certainly be forced to endure the control of Japan's authorities. But the actual nature of this relationship with the Japanese state has posed a problem of interpretation for historians. Yokohama newspapers during wartime regularly printed articles showing that the Chinese engaged in marches and celebrations in support of Japan's war. But were these Chinese truly converted to Japan's cause? There is reason to believe that they were not, though archival sources cannot provide a definitive answer. Wartime surveillance by the Japanese police and postwar Chinese nationalism have both shaped the documentary record in ways that prevent clear assessment of the motivations of the Yokohama Chinese. On one hand, oppression by the Japanese state limited the range of opinions that could be expressed and recorded during wartime. On the other hand, Japan's defeat made it difficult to retrospectively admit to the possibility of sincere support during wartime.

Regarding the latter phenomenon, historian Timothy Brook and others critique the way that postwar Chinese nationalism has created a moral filter on the past and yielded a "resistentialist" master narrative—that is, a stark dichotomy between loyal resistance and moral failure. This master narrative has contributed to a myth that all true Chinese resisted Japan, a characterization that extended to *huaqiao* as well.[7] Indeed, postwar memoirs and histories by Chinese in Yokohama have emphasized the "fascist" coercion behind their wartime cooperation, implying the oppression of their innate, patriotic resistance to Japan.[8]

Japanese scholarship has offered correctives to this narrative, but these writings err in taking at face value sources produced in oppressive contexts. By relying heavily on records published or compiled by Japanese authorities during wartime—the Ministry of Foreign Affairs, the Home Ministry, and its subsidiary Foreign Police—these histories exaggerate the hegemony of Japan's wartime ideology. For instance, the official Yokohama city history takes the view that a significant pro-Japan faction existed among the Yokohama Chinese. Accordingly, these Chinese voluntarily cooperated with Japanese authorities after they were liberated from the hegemonic influence of the Chinese consulate.[9] Kikuchi Kazutaka's 2011 monograph, *Sensō to kakyō: Nihon, kokumin seifu kōkan, kairai seiken, kakyō kan no seiji rikigaku* (Overseas Chinese and the Asia-Pacific War 1937–45: The political dynamic among Japan, China, and the puppet regimes), reaches a similar conclusion. Kikuchi eschews the subjective record of memoir in favor of newspaper articles and government documents, and argues that *huaqiao* in Japan "greatly welcomed" the new puppet regimes and, "objectively speaking, supported Japan's policy of invasion."[10]

-----

7. Brook, *Collaboration*; Margherita Zanasi, "New Perspectives on Chinese Collaboration."

8. *BX*, pp. 78–90; CKK and YKS, *Yokohama kakyō no kioku*.

9. *YSSII*, 2:943–49.

10. Kikuchi, *Sensō to kakyō*, pp. 479–80.

However, official documents in wartime do not provide compelling evidence of actual political commitments. In other words, the appearance of Chinese compliance should not be treated as definitive proof of Japan's ideological hegemony. James C. Scott's concepts of public and hidden transcripts offer a perspective that avoids both the notion of Japanese hegemony as well as the a priori nationalist myth of resistance. By expressing support for Japan's war mission, the Yokohama Chinese were constructing a public transcript, what Scott defines as "the open interaction between subordinates and those who dominate" designed to "affirm and naturalize the power of dominant elites." But where there is domination, we may also posit a hidden transcript—that is, conversations "beyond the direct observation of powerholders"—that sustains a reservoir of resistance. This form of resistance, as Scott reminds us, is absent from the historical record, not just because those who dominate choose not to record it, but because subordinates have concealed it for their own protection.[11] A critical reading of wartime records and postwar memoirs sheds light on the hidden negotiations that complicate the appearance of support by the Yokohama Chinese for Japan's war.

As we will see from the gap between public and hidden transcripts, Yokohama Chinese leaders did not necessarily accept the mission of Sino-Japanese amity on the terms offered by Japan's wartime authorities. Moreover, the decision to cooperate was inseparable from the decision to remain in the city during the war, and therefore their social and economic integration. By weathering the war years in Yokohama, the Chinese community proved their commitment to a *hamakko,* or Yokohama-ite, identity. As in the Sino-Japanese War of 1894–95, the dilemmas created by the war serve as a prism to refract and reveal the contradictions between national and local identities.

Huaqiao *Identity and the Japanese State*

By the late 1930s, Chinese in Yokohama had overwhelmingly accepted a diasporic national identity as *huaqiao*.[12] This transition was enabled by the

---

11. Scott, *Domination and the Arts of Resistance*, pp. 2, 5, 18, 119, 183. This theory does not intend to set up a dichotomy between falsity and truth, domination and freedom; as Scott reminds us, the hidden transcript is also a social product of power relations.

12. In Yokohama, the use of the term *huaqiao* only became widespread in the 1930s, approximately two decades later than the communities of Southeast Asia.

regulations and activities of institutions created by the ROC from the 1920s. Japanese government institutes and independent authors concurred with these ROC policies. Japanese research and publishing in the 1920s and 1930s on the subject of *huaqiao* confirmed the identity as real and significant to Japan's security and interests. These works issued from both governmental institutes, such as the South Manchuria Railway East-Asian Economic Investigation Bureau (Minami Manshū tetsudō Tōa keizai chōsakyoku) and the Ministry of Foreign Affairs Commerce Office (Gaimushō tsūshōkyoku), as well as individual authors.[13] They consistently sounded the alarm that *huaqiao* in Southeast Asia posed a threat to Japanese interests as economic competitors and sources of anti-Japanese agitation. The strategic imperatives implicit in these studies forced them to define the *huaqiao* in the broadest terms possible. Today the term *huaqiao* denotes overseas Chinese who have maintained Chinese nationality, in contrast to *huaren* (ethnic Chinese), which denotes those with host-country nationality. Japanese works from this era, however, defined the *huaqiao* as *all* individuals who might be involved in activities supporting the ROC. They included even those with mixed blood and those who had naturalized, and thus aided in the imagining of an expansive community of like-minded and patriotic overseas Chinese.[14]

These publications claimed that the *huaqiao* posed a threat to Japan's economic and diplomatic interests because of their ability to conduct coordinated economic boycotts against Japan. These were, it was claimed, orchestrated by the GMD, allowing a 1928 boycott to cut Japanese exports to the Straits Colony, the Dutch East Indies, French Indochina, and Siam by 50 to 80 percent. These and similar actions demonstrated *huaqiao* dominance of retail distribution in the Southeast Asian economy.[15] A Japanese investigation

---

The term's use was linked to the rising prominence of the second generation who sought a way to differentiate themselves from parents who thought of themselves as simply Chinese (*Zhongguoren*). The term *huaqiao*, however, was not unknown before this, though it was used only sporadically. Most visibly, it was used in the name of the school founded in 1908 by Sun Yatsen's supporters, the Hengbin huaqiao xuexiao, as described in chap. 2.

13. Minami Manshū tetsudō Tōa keizai chōsakyoku, *Kakyō*; Nagano Akira, *Kakyō*; Kobayashi, *Kakyō no kenkyū*; Kobayashi, *Shina minzoku no kaigai hatten*; Tsūshō kyoku dainika, *Kakyō no gensei*.

14. Hayashi Teishirō, *Tōa kyōeiken to kakyō*, pp. 1–2.

15. Kobayashi, *Shina minzoku no kaigai hatten*, pp. 319–37; Minami Manshū tetsudō Tōa keizai chōsakyoku, *Kakyō*, pp. 211–17. Japanese authors argued that

in 1939 concluded that without the Chinese distribution network there, "the sale of most of our goods [would be] impossible."[16]

Although few of these works devoted more than a few pages to the *huaqiao* in Japan, they cited similarities with the *huaqiao* of Southeast Asia regarding economic, intermarriage, and naturalization patterns.[17] One of the main consequences of this consensus on *huaqiao* identity was that it convinced Japanese planners of the coextensiveness of the Chinese in Japan with this wider *huaqiao* community, and thus a latent threat within Japan's borders. In effect, these studies confirmed the ROC's own stance on its overseas citizens.

As the two countries moved toward war, the role of the Overseas Chinese Affairs Committee (OCAC) in Yokohama was bound to generate friction with the Japanese state. Chinese education in Yokohama became, once again, a locus of contention because the OCAC used the Yokohama Chinese Public School to politicize the local community.[18] They promoted homeland standards through the teaching of Mandarin and stipulated the use of textbooks produced in the motherland, reproducing a historical consciousness incompatible with that of Japanese society.

This problem was familiar to Japanese authorities. Since the 1910s, Japan's Ministry of Foreign Affairs and the research arm of the South Manchuria Railway Company had been monitoring what they considered to be anti-Japanese sentiments in Chinese textbooks. They described these as expel Japan (*hai Nichi*) or insult Japan (*bin Nichi*) education and protested them as harmful to Sino-Japanese relations.[19] When Japan's Foreign Police discovered similar content in textbooks used at Chinese schools in Japan, a wider

---

participation in this boycott derived from brute coercion by GMD operatives, including communists and secret society thugs.

16. Fukuda and Oates, *With Sweat & Abacus*, p. 228.

17. Kobayashi, *Kakyō no kenkyū*, pp. 181–82.

18. *BX*, p. 84. In 1935, the OCAC standardized the school name to match other overseas communities, changing it to Yokohama Chinese Public Elementary School (Hengbin zhonghua gongli xiaoxue).

19. Kantō butoku, "Hai-Nichi kyōkasho ni kansuru ken," 1914, DRMFA, ref. B03030217500, JACAR; Makino Nobuaki, "Chūnichi gakuin shiyō no kyōkashochū hainichi jikō toriatsukaikata," 1936, DRMFA, ref. Ref. B05015326500, JACAR; Tōa keizai chōsakyoku, *Shina kokutei hainichi dokuhon*; Naimushō keihōkyoku, *Gaiji keisatsu gaikyō*, 2:48–50; "Mata Chūka shōgakkō de hai Nichi kyōkasho," *Yomiuri shinbun*, evening edition, Nov. 20, 1936, p. 2.

set of organizations took action. On February 17, 1936, representatives from the Home Ministry, Ministry of Foreign Affairs, and Ministry of Education jointly resolved to ban these texts, order Chinese schools to reform their curricula, and admonish the Chinese ambassador to supervise school administrators more carefully.[20]

In subsequent months, the Foreign Police repeatedly investigated the Yokohama Chinese Public school.[21] As a school child Ling Yintang recalled that one day his teacher Wu Bokang collected their textbooks and burned them in the schoolyard to prevent their discovery by Japanese police. Nevertheless, the Japanese police and the Ministry of Education found objectionable material twice during this year, including condemnations of Japanese imperialism, the Twenty-One Demands, and other recent Sino-Japanese conflicts. Each time, they confiscated the offending books and demanded the use of revised texts.[22]

With the start of the war in July of 1937, Japanese authorities executed a more forceful investigation and suppression of Chinese organizations, particularly those affiliated with the GMD. During these months, the GMD branch office and consulate general in Yokohama executed some final attempts to oppose Japan. On August 10, 1937, the central executives of the GMD obligated all overseas members to pledge to an emergency party member loyalty oath.[23] However, Japanese police investigation and surveillance convinced many prominent members of the community to avoid meetings held by Shao Yulin, the Chinese consul general.[24] Then, in a crackdown on the GMD in December, police deported nine GMD members and jailed teachers with party affiliations.[25] Wu Bokang, acting principal of the Chinese school, was

---

20. "Chūgoku ryūgakusei shiyō kyōkasho oyobi kyōiku ni kanshite gaimu-monbu-naimu sanshō kyōgi no ken," 1936, DRMFA, ref. B05015408000, JACAR.

21. Naimushō keihōkyoku, *Gaiji keisatsu gaikyō*, 2:48–50.

22. "Shingakki kara teiseiban, bin Nichi kyōkasho mondai osamaru," *YBS*, Apr. 2, 1936, p. 2; "Chūka shōgakkō dokuhon saido hatsubai o kinshi," *YBS*, June 21, 1936, p. 2.

23. Naimushō keihōkyoku, "Hokushi jihen ni kansuru jōhō," 1937, RHM, ref. A06030016600, JACAR.

24. Naimushō gaijika, "Shina jihen ka ni okeru gaiji keisatsu no ippan jōkyō," 1939, RHM, ref. A07040002700, JACAR; Naimushō keihōkyoku, "Hokushi jihen ni kansuru jōhō."

25. CKK and YKS, *Yokohama kakyō no kioku*, p. 58; Naimushō keihōkyoku, *Gaiji keisatsu gaikyō*, 4:83, 290–91.

among them; Japanese police arrested him on suspicion of espionage and interrogated him for three months.[26] Wu was only released through the determined efforts of his friend Bao Bogong, but the school was thereafter closely watched by Japanese police.[27] In this fashion, Kanagawa prefectural police persecution led GMD sympathizers to either leave or conceal those ties.

Japan's Home Ministry had no intention, however, of dislodging the Chinese population from Yokohama; it only sought to crush the influence of the GMD. After Japan's North China Area Army established the Beijing Provisional Government, the Foreign Police coerced Chinese institutions in Yokohama to recognize the regime's authority. ROC diplomatic officers, however, resisted this appropriation to the extent that they could. According to the January 15, 1938, *Yomiuri shinbun,* representatives from eighteen Yokohama Chinese associations met on January 14 and resolved to fly the five-color flag of the Beijing Provisional Government. At this meeting, Consul General Shao Yulin stood before the gathered community leaders in tears, calling for those who did not wish to fly the five-color flag to join him in walking out of the meeting. Several did.[28] The first organization to fly the new flag in defiance of the Chinese consulate was the Fujian Federation (Fujian lianhehui), whose president He Naojirō raised the flag at noon on January 14. Although supporters of the Chinese consulate promptly snatched down this flag, they could not prevent the Fujianese from flying another flag from their building's second floor.[29] These actions suggest differences in opinion among Chinese subnational groups, particularly those marginalized by the community's Cantonese majority.[30]

ROC Ambassador Xu Shiying faced a similar situation when he visited Yokohama on January 18, 1938, shortly before his departure from Japan.

---

26. Wu, "Yi Hengbin huaqiao xuexiao," p. 133.

27. Ye, "Chūgoku daidō gakkō-shi," pp. 87–90; Wu, "Yi Hengbin huaqiao xuexiao," p. 133.

28. Kikuchi, *Sensō to kakyō,* p. 108.

29. "Goshokuki ketsugi o sōryōji jūrin," *Yomiuri shinbun,* Jan. 15, 1938, morning edition, p. 7; "Hama no goshokuki ihen," *Yomiuri shinbun,* Jan. 15, 1938, evening edition, p. 2; Naimushō gaijika, "Gaiji keisatsu no ippan jōkyō."

30. The Fujian Federation may have sought external Japanese affirmation as a lever against Cantonese dominance over the community, though it is impossible at this point to determine their precise motivation. Naojirō, a Japanese name, also suggests an acculturated status.

While delivering a fiery speech at the Chinese Guild, a Japanese policeman strode up to the podium, took down the two ROC flags that stood beside the ambassador, and attempted to hang the five-color flag in their place. Xu thundered, "This is absolutely impermissible. You can take them down after I leave, but while I am here you are not to touch them." Xu's prerogative as ambassador prevailed, but only for the moment.[31] Soon thereafter, most Chinese buildings in Yokohama flew the five-color flag, even the Yokohama Chinese Public School, a former bastion of anti-Japanese sentiment.[32]

Japan's Foreign Police described these developments in its records as the conversion of the *huaqiao* community to the goal of Sino-Japanese harmony through liberation from GMD and consular constraints.[33] The Japanese government then sponsored the establishment of a new umbrella organization in January 1938, the Federation of Huaqiao in Japan (Lüri huaqiao lianhehui). The Beijing collaborationist regime then set up a *huaqiao* affairs office in Tokyo in April 1938.[34] And in December 1939, Japan's Home Ministry began preparations to establish a new umbrella organization called the General Assembly of Huaqiao in Japan (Quanri huaqiao zonghui). This organization would serve as a liaison with Wang Jingwei's Reorganized National Government, but operated under the auspices of Japan's Kōain, a high-level governmental body established in 1938 to administer occupied China.[35] According to its bylaws, the General Assembly sought to coordinate *huaqiao* organizations, "unify the *huaqiao* living in all regions of the Great Japanese Empire, promote Sino-Japanese amity and cooperation, support the construction of the New Order in East Asia, and further the overall welfare of the *huaqiao*."[36] The Kōain provided funding for the General Assembly, and the January 1943 roster illustrates the degree of Japanese supervision over its

---

31. CKK and YKS, *Yokohama kakyō no kioku*, p. 145.

32. "Goshokuki mantenshoku, wakitatsu Hama no Nankinmachi," *YBS*, Jan. 18, 1938, evening edition, p. 2.

33. Naimushō Gaijika, "Gaiji keisatsu no ippan jōkyō."

34. Kikuchi, *Sensō to kakyō*, p. 32.

35. Naimushō keihōkyoku, *Gaiji keisatsu gaikyō*, 5:12; Chen Jicheng, "Qiaowu gongzuo," p. 11. In 1942 the Kōain was integrated into the newly established Ministry of Greater East Asia (Daitōashō).

36. Naimushō keihōkyoku, *Gaiji keisatsu gaikyō*, 5:12–13.

activities; three posts were occupied by Japanese police representatives: counselor (*sanji*), superintendent (*shuji*), and secretary (*shoki*).[37]

In this way, Japan's Foreign Police presided over the nominal conversion of existing Chinatown institutions to a pro-Japan stance, and even helped establish a new nationwide network of *huaqiao* associations. This was consistent with the Japanese state's strategic vision, which acknowledged the strength of Chinese national sentiment and sought to appropriate it. Only as Chinese could their support bolster the legitimacy of the conflict as a pan-Asian war of liberation. These activities by the Chinese in Japan are best described by the term "collaborationism," which Timothy Brook defines as "supportive engagement in the tasks and ideology of the occupier," rather than collaboration, which denotes "the continuing exercise of power under the pressure produced by the presence of an occupying power." These Chinese did not live in the occupied homeland, and the mundane activities of community leaders provided little direct aid to that occupation.[38] Coerced collaborationism was one way for Japanese authorities to square the ideal of national self-determination with the imperatives of Japanese imperial expansion.[39]

Thereafter, Chinese patriotism and collaborationism were conjoined and justified by the familiar slogan of Sino-Japanese amity.[40] In wartime, even if few took such messages of friendship seriously, the rhetoric had material effects. The Yokohama Chinese community became a symbolic exemplar of Sino-Japanese relations, and Japan authorities left the community intact and largely in peace; they would remain Chinese, neither forcibly excluded from

---

37. Chen Kunwang, *Nihon kakyō, ryūgakusei undōshi.*

38. Brook, *Collaboration*, pp. 2, 10.

39. Doak, "Concept of Ethnic Nationality," pp. 168, 172–78; Weiner, "Invention of Identity," pp. 99–100. This element of Japan's wartime ideology was the culmination of a shift in Pan-Asianist discourses since World War I, away from an emphasis on shared race (*jinshu*) toward an acceptance of ethnic nationality as the superordinate principle of identity. Although this shift appears at first glance to vitiate the regionalist imaginings that underlay Japanese colonialism and territorial expansion, during the 1920s and 1930s a variety of Japanese social scientists and politicians reconciled Asian solidarity and ethnic national distinctions by arguing for either a hierarchical league of Asian nations led by Japan or an organic body of complementary Asian nations described as an East Asian community (*Tōa kyōdōtai*).

40. The term was variously written as *Nikka, Nisshi,* or *Nicchū shinzen,* using the various terms available to denote China.

Japanese territory nor forcibly included in the Japanese polity like Taiwanese and Koreans.[41] Nor did Japanese authorities sequester the Chinese in internment camps, as the United States did to 110,000 ethnic Japanese after the attack on Pearl Harbor.[42] In return, Japan's foreign police demanded their participation in parades, celebrations, and propaganda broadcasts in support of Japan's war.

Moreover, some Japanese researchers believed that the *huaqiao* in Japan could aid in the construction of the Greater East Asia Co-Prosperity Sphere. One such advocate was Matsumoto Otō, one of the trustees of the Southern Society (Nanpō kyōkai), a research and planning organization involved in Southeast Asia and Taiwan. In the Chinese-language magazine *Huawen Daban meiri* (*Kabun Osaka mainichi*), he argued that the "pernicious and meaningless" support of Chiang Kaishek's regime among *huaqiao* in Southeast Asia derived from their years under the "authority of the white man," which had destroyed their Asian consciousness and bequeathed them a faulty view of Japan. Matsumoto believed that *huaqiao* in Japan would be useful in rectifying this situation because they "have seen more than any other Chinese the sincerity of the Japanese, have already put Sino-Japanese cooperation into practice and have contributed to the reconstruction of a revived China."[43]

By the end of the war, Japanese government policy makers proposed similar roles for the Chinese in Japan. For instance, in April 1944, the Japanese Ministry of Greater East Asia (Daitōashō) produced a secret plan outlining the exploitation of *huaqiao* in Japan for three main purposes: to aid in propaganda, shipping, and the investigation of enemy territory; to recruit

---

41. *YSSII*, 1:36; M. Lin, "Overseas Chinese Merchants and Multiple Nationality," p. 992; Ching, *Becoming "Japanese."* Japanese colonial rule in Korea and Taiwan ranged from the brutal suppression of independence movements to efforts to build harmony (*kyōwa*) between colonial subjects and Japanese. By 1936, the imperatives of war mobilization led Japanese colonial policies to shift toward explicit assimilation (*dōka*), including prohibitions on native language and clothing, as well as the adoption of Japanese surnames and enforced worship at Shintō shrines.

42. Yang Murray, *Historical Memories of Japanese American Internment*, p. 27.

43. Matsumoto Otō, "Nanyang huaqiao wenti," p. 11; CKK and YKS, *Yokohama kakyō no kioku*, pp. 94–95. The *Huawen Daban meiri* was a monthly magazine published by the Ōsaka Mainichi newspaper company and heavily subsidized by the Japanese army. It employed around eight Chinese authors and translators, and was distributed in Manchukuo and North China.

and supervise Chinese coolies at mines and ports in Japan; and to engage in the "enlightening" of Chinese inside and outside the Greater East Asia Co-Prosperity Sphere.[44] It is unclear to what extent the ministry implemented this plan. It is also doubtful such operations would have been effective, given Japan's deteriorating military situation and the atrocities they inflicted on China and ethnic Chinese populations across Southeast Asia. Nevertheless, the ministry's plan demonstrates that the Japanese government did not attempt to assimilate the Chinese in Japan as imperial subjects; to the end of the war they saw them as useful for the roles they could perform as "true Chinese."

Huaqiao *Imperatives,* Hamakko *Commitments*

To understand what cooperation with the wartime Japanese state meant to the Yokohama Chinese, it is crucial to examine who chose to stay and who opted to leave. Over the first two years of the war, approximately 40 percent of the Chinese in Kanagawa Prefecture departed for the homeland, most leaving in the latter half of 1937.[45] This development was driven by both political protest against Japan's invasion of China and an economic collapse. Starting in mid-August 1937, the Chinese consulate general in Yokohama, following an August 3 ROC policy directive, began encouraging the voluntary return of its compatriots on commissioned Japanese postal and P&O Line steamships.[46] In the autumn of 1937, uncertainty, shipping disruptions, and Japanese commercial restrictions reduced Chinese financial transactions and sales of general goods by 90 percent, sales of food and textiles by 50 percent, and exports by 70 percent. Imports dropped to next to nothing.[47] As in 1894 and 1931, many businesses closed their doors, including some venerable and well-known restaurants.[48]

---

44. Daitōashō Shina jimukyoku sōmuka, *Nihon kakyō no katsuyō men.*

45. *YSSII,* 1:36.

46. "Zai-Hama Shinajin gun ni sōryōji yori hikiage junbi tsūchō," *YBS,* Aug. 15, 1937, p. 1; Kikuchi, *Sensō to kakyō,* pp. 19–20. Peninsular and Oriental Steam Navigation Company (P&O) was a British shipping company.

47. Naimushō gaijika, "Gaiji keisatsu no ippan jōkyō."

48. "Minkoku kokumintō kaisan," *YBS,* Sept. 1, 1937, p. 5; "Zairyū Shinajin sanbyaku kinō no fune de Shanhai e," *YBS,* Aug. 4, 1937, p. 5; "Yokohama zairyū Shinajin tairyō kikoku o junbi," *YBS,* Aug. 31, 1937, p. 4.

The Chinese community also confronted antagonism from Japanese society. As in past Sino-Japanese conflicts, a marked decline took place in Japanese commerce and consumption in Chinatown. Before July 1937, the top restaurants in Chinatown pulled in 5,000 to 8,000 yen a month; by the fall, their earnings had plummeted to 1,500 to 2,000 yen per month. Worse, isolated cases of violence occurred. A Japanese was arrested for throwing a cement block through a window at the Chinese consulate.[49] Japanese police records state that Chinatown became a "desolate place" in 1937–38 through a combination of these departures and social ostracization from Japanese society.[50]

Japanese police suppression of the GMD contributed to the anxieties felt by the community. One of those deported was recent Waseda University graduate Mo Boxian, who was forced to leave a wife and child behind in Yokohama.[51] Many were kept in custody, however, suffering cruel interrogation and torture for months. Some killed themselves by jumping from the top of police stations, and among those deported, some were so mentally disordered that they hanged themselves on the voyage back to China.[52] Another anecdote can illustrate the particular vulnerability of the Yokohama *huaqiao* in wartime. Bao Shengchang, a Yokohama resident since around 1900, was arrested by the Japanese police for serving as a member of the GMD. He then lost his personal property and assets when he and his family were deported in early 1938. Disillusioned by the inability of the Chinese government to care for him during the war, and receiving no postwar compensation from Japan for his suffering, he turned his back on the GMD and warned his children never to participate in political organizations.[53]

Apart from the deportees, the immediate returnees were by and large short-term residents such as immigrant laborers, itinerant peddlers, and students. These groups had a weak economic base in Japan and were relatively

---

49. Naimushō keihōkyoku, *Gaiji keisatsu gaikyō*, 4:23.

50. Naimushō gaijika, "Gaiji keisatsu no ippan jōkyō," p. 36; Naimushō keihōkyoku, *Gaiji keisatsu gaikyō*, 3:77–78. Conflicts between Chinese and Japanese were taking place nationwide. In Tokyo, an unemployed Japanese youth named Komiyama Noboru was arrested on October 4 for plotting to assassinate the Chinese ambassador.

51. Sugawara, *Nihon no kakyō*, p. 319.

52. Naimushō gaijika, "Gaiji keisatsu no ippan jōkyō."

53. Bao Guanming et al., "Jiti zonghe jishi," pp. 230–31.

free to act on their political consciousness. For instance, on August 20, the *Asama-maru* left Yokohama bound for Hong Kong. It carried 170 Chinese, including 100 students.[54] For Chinese with deeper familial or commercial roots in Yokohama—precisely those who faced a contradiction between their national and local attachments—the decision to return to the homeland could be traumatic. The Chinese who left during Japan's invasion of Manchuria from 1931 to 1932 suffered immense economic losses and were loath to repeat that experience. In 1937, many apparently felt they would rather ride out the war, which they felt would be short-lived, than lose a lifetime's worth of property and savings.[55] Demographic data through the end of the war indicate that the population who chose to remain indeed displayed a more permanent form of settlement than the bachelor and sojourner community that existed at the turn of the century. They were relatively balanced between the genders and often had sizeable families.[56]

Personal stories bear out how the war could tear apart families. Ye Xiaolin (b. 1915) recalled that in 1937 many Chinese men left their children and Japanese wives behind in Yokohama. She saw those wives "crying and crying, standing in front of the Chinese Guild" as their husbands prepared to board a ship for China. Ye's mother brought her younger brother back to China on that ship, but Ye and her husband remained.[57] Ling Yintang's father also departed for Hong Kong in 1937, leaving the college-age Yintang

---

54. YSSII, 2:940; Kikuchi, *Sensō to kakyō*, pp. 19–20.

55. Murakami, *Yokohama Chūkagaiteki kakyōden*, p. 140; Kikuchi, *Sensō to kakyō*, p. 19. These sentiments were corroborated by the testimony of Ling Yintang (b. 1925) and Lin Guangwei (b. 1904).

56. Yokohama-shi, *Yokohama-shi tōkei sho*, 2:34; Kanagawa-ken, "Zairyū gaikokujin meibo," Aug. 25, 1945, RHM, ref. A06030109400, JACAR. In 1902, Chinese men outnumbered women by a proportion of greater than 3 to 1. By war's end in August 1945, that proportion in Kanagawa Prefecture was 1.5 to 1. The average Chinese household size in Kanagawa Prefecture was then 3.65 people. One extreme case was Bao Bogong's household of eight, including his wife, three sons, two daughters, the wife of one of his sons, and a 65-year-old chef who worked for his restaurant. Although smaller than the Japanese average at the time of around 5 people, it was significantly higher than that of the next largest group of foreigners in Kanagawa, the Germans, who averaged only 2.42 people per household.

57. CKK and YKS, *Yokohama kakyō no kioku*, p. 41.

behind.[58] The conflict divided families in other ways as well. As noted in the introduction, two brothers of restaurateur Bao Bogong elected to enter the Japanese army, one as an army doctor, and the other as a Chinese-language interpreter. The latter brother died in the fighting on the Chinese mainland. Another brother served as a doctor for the Chinese Nationalist army.[59]

Despite the outbursts of anti-Chinese sentiment at the start of the war, Yokohama organizations encouraged Chinese to stay, acknowledging their importance to the local economy and community. The Yamashita-chō Association, the Hygiene Cooperative, and Kanagawa Prefecture all urged the Chinese to remain in Chinatown and continue operating their businesses, even distributing pamphlets promising consistent treatment as the war escalated.[60]

Memoirs moreover suggest that relations between Chinese and Japanese in Yokohama Chinatown did in fact return to normal during the war, at least in comparison to other regions in Japan. Liu Xinglan (b. 1906) recalls that her family was helped during the lean years of the war by a Japanese friend who worked at a noodle factory and could procure a little extra on the side. This generosity ended, unfortunately, when the friend was sent to the front.[61] Other elderly Chinese noted that Japanese and Chinese children continued to play together in the streets, and Chinese both participated in air-raid drills and received food rations in the war's later stages.[62] The localized culture of the Chinese community was still expressed at the school, where children often spoke a mixture of Cantonese and Japanese, the languages used at home. The school song, sung in Cantonese, invoked the local specificity of their community: "Faint Mt. Fuji in the distance, the expansive water of Yokohama harbor, let our Chinese Public School live forever."[63]

Chinese cuisine remained an important element of daily life in Yokohama as many of Chinatown's Chinese restaurants remained open despite

---

58. Ceng, "Ou," p. 7.
59. Sugawara, *Nihon no kakyō*, pp. 20–21.
60. *YSSII*, 2:938.
61. *FNWS*, p. 98.
62. Miao Shunxin, conversation with author, Sept. 10, 2005.
63. Li, "Shisso de kenjitsu na shōgakkō," p. 142; Chen Xiaoyin, "Yokohama Chūka kōritsu shōgakkō no omoide," p. 143.

persistent food shortages that shut down most other restaurants. There was even a small boom in business for Chinese restaurants from 1938 to 1941 as the larger establishments provided farewell banquets for Japanese soldiers and their families. Under tightened economic conditions, the Chinese restaurants managed to continue serving customers, relying on black-market procurements, and when these failed, debasing their sweet-and-sour pork with whale or horse meat.[64] They were hardly prospering; at the later stages of the war, Chinese restaurants only had enough ingredients to remain open for two and a half hours each day. But, by the end of the war, upwards of 54 percent of working Chinese were employed in Chinese restaurants. The next most common work was tailoring and clothing sales, which only employed 11.1 percent of the working population.[65] This shift was pivotal and led to the predominance of Chinese restaurants in the commercial life of the district, providing the recipe for Yokohama Chinatown's postwar economic prosperity and social integration.

Traders, meanwhile, found their activities constrained by onerous regulations and import-export restrictions. Even though Japanese planners attempted to expand trade into occupied China and Southeast Asia with the help of *huaqiao* in Japan, these efforts did not provide much benefit for the Yokohama community. The port primarily handled exports to Europe and America.[66] This was the reason that there were few carpetbagging Chinese newcomers in wartime Yokohama. Kobe, in contrast, saw the arrival of a new cohort of Chinese merchants who exploited textile export opportunities created by Japan's imperial expansion into North China and the Dutch East Indies.[67]

The Chinese who elected to remain in Yokohama during the war were acculturated and socially integrated into the local community. Some Chinese leaders in Japan lamented that many of their compatriots had married

---

64. Yokohama Chinatown Official Website, "Sonrō keirō intabyū: Kakyō issei no jidai," accessed Sept. 26, 2007, http://www.chinatown.or.jp/lovechinatown/talk /respectolder.html. Liang Zhaohua (1905–2007) recalled that police often came to search their freezers, confiscating any black market meat they found.

65. Fukushima, "Shōwa-ki Chūkagai no seisui," p. 17; Kanagawa-ken, "Zairyū gaikokujin meibo."

66. Kikuchi, *Sensō to kakyō*, pp. 112–13; Iriyama, "Honpō ni okeru kakyō o ronzu," p. 196; Kagotani, "Chinese Merchant Community in Kobe," p. 50.

67. Kagotani, "Chinese Merchant Community in Kobe," pp. 67–69.

Japanese, forgotten how to speak Mandarin, and were willing to naturalize if the situation demanded it.[68] It was this integration into local society, in fact, that motivated them to stay. But such motivations were at odds with the vision of discrete national communities promoted by both Chinese and Japanese state rhetoric, especially the Japanese invocation of Sino-Japanese amity. Nevertheless, the Japanese state would compel the Yokohama Chinese to publicly affirm this wartime ideology.

The Public Record of Amity

Accounts published in Japan during the war portrayed the Yokohama Chinese as willing supporters of Japan's military actions. From early 1938 until the end of the war, Yokohama newspapers indeed publicized a variety of collaborationist activities carried out by Yokohama Chinese leaders and organizations—celebrations, radio broadcasts, political rallies and parades, interviews, Buddhist ceremonies, and other gatherings between Chinese and Japanese residents. Even as wartime shortages decreased page counts, newspapers continued to print such articles, often with photographs.[69] These articles suggest a range of cultural events intended to build solidarity between Chinese and Japanese residents. On January 25, 1939, the *Yokohama bōeki shinpō* reported plans for a Buddhist ceremony to memorialize Chinese *and* Japanese soldiers killed by that point in the war. And on May 30, 1940, the newspaper reported that trustees of the Chinese Guild had organized an evening of traditional Chinese music. These activities and practices had abundant precedent in Yokohama, but under conditions of war were redirected to support Japanese policy.

Propaganda invested ordinary social exchanges with meaning for Sino-Japanese amity. Even an exchange meeting between Chinese and Japanese children, as reported in the above *Yokohama bōeki shinpō* article, furthered this very purpose. The Yokohama Chinese school also promoted the ideology of

---

68. Lu Feng, "Quan Riben huaqiao zonghui," pp. 23–25. Lu Feng observed that Chinese who spoke their provincial dialect at home were losing their ability to use the Chinese national language, Mandarin, in favor of another national language, Japanese.

69. We may understand the priority that newspaper gave to these stories as justified by a desire to prove the authenticity of Sino-Japanese amity for a Japanese reading public and to document and provide photographic evidence of Chinese complicity with Japan's war aims.

peace and amity, as a Dalian-born Japanese named Haga Hideo (b. 1922) discovered. When Haga visited the school in October 1942, he photographed students practicing their calligraphy with the phrase "Sino-Japanese peace [*Zhong-Ri heping*]" (fig. 4.2).[70] Intermarriage between Chinese men and Japanese women, a long-standing social phenomenon, was likewise heralded in a 1939 *Huawen Daban meiri* article as "Sino-Japanese amity marriage."[71] Previously, such marriages between Chinese men and Japanese women were attended by anxieties over miscegenation and national betrayal because the wife was assumed to become Chinese.[72]

In Japan's mass media, the most visible Yokohama Chinese supporter of Japan's war mission was the Yokohama-born Chen Dongting (1895–1966).[73] Chen was a graduate of the Datong xuexiao and attended the Japanese university Meiji daigaku. In his adult life he took over his family's import-export business and by 1933 had become a trustee of both the Chinese Guild and the Chinese Chamber of Commerce. In 1937 he was elected to head the Chinese Guild, and it was from this leadership position that he

---

70. Haga, "Yomigaeru kioku," p. 137.

71. "Liu-Ri huaqiao xianfeng xuanyan: xieli jianshe gengsheng xin Zhongguo gongxian shenxin yu xingya daye," *Huawen Daban meiri* 2, no. 6 (1939), pp. 30–31.

72. Oguma, *Genealogy of "Japanese" Self-Images*, p. 43; Caprio, *Japanese Assimilation Policies in Colonial Korea*, p. 169. This view of Sino-Japanese couples was similar to the encouragement of intermarriage between Koreans and Japanese under Japanese colonial rule. The primary difference, however, lay in the fact that the mixing of Japanese and Korean blood was intended to obliterate any ethnic distinctions between the two populations and irreversibly integrate Korea into Japan. In the case of this article for a Chinese audience, there was no hint of such motives; the categories of Chinese and Japanese were described as discrete entities, and presumably expected to remain so.

73. Wang Liang, *Zhonghua minguo liu-Ri Hengbin huaqiao zonghui*; Chen Tien-shi, "Chin Dōtei (Chen Dongting)," in *Kakyō-kajin jiten*, ed. Kani Hiroaki, Shiba Yoshinobu, and You Zhongxun (Tokyo: Kōbundō, 2002), p. 717; "Chin Dōtei kōseki chōsho," enclosure to Kanagawa Prefectural Governor to Home Ministry, Chief of Personnel Division, Nov. 10, 1939, ref. 1199405393, KPA. Chinese and Japanese sources disagree over Chen's place of birth. Kanagawa Prefecture documents and a Sept. 6, 1940, article in the *YBS* claim that he was born in Yokohama. More recent writings by Chinese authors claim he was born in Zhongshan Prefecture, Guangdong Province.

FIG. 4.2. Children at the Yokohama Chinese school practicing calligraphy by writing "Sino-Japanese peace" (*Zhong-Ri heping*), 1942. Courtesy of Haga Hideo/Haga Library.

helped engineer the break with the Chinese consulate.[74] Responding to the consul's criticism of the Yokohama *huaqiao* for failing to demonstrate patriotism, Chen countered that the international and local situations were incomparable and that they have their own sense of patriotism.[75] As Chinese patriotism was transformed by the goal of Sino-Japanese amity into collaborationism, Chen was at the forefront, lending his opinions and visage to Yokohama newspaper articles.

In this way, Chen helped define a localized Chinese identity that was reconciled to collaborationism. In a September 6, 1940, interview in the *Yokohama bōeki shinpō,* he argues: "We *huaqiao* who reside in Yokohama are real *huaqiao,* but our relationship to Japan is like that between close relatives.

---

74. Naimushō keihōkyoku, "Hokushi jihen ni kansuru jōhō."
75. Ibid.

It's because our shared history is so long, and many here have Japanese wives." The journalist describes Chen as "the strong nail that binds China and Japan together," and "a pure Yokohama-ite [*kissui no hamakko*]." This was the first recorded usage of the term *hamakko* to refer to the Yokohama Chinese and implied an ironic acceptance of ethnic heterogeneity within a "pure" local identity.[76]

Chen's activities as the "boss" of Chinatown earned him further praise from Japanese authorities. On July 7, 1939, the second anniversary of the outbreak of war, he invited professors to lecture in Chinatown on the importance of Sino-Japanese unity. Later that month, he led a contingent of Yokohama *huaqiao* to participate in an anti-British rally.[77] As vice president of the General Assembly of Huaqiao in Japan, he represented the Yokohama Chinese community in national meetings. He also promoted donations to various Japanese governmental organs and military associations. These donations came from resident Chinese in all sizes; at one extreme, Bao Bogong contributed an astounding 80,000 yen, and at the other, a Chinese cook donated a modest 50 yen.[78] For these leadership activities Kanagawa Prefecture lauded Chen as a model for both foreigners and Japanese in 1939.[79]

In addition, Chen contributed to propaganda messages directed at international audiences. In 1938, Yokohama Chinese performed three short-wave radio broadcasts from Tokyo Broadcasting Station (JOAK) to ethnic-Chinese communities worldwide.[80] Chen Dongting took the lead with a Cantonese address on August 2, introducing the secure and prosperous life enjoyed

---

76. The content of the Yokohama-ite identity was left vague in this and other publications, suggesting that its meaning for the local community was implicitly understood. Its primary basis was pride in Yokohama's port-city cosmopolitanism and a conscious differentiation from the culture of the capital city of Tokyo.

77. "Chin Dōtei kōseki chōsho."

78. Naimushō gaijika, "Gaiji keisatsu no ippan jōkyō"; "Kanshin na Shinajin kokku," *YBS*, Jan. 31, 1939, p. 2; Yokohama-shi, *Yokohama-shi tōkei sho,* 33:15. Bao's massive donation appears to have been calculated to push the Chinese donation total (102,180 yen) past that of all Western residents of Yokohama combined (102,000 yen). At the time, this sum of money could have purchased 1.3 acres of high-quality (rice) paddy field, or 32.5 acres of poor-quality land in Naka Ward.

79. "Chin Dōtei kōseki chōsho."

80. This station was a precursor to Japan's public broadcasting company, NHK. JOAK was the station's call sign.

by *huaqiao* in Japan. Next, on September 19, Chinese Guild trustee and Datong xuexiao graduate Bao Qikang delivered a fifteen-minute English-language broadcast to *huaqiao* in the Americas and Southeast Asia. Finally, on November 24, two twelve-year-old students from the Yokohama Chinese school, Wang Jinzhou (b. 1925) and Chen Huicai, reached out to Chinese children with songs in both Chinese and Japanese.[81] A similar message was printed onto leaflets and spread on the Chinese mainland in 1940. Entitled "Liu-Ri huaqiao de heping shenghuo yu jianshe Dongya xinzhixu yundong de zhaopian" (Photographs of the peaceful life of *huaqiao* in Japan, and the construction of the New Order in East Asia), these leaflets declared that allying with America and the Soviet Union against Japan was idiocy, and highlighted the model behavior of the *huaqiao* in Japan.

Another venue for the performance of Chinese collaborationism was the Establishing the Nation Gymnastics (Kenkoku taisō) movement. Brainchild of Matsumoto Gaku, former police section chief in the Home Ministry, this movement was developed in late 1937 as a patriotic form of radio gymnastics incorporating fifteen "thrusting, striking, cutting" motions derived from traditional martial arts. Matsumoto intended the exercises to strengthen the physique and spirit of the Japanese people in order to endure a long culture war (*bunkasen*).[82] However, Police Chief Sakamoto Seigō in Yokohama eagerly included Chinatown's Chinese as well, implying perhaps that "the nation" to be established was not specifically Japan, but rather the very principle of ethnic nationality. In fact, similar social engineering exercises in the Japanese puppet state of Manchukuo had been used to promote Manchukuo nationalism.

Chen Dongting introduced Kenkoku taisō to the Yokohama Chinese school on December 15, 1938.[83] The following month, Chen Dongting and Wu Bokang, now the Chinese school's director of moral education, led forty Chinese students in a public performance of Kenkoku taisō. Wu was then invited by Bao Bogong, the education affairs trustee of the Chinese Guild, to a celebratory banquet to honor the police sponsors of Kenkoku taisō on December 26, 1938. We may imagine his trepidation at having to greet, as

---

81. Naimushō gaijika, "Gaiji keisatsu no ippan jōkyō"; "Zairyū kakyō futatabi hōsō," *Yomiuri shinbun*, Sept. 8, 1938, evening edition, p. 2; "Kono koe o kike, Shinaji jidō ga sokoku e hōsō," *Yomiuri shinbun*, Nov. 25, 1938, evening edition, p. 2.

82. Matsumoto Gaku, "Kokumin taii kōjō to kenkoku taisō," p. 1.

83. "Chin Dōtei kōseki chōsho."

well as thank, his former jailers; but the record of this encounter published in the journal *Kōsei jidai* (Age of public welfare) indicates that Wu toasted these gymnastics as "the best way to initiate Sino-Japanese amity." He noted with approval that his young son and daughter cheerfully braved the early morning cold to begin their day with these exercises.[84]

Wu Bokang's praise of Kenkoku taisō should be understood in light of his previous incarceration and the oppressive atmosphere that hung over the Chinese in Yokohama. Given this context, we may even detect some disguised ambivalence in his toast to Sakamoto Seigō and the Yokohama police; he declared that "right now, we must bring Sino-Japanese amity into being through the education of both countries' children," and "if we do so, I believe that in twenty or thirty years time, we will have a true Sino-Japanese amity."[85] By deferring true Sino-Japanese amity several decades into the future, Wu implicitly questioned both the legitimacy of the collaborationist regimes being installed in China and the sincerity of the rituals performed in Yokohama and elsewhere in support of Japan's war mission.

Genuinely believed or not, slogans of Sino-Japanese amity were essentially performative. Repeated enunciation allowed Chinese to remain in Yokohama, unmolested by the police. After the establishment of the collaborationist regimes, they were classified as allied nationals and not subjected to the draconian policies later applied to American, British, Canadian, or Australian nationals.[86] Japanese authorities, by participating in this narrative, were also compelled to live up to it. They publicly praised exemplary *huaqiao*, as Kanagawa Prefecture did for Chen Dongting. In a January 1939 case, Yokohama police even used Sino-Japanese amity to justify leniency when they arrested eighteen *huaqiao* for mahjong gambling. In light of the

---

84. Fujino, *Kyōsei sareta kenkō*, pp. 58–61; Wu, "Enkaichū hitokoto mōshiagemasu," p. 8.

85. Wu, "Enkaichū hitokoto mōshiagemasu," p. 8.

86. *YSSII*, 1:37–38; Shibata, "Tekisan shori to tokushu zaisan," pp. 426–34. In July 1941, the Japanese government prohibited all financial and business activities for American, British, Australian, and Canadian citizens. All company assets, properties, and cargo left at port were also confiscated. The Western-established mission schools on the Bluff were given over to Japanese principals, and their curricula shifted toward Japanese patriotism. Finally, with the declaration of war against the United States and Britain on December 8, 1941, enemy nationals in Yokohama were separated by sex and placed in camps to await repatriation.

"increasingly harmonious" relations between Chinese and Japanese, the arresting officers did not deport the offenders. They simply summoned Chen Dongting and other community representatives to receive along with the guilty parties a lecture on Sino-Japanese cooperation and behaving as "Japan's finest *huaqiao*."[87] In contrast, Chinese in outlying areas could not always rely on the rhetoric of Sino-Japanese solidarity to secure good treatment from their neighbors. During the war, Fujian-born Lin Tongchun (b. 1925) endured taunts and slurs by classmates in a Japanese school in the city of Tsuyama in western Japan. In addition, his father was once assaulted by a Japanese man whose son had been killed in China. Lin's worst experience was being forced by his teacher to stand among the straw dummies during his school's bamboo-spear drills so the students could get a look at "a real Shinajin."[88]

Hidden Transcripts of Ambivalence

The public transcript of Sino-Japanese amity downplayed the coercive power of the Japanese state and portrayed Chinese collaborationism as voluntary and sincere. However, records of a more private nature—oral histories, police and diplomatic records, and the confidential minutes of two meetings between Chinese leaders and Japanese government representatives—reveal relations that were far less harmonious. These sources challenge the appearance of Sino-Japanese amity in three ways: first, they reveal to us doubts and suspicions held by both Japanese and Chinese about the actual practices of collaborationism; second, they show Chinese motivations to be economic and instrumental; finally, they document Chinese articulations of identity that made their role in collaborationism ambiguous.

First, it is difficult to sustain the conclusion that Chinese initiated, of their own volition, the displays of support for Japan's war mission carried in newspapers. Available evidence suggests that such activities were instigated by Yokohama advisers, often through the puppet regimes or the General Assembly. For instance, the *Kanagawa-ken shinbun* reported that on March 27, 1941, Yokohama's Chinese Guild celebrated the one-year anniversary of the

---

87. Naimushō gaijika, "Gaiji keisatsu no ippan jōkyō"; "Daijōteki kanten kara Kaga-chō sho no hogaraka sabaki," *YBS*, Jan. 10, 1939, p. 2. Thirty individuals had been deported for similar offenses in April of the previous year.

88. Lin Tongchun, *Hashi wataru hito*, pp. 42–43, 56–57.

founding of Wang Jingwei's regime. Records of Japan's Foreign Police reveal that it was Feng You, Yokohama consul general of the Reorganized National Government, who ordered the community organizations to commemorate the event.[89] Typically, the chain of command originated in the embassy and consulates of Wang Jingwei's government and reached the local *huaqiao* organizations via the General Assembly, which also mediated between the local community and Japanese authorities.[90] In addition, according to a document authored by Japan's Army Ministry (Rikugunshō), the Kōain funded and exercised control over the General Assembly. The Kōain in fact orchestrated the General Assembly's inaugural conference on March 6, 1940, directed it to host a representative from Wang's regime, and arranged far in advance the congratulatory telegram the General Assembly would send to Wang Jingwei on March 30.[91] In other words, the political pageantry sponsored by the General Assembly in support of Sino-Japanese amity derived from outside directives.

Japanese police, moreover, distrusted the Chinese population. Despite the lofty language of friendship used by Japanese authorities, they treated the Yokohama Chinese as potential threats to security. The Kanagawa Foreign Police sequestered the Chinese in Chinatown and forced those living outside of its precincts to relocate to the city center.[92] Huang Lixiang (1912–1999) recalled that in 1943 police forced him to abandon both home and restaurant in the municipality of Honmoku.[93] Police also restricted their right to travel; Ye Xiaolin recalled that her family had to apply for permission to visit the family grave at the nearby Chinese cemetery.[94] Even Wang Jinzhou, one of the children who participated in the 1938 JOAK propaganda broadcasts, was not free from suspicion. He commuted for a time to St. Joseph's Academy, a mission school on the Bluff overlooking Yokohama harbor. As a result, the Special Higher Police (Tokkō) detained him several

---

89. Naimushō gaijika, *Gaiji keisatsu gaikyō*, 7:54.
90. Kikuchi, *Sensō to kakyō*, pp. 55–56.
91. Naimushō gaijika, *Gaiji keisatsu gaikyō*, 7:54.
92. Chen Changhao, "Huiyi yu qipan," p. 276; Murakami, *Yokohama Chūkagaiteki kakyōden*, p. 100; *BX*, p. 87. This situation was confirmed by the testimony of both Matsumura Noboru (born Liang Yourong) and Chen Changhao.
93. CKK and YKS, *Yokohama kakyō no kioku*, pp. 29–30.
94. Ibid., p. 40.

times, pointedly asking why he was both studying the enemy language of English and watching ships arriving at port.[95]

Wang's experience was relatively mild compared to others. Zheng Huagui recalled that the Special Higher Police came to search his house on suspicion of signaling to enemy planes.[96] Speaking in Chinese did not necessarily provide safety. Liang Zhaohua (1915–2007) recounted that many Chinese feared their Japanese neighbor, a man who understood both Mandarin and Cantonese and served as an informant for the Japanese police.[97] A piano tuner named Zhou Rangjie was indeed arrested for praising Chiang Kai-shek at his father's piano factory in the spring of 1945. On suspicion of espionage, Japanese police tortured and interrogated Zhou until the end of the war.[98] Other memoirs assert that Japanese police jailed at least ten other Yokohama Chinese before the end of the war for similar crimes.[99] Police surveillance and repression thus implied an assumption that many in the Chinese community continued to hold anti-Japanese, pro-GMD beliefs.

In private venues, the same Chinese leaders who received credit for steering the community toward collaborationism also deviated from the public script of Sino-Japanese amity. Under the auspices of the Society for the Promotion of Diplomacy (Nihon gaikō kyōkai), Chinese representatives from Tokyo and Yokohama met with Japanese China experts in November 1938 and March 1939 to discuss *huaqiao* contributions to Japan's war effort. Records from these meetings offer insight into how they construed their relationship with Japanese authorities and how they wished to frame their motivations. It is telling that Japan's Ministry of Foreign Affairs sealed these discussions from public view by classifying both documents as top secret (*gokuhi*). The preface of the first meeting's minutes warned that the document should be treated with care, lest the unguarded words of the speakers lead to unfortunate misunderstandings.[100] The record of the second meeting also noted that the *huaqiao* representatives themselves requested that

---

95. Ibid., p. 146.
96. Murakami, *Yokohama Chūkagaiteki kakyōden*, p. 130.
97. CKK and YKS, *Yokohama kakyō no kioku*, p. 89.
98. Sugawara, *Nihon no kakyō*, pp. 81–82.
99. *FNWS*, p. 98.
100. Nihon gaikō kyōkai, "Honpō zaijū kakyō no Nisshi jikyoku kondan (dai-ikkai)," 1938, DRMFA, ref. B02030924400, JACAR.

their candid impressions remain private.[101] Much of what they said, indeed, suggests that the cooperation between the *huaqiao* and Japan was little more than a veneer.

At these two meetings, several Chinese leaders acknowledged that exchange students and the rank and file did not fully accept invocations of friendship and unity between the two countries. Regarding the average *huaqiao* in Japan, Japan-born Zhang Zhaoxiu admitted that "few actually believed in the noble ideals that justified the conflict" but remained in Japan because they expected a quick resolution. Moreover, he predicted that *huaqiao* in Japan might increasingly question the pro-Japan spirit and fall into the trap of pure opportunism if the war of resistance dragged on.[102]

Chinese leaders themselves averred sincere support for the goal of Sino-Japanese amity. Many, however, insinuated an ambivalence toward its practice, at least in the present, by offering their opinion on what *real* Sino-Japanese amity (*shin Nisshi shinzen*) would be. Chen Dongting proposed that schools begin inculcating the message of Sino-Japanese amity from elementary school so that "true amity between the two countries can come into being . . . by the time students reach college."[103] These statements echoed the sentiments of Wu Bokang, whose statements in *Kōsei jidai* similarly deferred authentic Sino-Japanese amity far into the future.

Seventy-seven-year-old Wen Bingchen offered more direct criticism of past and present Japanese policy.[104] Wen declared that Japan was as responsible as China for the current conflict and that neither had been living up to the principle of Asian solidarity. Japan, he argued, "claims to be a leader in Asia, but its autonomy is but a pale shadow. . . . If Japan continues to rely on the power of Germany and Italy . . . then no matter how much you repeat the slogan of Sino-Japanese amity, you will not convert the hearts of Chinese to true Sino-Japanese amity."[105]

---

101. Nihon gaikō kyōkai, "Ryūnichi kakyō no Nisshi jikyokukan (dainikai)," 1939, ref. 4338, Tōyō Bunko.

102. Nihon gaikō kyōkai, "Nisshi jikyokukan (dainikai)," pp. 44–45.

103. Nihon gaikō kyōkai, "Nisshi jikyoku kondan (daiikkai)," p. 33.

104. Ogasawara, *Sonbun o sasaeta Yokohama kakyō*, pp. 22, 42–43. Wen's latitude to speak freely likely derived from his status as a community elder with unimpeachable Asianist credentials. In 1898 he sheltered Sun Yatsen in Yokohama, served as his translator and bodyguard, and as described in chap. 2, sparked the brawl at the Chinese Guild in 1899.

105. Nihon gaikō kyōkai, "Nisshi jikyoku kondan (daiikkai)," pp. 51–52.

Other Chinese representatives called for true Sino-Japanese amity in order to voice specific complaints. In that regard, they were admitting to impure economic motivations behind their cooperation, which was perhaps one of the reasons the representatives at these meetings wished to keep their discussions confidential.[106] Lin Jinci, trustee of the Tokyo *huaqiao* association, appealed for greater freedom to conduct business and travel in Japan, which he argued was "a matter of life or death for the *huaqiao*." A positive response from the Japanese government would thus be "the most direct path toward true Sino-Japanese amity."[107] Lin was reflecting on the formidable economic difficulties that Chinese in Tokyo and Yokohama were experiencing since 1937. In this context, Zhang Zhaoxiu argued that "*huaqiao* are economic warriors" who can promote Japan's message better than Japan's clumsy propaganda. He argued, "Show [the *huaqiao* around Asia that] they will profit more than they would under Western control. Our economic success will show [them] Japan's good intentions. So use *us*. Economic results will dispel Western propaganda like snow at sunrise."[108]

Economic motives were evident in many collaborationist activities by the Chinese, because these often arrived with appeals for assistance.[109] In June 1939, Tokyo and Yokohama *huaqiao* organizations jointly transmitted a petition to Japan's Ministry of Foreign Affairs. The leaders, Chen Dongting of Yokohama and Zhang Zesheng of Tokyo, promised their communities' cooperation, proposing even to send representatives to aid in pacification work in occupied China. In return, they requested that Japan loosen import and export restrictions and issue permits for travel to and from China. This type of economic instrumentalism mirrored the secret plans laid out by the Ministry of Greater East Asia in 1944. Nevertheless, at this early stage of the war, Japanese police rejected these requests, noting in their records that they should investigate *huaqiao* organizations more closely to forestall further appeals of this sort.[110]

---

106. Naimushō keihōkyoku, *Gaiji keisatsu gaikyō*, 4:28. This judgment of impure motives is not mine. The Japanese police observed that Chinese at times accused each other of self-serving motives. Sycophants were apparently not well tolerated in their communities.

107. Nihon gaikō kyōkai, "Nisshi jikyoku kondan (daiikkai)," pp. 62–64.

108. Nihon gaikō kyōkai, "Nisshi jikyokukan (dainikai)," pp. 40–44.

109. Kikuchi, *Sensō to kakyō*, p. 64.

110. Ibid., p. 109.

In addition, Chinese in Japan present at the two secret meetings were not ideal representatives of Sino-Japanese amity because they asserted complex identity positions. At the 1938 meeting, Zhang Jilai, a clothing merchant from Tokyo, argued that "viewed from the perspective of Japanese-Chinese-Manchurian cooperation, we do not want to be considered Chinese, but rather treated as Japanese, broadly defined [*hiroi imi ni okeru Nihonjin*]. Without this, there can be no true amity."[111] Chen Dongting similarly challenged the fundamental distinction between Chinese and Japanese, offering a statement that was nearly identical in substance to his subsequent newspaper interview in 1940. Intending, perhaps, to flatter his Japanese counterparts and establish the loyalty of the Yokohama Chinese, he inadvertently blurred the boundary between the two:

> Most of us who remain [in Japan] have the same feelings and lifestyles as our Japanese brothers. Most of us were born in Japan. My wife is Japanese and our children are practically the same as Japanese; there is no way that we could harbor any ill feelings toward Japan. On the contrary, we feel extreme gratitude toward Japan. . . . The very thought of having to go back to China makes us feel grateful to be allowed to stay in Japan.[112]

Bao Qikang, in turn, argued that he "no longer considers himself Chinese" because he has lived in Yokohama for thirty-one years. He then turned his personal identification with Yokohama into a challenge to the political and diplomatic terms in which Japanese authorities construed Sino-Japanese amity. To Bao Qikang, true amity was local and quotidian: "If we interact with each other sincerely in our daily lives, we can overcome differences in customs, naturally harmonize our feelings, and achieve true Sino-Japanese amity. . . . this would be far better than a Sino-Japanese amity imposed from above."[113]

Clearly, neither Chen nor Bao intended to deny a role for the Yokohama Chinese in promoting friendship between China and Japan. But by evoking their identification with Yokohama, they undermined their standing as representative Chinese. The friendship discourse, as part of wartime

---

111. Nihon gaikō kyōkai, "Nisshi jikyoku kondan (daiikkai)," pp. 13–16.
112. Ibid., p. 31.
113. Ibid., pp. 59–61. Bao was also echoing a defense of local autonomy that Chen Dongting had made in the fall of 1937 against ROC consular criticism. Chen had emphasized that even though the Yokohama Chinese defied the wishes of the consulate, they had their own, locally defined, sense of patriotism.

pan-Asianism, depended on the coherence of separate Chinese and Japanese nations. For the Yokohama Chinese, their local and national identifications both enabled and undercut their exploitation as propaganda tools by the Japanese government. Living as "pure Yokohama-ites," as the journalist called Chen in the 1940 article, aligned their interests with Yokohama society, and like it or not, Japan as a whole. Yet, this local integration separated them from Chinese in China and other *huaqiao* around the world.

Conclusion

When Allied firebombing campaigns on civilian targets in Japan began in the spring of 1945, the Chinese of Yokohama suffered the same fate as their Japanese neighbors. Those with Japanese relatives, mainly through marriage, were allowed to evacuate to familial homes in the countryside. Others with ties to Chinese in areas surrounding Yokohama, for instance Karuizawa or Hakone, were also allowed to evacuate there. Most, however, stayed in the city center, despite American-dropped leaflets warning them of the imminent bombardment, and awaited their fate.[114]

On the morning of May 29, 1945, more than 500 B-29 bombers dropped 2,570 tons of incendiary bombs on Yokohama, reducing it to smoking ruin.[115] Many died in their air-raid shelters; others fled the flames to the waters of the harbor. When the bombs fell, restaurant-owner Zhou Chaozong, along with his neighbors, outran the flames and jumped into Yokohama harbor for safety. Afterwards he was treated like any other resident and given blankets by the neighborhood association.[116] The bombing destroyed Chinatown completely, including Zhou Rangjie's piano factory, its restaurants, and the Chinese school. Wu Bokang had been living at the school and was severely injured when bombs struck the building. His wife, daughter, and son, however, perished in the collapsed structure. Wu's life thus epitomized three distinct phases of the war experienced by the Yokohama Chinese:

---

114. Yokohama Chinatown Official Website, "Kakyō issei no jidai."

115. *BX*, p. 88; *YSSII*, 2:1024–26. From the end of June 1943 until Japan's surrender, the number of Chinese living in Kanagawa Prefecture had dropped from 2,964 to 1,917. However, it is difficult to gauge how many Chinese were killed in the bombardment from population figures; many had evacuated to other regions before and after Yokohama was destroyed.

116. Sugawara, *Nihon no kakyō*, p. 60.

first oppression by the Japanese police, then coerced collaborationism, and finally personal tragedy in the firebombings of May 1945.[117]

With the end of the war and the beginning of the Allied Occupation of Japan, the Yokohama *huaqiao* returned to the control of the ROC and became Allied nationals—nominal victors in the Asia-Pacific War. Chinese Ministry of Foreign Affairs documents reveal that the Chinese Mission (Zhonghua minguo zhu-Ri daibiao tuan) exercised jurisdiction over Chinese nationals in Japan, from prosecuting postwar crimes—like firearms possession and black marketeering—to arresting suspected war criminals.[118] The Chinese Mission passed orders to the Allied Occupation to arrest Bao Qikang in August 1946 for working in the Wang Jingwei regime's central bank.[119] Despite his wartime assertion that he no longer considered himself Chinese, Chinese authorities saw things very differently. In April 1947, the Allied Occupation repatriated him to Shanghai to stand trial. The Shanghai Higher Court convicted him of aiding the enemy, but also acknowledged that his role in the collaborationist regime was subordinate and his duties mundane; on August 19, 1947, it passed the relatively light sentence of sixteen months imprisonment, minus time already served.[120] The other leaders who were not directly affiliated with the Chinese collaborationist regimes escaped prosecution entirely and reemerged after the war as ROC citizens with their influence fully intact.

The recategorization of the Yokohama Chinese as Allied nationals was one more reversal in a decade of similar contortions, demonstrating the unstable and constructed link between a state and a people. This experience, however, did not discredit the authenticity of Chinese national identity; on the contrary, it confirmed this identification as indelible and inevitable. These political machinations would not have had much effect without the universal acceptance of nationhood as the public identity that mattered most. From the 1920s, Chinese and Japanese governments cooperated in constructing the national subjectivity of the Yokohama Chinese. The ROC built a network of national representatives through its OCAC, and Japanese

---

117. *BX*, p. 90.

118. Waijiaobu, "Woguo zhu-Ri daibiao tuan falüchu gongzuo baogao," 1947–48, ref. 020-010121-0004, AH.

119. Otis Luckman to Commanding Officer, Sugamo Prison, APO 181, Apr. 17, 1947, box 125, folder 26, RG 554, NACP.

120. Waijiaobu, "Falüchu gongzuo baogao," pp. 174–75.

researchers conducted volumes of research on *huaqiao* that promoted the vision of a global community of diasporic Chinese. Wartime imperatives then elevated nationality as the overriding modality of identity. Japanese propagandists wanted Chinese spokespersons for Japan's war mission and crafted pluralistic, nonassimilationist policies. Participation in the discourse of Sino-Japanese amity in its various guises—gymnastics, parades, propaganda—helped construct Chineseness even as it buttressed Japan's legitimacy in the conflict.

These Chinese tolerated Japanese government interventions into their community, however, because they were also socially invested in Yokohama. Contrary to the typical characterization of wartime collaborators as motivated by greed or political opportunism, the Yokohama Chinese could anticipate few economic gains from Japan's invasion of China and Southeast Asia. Their niches in the city's economy collapsed with the outbreak of hostilities in 1937, and the only line of work that recovered to any major extent was restaurants. Their community leaders articulated economic appeals to the Japanese authorities to ameliorate their desperate straits while they waited for the return of peace. Moreover, these leaders were not mercenary interlopers or marginal elites, as often seen in Japanese-occupied China.[121] Rather, they were the same men who guided community associations prior to the war—second-generation Chinese in Japan like Chen Dongting, Bao Bogong, and Wu Bokang. In their daily lives, their economic privation, enforced frugality, and participation in local defense activities was little different from other local residents.

Collaborationism was therefore a method to resolve competing attachments to Yokohama and China—in other words, to continue living as Yokohama Chinese. It was, however, an imperfect solution. They did not have the ability to break the core script of Sino-Japanese amity, much less reject Japanese wartime ideology. Living as Yokohama-ites, moreover, contradicted their deployment as model, representative Chinese. The ambivalent and contradictory terms used by Chinese leaders reveal a yawning gap between their national and local identifications. By war's end, they nevertheless paid the price for their local affiliation when Allied bombardment destroyed Yokohama.

---

121. Brook, *Collaboration*, pp. 48–49, 75.

Collaborationism exercised a complex influence on the postwar subjectivities of the Yokohama Chinese, which may be generalized in two antithetical ways. First, the acceptance and respect for cultural difference that was embedded in Japanese wartime discourse strengthened the long-term coherence of Chinese identity. In the postwar era, as in wartime, Chinese welcomed the pluralistic acceptance of their national difference. Many did not perceive it as unwanted *exclusion* from Japanese society, but rather as protection from a repressive state apparatus that had attempted to assimilate Koreans and Taiwanese through the obliteration of their cultures. Japanese laws made the naturalization process onerous, but there were also psychological barriers against becoming Japanese. Second, joint action with their Japanese neighbors opened up avenues to local integration. Chinese did not experience similar psychological barriers against embracing Yokohama as their hometown. Even during wartime, they expressed this localism in defiance of state imperatives and contributed to the commonsense acceptance of the Yokohama Chinese as Yokohama-ites. The ways in which diasporic nationalism developed alongside this acculturation and local integration is the story of the postwar years.

CHAPTER FIVE

A Town Divided:
The Cold War in Yokohama Chinatown,
1945–72

Yokohama Chinatown experienced enormous social, cultural, and economic transformations in the three decades from the end of the Asia-Pacific War to the normalization of diplomatic relations between Japan and the People's Republic of China (PRC) in 1972. These were decades when their homelands and host lands emerged from a devastating war into the unstable power dynamics of a global Cold War. These geopolitical circumstances shaped Yokohama Chinatown's relationship to China, the legal status of Chinese in Japan, and their role in the local economy. Most visibly, this era saw the rising economic fortunes of the Yokohama Chinese, which can be adduced by transformations in the cityscape itself: from a smoldering ruin after the Allied firebombing campaigns of spring 1945, to a shanty town of barracks and black markets during the Allied Occupation, to a district of seedy bars and cabarets in the 1950s and 1960s, and then to a gourmet destination for Japanese tourists by the 1970s (fig. 5.1).

This latter transition was the product of long-term but accelerating commercial trends. By war's end, some thirty Chinese restaurants employed a majority of the working population; by 1976, the district had over ninety-five.[1]

---

1. Sugawara, *Chainataun*, p. 149.

FIG. 5.1. Yokohama Chinatown in ruins in 1945 (above) and as a bustling tourist destination in 1975 (below). Courtesy of Yokohama shishi shiryō shitsu.

In other ways, however, the Yokohama Chinatown community remained the same. The Chinese population of Yokohama rebounded after the war, but did not grow much beyond its prewar size. In December 1960, 5,546 Chinese nationals lived in Kanagawa Prefecture, with a dominant proportion (3,418) residing in Chinatown and the surrounding Naka Ward. Long-term residents and their descendants comprised the majority; a July 1962 survey indicated that 63.8 percent were born in Japan, and 89 percent were permanent residents. Moreover, the majority of the community remained Cantonese (55.1 percent) with only a minor fraction (10.4 percent) originating from Taiwan. Taiwanese were recently divested of their Japanese citizenship and comprised more than half the total population of Chinese nationals in Japan; but they did not settle in significant numbers in Chinatown.[2] On the other hand, Chinese did not comprise the majority of residents in Chinatown; it continued to be a mixed community whose residences and businesses were 58.4 percent Japanese.[3]

Continuity of settlement and ethnic mixing were important factors that promoted the cultural and economic integration of these Chinese into the wider Yokohama community. This integration, ongoing since the nineteenth century, had gradually granted the Yokohama Chinese self-awareness as Yokohama-ites. By the 1970s, Yokohama Chinese were identifying, and being identified, as city residents (*shimin*) to a greater degree than ever before. One indication of this development was their contributions to *Shimin to bunka* (City residents and culture), a magazine that launched in 1979 to introduce Yokohama society and culture to a local readership; the magazine included articles on the history of Chinese settlement, as well as Chinese recipes by Yokohama-born Huang Chengwu. These articles and the reader letters they inspired suggest the degree to which Yokohama society had come to accept the Yokohama Chinese as fellow residents.[4] Such publications also illustrate how important cuisine was to this shared local culture; a 1976 work entitled *Yokohama no aji* (The taste of Yokohama) devoted a full

---

2. Nagano Takeshi, *Zainichi Chūgokujin*, p. 209. In 1946, there were 14,921 Chinese nationals and 15,906 Taiwanese in Japan.

3. Yamamuro and Kawamura, "Yokohama zairyū kakyō," pp. 3, 7, 11, 16, 26. These population figures exclude the thousands who returned home in the repatriation programs after the end of the war.

4. Ryū, "Hitsugi bune," pp. 30–31; Huang, "Kō sensei ga tsukuru," pp. 48–49; Fujisawa, "Yokohama umare," p. 39.

third of the volume to Chinese restaurants, followed by French, Italian, Mexican, American, and finally Japanese restaurants.[5] During these decades, the popularity of this multicultural gastronomy allowed Yokohama Chinese to join with administrators in Yokohama City and Kanagawa Prefecture to promote Chinatown's restaurants as a premier tourist attraction in the city.

However, this localism emerged from an era that also saw the universalization of the ethnic nation as an individual's terminal identification. The years after 1945 witnessed the rise of a global order in which national identity surged on waves of decolonization.[6] After defeat in the Asia-Pacific War, Japan lost its multiethnic empire and turned instead toward a monoethnic (*tan'itsu minzoku*) determinant of national identity. *Jus sanguinis* nationality laws continued to define formal citizenship and enacted social closure according to a community of shared descent—an ethnic people (*minzoku*) in both popular understanding and government policy.[7] This definition of the Japanese nation was reinforced by both left- and right-wing opinions; it was as much a liberal and leftist repudiation of the multinational empire as an expression of conservative notions of Japan's cultural uniqueness.[8] Moreover, in the postwar era of high-speed economic growth, Japanese eagerly created and consumed popular writings theorizing the Japanese national character (Nihonjinron), which reinforced a sense of ethnic and cultural unity.[9]

Japanese government policies implemented this monoethnic understanding of the nation by stripping Japanese citizenship from former colonial

---

5. Shiragami, *Yokohama no aji*.

6. Morris-Suzuki, *Re-inventing Japan*, p. 172.

7. Ibid., p. 190; Doak, *History of Nationalism in Modern Japan*, p. 250. To be clear, the Japanese people were defined according to different terminology in Japan's American-imposed postwar constitution. In that document, members of the political community were defined as nationals (*kokumin*) who naturally enjoyed rights in the nation-state, no longer as imperial subjects (*shinmin*) with rights bestowed by the emperor. The term *kokumin*, however, usually implies a people defined through civic participation rather than ethnic belonging. The choice of wording likely derived from the fact that Americans often mistook *minzoku* for "race."

8. Doak, *History of Nationalism in Modern Japan*, 252; Doak, "What Is a Nation?," p. 300; Oguma, *Genealogy of "Japanese" Self-Images*, p. 298.

9. Befu, *Hegemony of Homogeneity*, pp. 139–40; Lie, *Multiethnic Japan*, pp. 150–51; Yoshino, "Rethinking Theories of Nationalism, pp. 9, 17, 23.

subjects. In May 1947, Japan's Alien Registration law abruptly redesignated Taiwanese and Koreans as resident aliens.[10] But this move was not based on a unilateral understanding of ethnic difference. Under Japanese rule, Korean and Taiwanese independence activists had deployed ethnic nationalist discourses to resist colonial assimilation. And with the end of Japanese empire, the leaders of these territories accepted such ideas of nationhood. In June 1946, the Republic of China (ROC) decreed that Taiwanese living overseas would be redesignated Chinese citizens, based on the principle that Taiwan was territorially part of China and its people ethnically Chinese. Those who did not wish to revert to Chinese nationality were requested to apply at their local diplomatic office by the end of December.[11] Meanwhile, massive military demobilization and civilian repatriation in East Asia aligned ethnic identities with territorial boundaries. Almost seven million ethnic Japanese returned to Japan from the former empire and one and a half million ethnic Koreans returned to Korea in the years following the war.[12] Nearly all of the surviving thirty-two thousand Chinese forced laborers in Japan, dragooned by various Japanese military units and government agencies to work in mines and docks in wartime, also returned home.[13]

For Chinese residents of Japan, this historical transition meant a continuation of their position within Japanese society as ethnically marked but socially accepted resident aliens. But they were not alone in this regard. In postwar Japan, former colonial subjects from Korea numerically overshadowed the Chinese. According to registration records, this *zainichi* (residing in Japan) Korean population was 647,006 in 1946.[14] The term *zainichi* meant at one time temporary residence in Japan; gradually, however, it came to connote permanent settlement in Japan and a clear distinction from both

---

10. C. Lee, "Legal Status of Koreans in Japan," pp. 138, 151–52; Herzog, "Minorities," p. 554.

11. Nagano Takeshi, *Zainichi Chūgokujin*, p. 184. The economic incentive of securing the benefits of Allied nationals led most Taiwanese to accept the reversion of their nationality.

12. Gordon, *Modern History of Japan*, pp. 229, 261.

13. Nozoe, *Hanaoka jiken*, p. 14; Nagano Takeshi, *Zainichi Chūgokujin*, pp. 207–9. Nozoe Kenji attests that 38,935 Chinese forced laborers, including prisoners of war, were brought to Japan from 1943 to the end of the war. Nearly 7,000 perished due to maltreatment and harsh working conditions.

14. Nagano Takeshi, *Zainichi Chūgokujin*, pp. 208–9.

Japanese and Koreans in Korea.[15] Classified by Japan as resident aliens, they would face the same patterns of national exclusion and local inclusion that Chinese had experienced since the late nineteenth century, and would craft similar forms of identity.

This chapter examines the way the Yokohama Chinatown community mediated their national and local identities in the three decades after the end of the Asia-Pacific War. It deals first with the ideology of Japanese monoethnicity, and its congruence with efforts by the two Chinese claimant regimes to maintain Chinese patriotism in Yokohama. The interventions by these competing governments reached a crescendo in the 1950s when the community split into two factions supporting either the ROC or the PRC. This moment thus signified the peak of *huaqiao* consciousness in Yokohama, as the community reproduced the politics of a divided homeland in the streets of Chinatown. Nevertheless, subsequent years saw a Yokohama-ite identity rise to prominence from these very conditions. For the Yokohama Chinese, the ideological bifurcation of the community undermined the principle of ethnic unity, and meanwhile, economic imperatives further integrated them into the local community and legitimated their belonging as bona fide *shimin* or *jūmin* (local residents).

The Apotheosis of Huaqiao Identity

After the Japanese emperor's surrender broadcast on August 15, 1945, and the capitulation of wartime collaborationist regimes in China, the ROC under Chiang Kaishek reasserted representation and jurisdiction over Chinese in Japan; this reversion meant that they were now Allied nationals, with all the benefits that status conferred. Moreover, the Allied Occupation did not interfere with life in Chinatown; from the perspective of Japanese observers, the district returned to a de facto state of extraterritoriality.[16]

Although ROC representatives and the Allied Occupation sought Bao Qikang and other Chinese who worked for Wang Jingwei's collaborationist regime, members of civilian bodies such as the Chinese Guild were left unmolested. Despite their open support for the war, these leaders of Yokohama's Chinese community reemerged after the war with their influence

---

15. Chapman, *Zainichi Korean Identity and Ethnicity*, pp. 4–5.
16. Waijiaobu, "Woguo zhu-Ri daibiao tuan falüchu gongzuo baogao," 1947–48, ref. 020-010121-0004, AH, pp. 1–27.

intact. In September 1945, a provisional Yokohama Chinese Association was established on the site of the former Chinese Guild. Its elections were democratic and conducted as town-hall meetings; the community would gather on the steps of the newly reconstructed Guandi Temple to hear speeches before voting.[17] Bao Bogong was elected president for the first term from March 1946 to March 1947. Chen Dongting was elected president in June 1950 and served until March 1952. Their legitimacy seems not to have been damaged by their cooperation with the Japanese authorities. In light of their shared wartime experiences, the local community likely understood the unpleasant but unavoidable compromises that they made.

In March 1946, the Chinese Mission in Tokyo, which represented the ROC, ordained the Yokohama Chinese Association as an official node of its worldwide network of *huaqiao* associations.[18] Registration by the association then served in lieu of passports until the normalization of diplomatic relations with the ROC in 1952.[19] As Allied nationals, *huaqiao* acquired economic benefits, including preferential access to rations and free travel by rail. According to a February 28, 1947, *Jiji shinpō* article, registration also had a disciplinary function based on the association's ability to punish misbehavior by denying ration coupons.

These advantages made the pre-1952 era the economic "golden years" for the *huaqiao* in Japan, an age when *huaqiao*-owned enterprises and Sino-Japanese joint ventures flourished. *Huaqiao* trading firms in Tokyo, Kobe, and Osaka leveraged their Allied status and connections with China, Taiwan, and Hong Kong to expand vigorously. *Huaqiao* were also hired in large numbers to conduct international trade by Japanese corporations stifled by Occupation restrictions placed on Japanese dealings with foreign countries.[20] The accumulation of capital in *huaqiao* hands, combined with preferential access to sugar, food, and paper rations, allowed *huaqiao*-owned

---

17. Sugawara, *Nihon no kakyō*, p. 61; Wang Liang, *Hengbin huaqiao zonghui*, pp. 101–8.

18. In the process, it was renamed the Republic of China Federation of Huaqiao in Yokohama, Japan (Zhonghua minguo liu-Ri Hengbin huaqiao lianhehui). Throughout its many official name changes, the English sign above the building remained "Chinese Association." For the sake of consistency, I will refer to it as such.

19. Memorandum from John B. Cooley to Imperial Japanese Government, APO 500, Feb. 25, 1947, box 3429, folder 27, RG 331, NACP.

20. Osada and Tanaka, "Ryūnichi kakyō keizai no dōkō (3)," p. 37.

confectionaries, restaurants, newspapers, and magazines to flourish across Japan.[21]

The Chinese of Yokohama, in contrast, did not rebuild large-scale import-export businesses because the Allied Occupation had appropriated much of the city's port facilities. Instead, Yokohama *huaqiao* prospered in legal and illegal markets adjoining the zones requisitioned by the U.S. military. Much of their merchandise passed directly from Occupation personnel into Chinese hands or arrived from Taiwan and the Chinese mainland. Stories abounded about the mysterious powers of procurement exhibited by the Chinese merchants of Yokohama, who could produce scarce products such as penicillin in quantities unimaginable elsewhere.[22]

Huaqiao identity thus achieved new and concrete meaning as a result of compulsory registration and economic incentives. But it was also an expression of the consensus that, for both Chinese and Japanese, ethnic, territorial, and political unity were conceived as corresponding conditions. However, this congruity was disrupted by China's civil war and the establishment of the PRC in October 1949, an event that divided China's territory and introduced a competing set of political institutions seeking to represent the overseas Chinese.

THE COLD WAR AND THE YOKOHAMA CHINESE

Even after Chiang Kaishek lost the Chinese civil war and retreated to Taiwan, his Cold War allies, which included Japan, regarded his regime as the legitimate government of China. The ROC's agents thus continued to dominate overseas Chinese communities around the world, though their influence was contested, often violently, by supporters of the PRC. This rivalry between the two Chinese claimant states did not play out in the same manner in all overseas Chinese communities. Studies of Chinatowns in the anticommunist states of the United States, Vancouver, and Panama suggest the overwhelming dominance of the Chinese Nationalists in the early decades of the Cold War, often accompanied by overt suppression of pro-PRC

---

21. Osada and Tanaka, "Ryūnichi kakyō keizai no dōkō (1)," p. 55; Chen Efang, "Zainichi kakyō genron shuppan kai," pp. 16–17. By 1948, some nineteen newspapers were published in Japan by *huaqiao* compared to none in the period immediately preceding the war.

22. Naka-ku 50 shūnen kinen jigyō jikkō iinkai, *Yokohama Naka-ku shi*, p. 344; Sugawara, *Nihon no kakyō*, p. 115.

groups.[23] In contrast, the pro-PRC faction in Japan remained a viable opposition group with significant local support. The group's persisting influence derived from both the legacy of the Asia-Pacific War in Japan and local conditions in Yokohama.

In Japan, rival factions imposed their conceptions of Chinese identity through publishing and education, much like the battles over representation at the turn of the twentieth century. In 1948, there were two *huaqiao*-owned newspapers boasting circulations of half a million copies each, and at least twenty-five active *huaqiao* magazines. The largest were capitalist ventures, published in Japanese for a Japanese audience. Their titles were often generic, such as *Kokusai shinbun* (International newspaper) and *Seiji keizai shinbun* (Politics and economy newspaper), giving little indication of the nationality of their publishers.[24] After 1949, however, periodicals with clear affiliations with either Chinese Communist or Nationalist factions proliferated; these typically incorporated the word *huaqiao* in their titles and attempted to intervene in the way their readership understood their Chinese identity.

One pro-Communist paper was *Kakyō minpō* (Huaqiao people's news), established in July 1949 by the Huaqiao Association for the Promotion of Democracy (Huaqiao minzhu cujinhui). As a house organ, the paper strongly promoted the cause of the Chinese Communists in the Chinese civil war that was then drawing to a close.[25] This and other pro-Communist journals attempted to assert their ideological leadership by attacking the commercial orientation of the other *huaqiao*-run papers.[26] Publications serving the ROC,

---

23. Nee and de Bary Nee, *Longtime Californ'*; Kwong, *New Chinatown*; Ng, *Chinese in Vancouver*; Siu, *Memories of a Future Home*.

24. Chen Efang, "Zainichi kakyō genron shuppan kai," pp. 17–19; Statistics Bureau, *Registered Aliens by Nationality*. These circulation numbers indicate a Japanese readership because in 1948 there were only 36,932 registered Chinese in Japan, including those from Taiwan.

25. Chen Kunwang, *Nihon kakyō, ryūgakusei undōshi*, pp. 272–73. This organization was closely watched by the Allied Occupation for its involvement with the Chinese Communist Party.

26. Ibid., pp. 274–75. The *Kakyō minpō* lambasted the daily *Chūka nippō* (est. October 1945) for firing all of its editors and writers and selling off its paper allotment under the rationing system to the Japanese newspaper *Yomiuri shinbun*. By exposing this instance of ration misappropriation, *Kakyō minpō* decried the betrayal of its *huaqiao* constituency.

such as the simply titled *Huaqiao* published from 1956, were equally active in mobilizing their constituency and confirming *huaqiao* as the dominant modality of Chinese identity.

A new Yokohama Chinese school was built in September 1946 through the efforts of Bao Bogong and Wu Bokang and was operated under the auspices of the Chinese Mission of the ROC. This body decreed that classes would be conducted entirely in Mandarin, a first for Yokohama, and with textbooks selected by the Chinese Ministry of Education. These materials included patriotic lessons to inculcate affective attachment to China and partisan pieces on leaders of the ROC.[27] At the time, its elementary, middle-school, and night-school divisions enrolled 1,000 people, nearly 20 percent of Kanagawa Prefecture's Chinese population.[28] The school therefore wielded extraordinary social importance for the community, and the unfolding Cold War in Asia sparked an all-out struggle for its control. The Korean War began in June 1950, and in late October troops from the PRC entered the conflict against the United States and South Korea. Consequently, the loyalties of the Chinese in Japan, particularly educators, became a critical concern for the Chinese Mission, the Allied Occupation, and Japanese government. Most of the Chinese teachers whom the Yokohama Chinese school hired from Tokyo for their Mandarin-language skills were staunch supporters of the PRC and organized reading circles about the newly established state. This fervor for the Communist regime extended to the school's principals as well, two of whom resigned to return to the mainland and aid in the construction of what they called "New China."[29]

During these years, the PRC reached out to and encouraged the return of overseas Chinese to China in accordance with a diasporic myth of return. However, this policy led to fears in host countries that the Chinese Communists were mobilizing the *huaqiao* as a fifth column, which led to repressive

---

27. Guoli bianyiguan, *Gaoji xiaoxue guoyu keben*, 4:1–11. This 1947 Mandarin textbook opened with the lesson "Ke ai de Zhonghua" (Lovable China). Another lesson described Chiang Kaishek's heroic fortitude when he was an exchange student in Japan, even confronting a Japanese professor for insulting China.

28. *BX*, p. 99.

29. *BX*, pp. 101, 107. In July 1950, Principal Wang Ying and several teachers left Yokohama for the mainland, hoping to aid its development. The next principal, Li Xijing, returned to the motherland in July 1951.

responses by noncommunist host countries.[30] In the United States, investigations into domestic communist sympathizers launched by Senator Joseph McCarthy dovetailed with a crackdown on Chinese immigration fraud. Because fraudulent—so-called "paper son"—immigration applications were endemic among Chinese Americans, the Federal Bureau of Investigation and the Immigration and Naturalization Service were able to selectively threaten leftists with deportation.[31]

The activities of left-leaning Yokohama *huaqiao* were also seen by the governments of Japan and the ROC as a precursor to Communist Chinese-led infiltration and insurrection. Organizational linkages between the Japan Communist Party (JCP) and Chinese and Korean radicals in Japan made this danger seem quite real.[32] When the Allied Occupation shuttered the JCP house organ *Akahata* (Red Flag) in June 1950 during the Red Purge, its

30. Fitzgerald, *China and the Overseas Chinese*, pp. 69, 102–3, 142. Hoping to gain investment, technical expertise, and prestige at the expense of the ROC, the PRC initially welcomed overseas Chinese with generous resettlement packages. As a result, some half a million overseas Chinese settled in the PRC from 1949–66. This active courting came to an end after 1957, when a policy shift in the PRC denied dual citizenship and began advocating naturalization among overseas Chinese to mitigate suspicions of communist infiltration. The PRC government's involvement with overseas communities, however, did not end in that year. Wherever Chinese remained Chinese nationals, as in a *jus sanguinis* country like Japan, the PRC still sought to compete with the ROC for the hearts and minds of patriotic *huaqiao*.

31. Ngai, "Legacies of Exclusion," pp. 3, 21; Nee and de Bary Nee, *Longtime Californ'*, pp. 211–12. From 1957 to 1965, the Immigration and Naturalization Service conducted its Chinese Confession Program that allowed Chinese immigrants to come clean on their participation in the widespread practice of entering the United States as a "paper son," that is, posing as a relative of a Chinese American. The ostensible justification was to bring to light fraudulent genealogies, used by an estimated 25 percent of Chinese immigrants in America at the time, and to grant proper residency and citizenship for those who cooperated. The Federal Bureau of Investigation employed the resulting information for a very different purpose.

32. "Report from Chinese Group of the Japan Communist Party to the Party Temporary Central Guidance Body," Mar. 8, 1952, box 2275GG, folder 61, RG 331, NACP; C. Lee, "Organizational Division and Conflict," p. 111. The JCP did not require Japanese nationality for membership. In 1948, Korean leftists participated in numerous cases of violent agitation under the leadership of the JCP. In 1952, eight Chinese JCP comrades in Yokohama funded the party through a general trading company.

writers and editors continued publishing under the auspices of *Kakyō minpō*.[33] However, Japanese authorities did not have the leverage of immigration law; moreover, the Chinese Communists enjoyed a significant amount of support from notable Japanese such as writer Takeuchi Yoshimi and Japan Socialist Party stalwart Asanuma Inejirō.[34] Another leftist organization that supported their cause was the Japan-China Friendship Association (Nitchū yūkō kyōkai, est. Oct. 1, 1950), which facilitated grassroots diplomacy between Japan and the PRC.[35]

The ROC sought to quash leftist inclinations among Chinese in Japan through its dominance of *huaqiao* institutions. The Nationalist government of China sent a military adviser to Tokyo in March 1950 to purify the leadership of the Chinese Mission and the Tokyo Chinese Association (Dongjing huaqiao zonghui).[36] In spring 1951, the Chinese Mission attempted to crush support for the PRC among the rank-and-file *huaqiao* by threatening to nullify their registration documents for political disloyalty. This loyalty clause and a clumsy attempt to influence the election of trustees at the Tokyo Chinese Association in May of that year incensed many in the community. When pro-Communist leaders were elected anyway, the Chinese Mission

---

33. "Monthly Trend of the Chinese in Japan (November)," Dec. 1, 1951, box 2275 GG, folder 60, RG 331, NACP. This example barely scratches the surface of Chinese involvement in leftist organizations in Japan. The Allied Occupation regarded the leaders of the student organization General Conference of Chinese Students in Japan (Ryūnichi gakusei dōgaku sōkai) as communist spies, and the Chinese Students' Hall (Chūka gakuyū kaikan) in Tokyo as the "base of operation of intelligence in connection with the smuggling carried out by the Communist China" ("On Wireless Equipments of Pro-Communistic Chinese Merchants in Japan," May 22, 1951, box 2275 GG, folder 64, RG 331, NACP).

34. In the wake of imperial Japan's defeat in the Asia-Pacific War, the pro-PRC stance appeared highly principled to many Japanese, and conformed with a desire to confront Japan's war responsibility.

35. Seraphim, *War Memory and Social Politics*, 108–34. The organization's aim was to create a foundation for postwar peace through Chinese-Japanese relations rather than the U.S.-Japan alliance. Its founding members included Itō Takeo, formerly of the South Manchuria Railway research department, and major Japan Socialist Party politicians like Ōyama Ikuo, Matsumoto Jiichirō, and the mayor of Yokohama.

36. "Clean-up operations of the Chinese National Government Mission in Japan," Apr. 14, 1950, box 2275 GG, folder 62, RG 331, NACP.

established a separate pro-ROC Tokyo Chinese Association in August of 1951.[37]

Two months later, as U.S. and Chinese troops were battling in a stalemate in Korea, representatives from the Chinese Mission came to inspect the Yokohama Chinese School. The divisive struggles in Tokyo during the spring and summer were still fresh in their minds, and they flew into a rage when they discovered the expression "Liberation" (*jiefang*) on a banner honoring the martyrs of the Nationalist Revolution of 1911. For them, this term called to mind the loaded terminology of communist revolution and the liberation of mainland China from capitalist and imperialist domination. The Chinese Mission immediately fired the school's principal, seized control of the board of trustees, and ignored a petition by the parent-teacher association to appoint a new principal from the community.[38]

On August 1, 1952, the Chinese Mission peremptorily installed a new principal from Tokyo named Wang Qingren and twenty new teachers. When angry parents, teachers, and graduates arrived in the school yard demanding the removal of the new school personnel, the mission called upon Japanese riot police to eject the crowd from the school grounds. Thus began the so-called school incident (*gakkō jiken*) that would bifurcate Yokohama Chinese institutions into two factions. Over the month of August, the majority in the community who either supported the PRC or opposed the Chinese Mission's tactics called several town meetings. They issued strong denunciations of the Chinese Mission's interference in the democratic management of their local community and condemned the school board for allowing it to happen.[39] The pro-ROC perspective, as recorded in a report compiled by the ROC consulate general in Yokohama, adopted the line that the communist bandit faction (*fei bang*) had usurped control of the school

---

37. "Trouble Caused by the Reelection of Officers of Tokyo Kakyo Sokai (Chinese General Association in Tokyo)," July 6, 1951, box 2275 GG, folder 71, RG 331, NACP; Chen Kunwang, *Nihon kakyō, ryūgakusei undōshi*, pp. 287–91. The new organization did not have an office of its own at the time, so its members and supporters attempted to storm and occupy the former association's building on Sept. 11, 1951. They failed to gain access to the building, but the incident foreshadowed events in Yokohama the following year.

38. *BX*, p. 107. This extreme response was also conditioned by the fact that the Chinese Mission had already accused the school of conducting red education and, moreover, considered as traitors the principals who had departed for the PRC.

39. *BX*, pp. 107–9.

and was conducting red education. *Mainichi* and *Yomiuri* newspaper articles similarly described the school incident as a battle against communism.[40] Nevertheless, the missives composed by the opposition movement did not dwell on ideology. Teachers, students, and parents phrased their objections to the new principal as interference (*kainyū*) by the state.[41] Memoirs of former students from this period also suggest that they supported their teachers against what they saw as the tyranny of outside interlopers. In short, the desire for local autonomy was prominent.[42]

As seen in the 1899 dispute over the Datong xuexiao, the factions were nominally defined by the politics of their leaders, but their bases of support were stitched together from more local concerns. The movement opposing the Chinese Mission went door-to-door to advocate self-determination and collective decision making. Participation was ethnically inclusive; proclamations were issued in both Chinese and Japanese, and one of its leaders was Egawa Taka, the Japanese wife of a Chinese resident.[43] The Chinese Mission's representative legitimacy in the community had been attenuated by the loss of the mainland to the Communists and further harmed by its reliance on the Japanese riot police, recalling to mind Japanese police oppression of the community during the war years.[44]

On September 1, the opposition went ahead with its plans to hold a separate opening ceremony under their elected principal, Wu Leji. The Chinese Mission responded by summoning a contingent of ROC sailors who then shut down the proceedings. When Wu Leji and the original teachers forced

---

40. Zhonghua minguo zhu-Hengbin lingshiguan, "Zhu-Hengbin lingshiguan fuguan hou xiaqu huaqiao linian zhongda shijian baogao," 1952–58, ref. 020000001993A, AH, pp. 47–49; "Chūka kō, akai kyōiku," *Yomiuri shinbun*, Aug. 31, 1952, morning edition, p. 3; "Futatsu no Chūgoku no nayami, rantō sawagai no chūkagakkō," *Mainichi shinbun*, Sept. 2, 1952.

41. Sugawara, *Nihon no kakyō*, p. 249.

42. Fu Xunhe (founder of cram school Terakoya) and Zeng Deshen (president of Shinkuang Trading Co., Ltd.), in discussion with author; Konuma and Chin, "Nihon no kakyō gakkō (2)," p. 41.

43. Sugawara, *Nihon no kakyō*, p. 191; *BX*, p. 110.

44. Konuma and Chin, "Nihon no kakyō gakkō (2)," p. 41. For most of the community, attachments to native place were still strong, perhaps even stronger than loyalty to nation. Since the ROC no longer controlled their native provinces of Guangzhou, Jiangsu, or Zhejiang, the regime became increasingly irrelevant to these affective ties.

their way into the classrooms, Japanese riot police were called in to evict them, leading to the arrest of Wu Leji and eight others.[45] When they were released the following day, they were greeted with a hero's welcome for standing up to both the Chinese Nationalists and the Japanese police. In many recollections and writings since 1952, this incident provided a dramatic birth narrative of a new Yokohama Chinatown community.[46] Naturally, the pro-ROC faction saw things very differently; the ROC consulate reported to their superiors that the bandit faction had violently seized control of the school at the behest of the Korean and Japanese Communist parties.[47]

Such views notwithstanding, the majority of Chinese in Yokohama rallied behind Wu Leji and the original teachers. Because the school was locked down by police order, parents in the opposition group found fourteen private homes in which to hold classes. This dispersed education continued until 1953 when a new school building was constructed in the Yamate district of Yokohama. Out of the approximately 830 students attending the Chinese school in 1952, some 600 continued with their original teachers at the new Yokohama Yamate chūkagakkō, whereas only around 70 remained with the ROC-controlled school, now called the Yokohama chūkagakuin.[48] The remaining 160 students, mainly children of affluent families, chose either Japanese schools or the American-run mission schools on the Bluff. As locals noted, "the cooks sent their children to the Yamate school, whereas the large restaurant owners sent their kids to American or Japanese schools."[49]

The struggle for independence against the Chinese Mission provided a compelling narrative, yet the opposition movement was operating in a field defined by the geopolitical situation. Their struggle tied them to the institutions of the PRC. Because they continued to receive monetary support both

---

45. These sailors were stationed on an ROC navy vessel that was anchored in Yokohama harbor.

46. *BX*, pp. 110–11. In contrast to the abundance of memoirs and retellings on the pro-PRC side, there are few narratives of the school incident from the perspective of ROC supporters.

47. Zhonghua minguo zhu-Hengbin lingshiguan, "Linian zhongda shijian baogao," pp. 47–49.

48. *BX*, pp. 112–13.

49. Konuma and Chin, "Nihon no kakyō gakkō (2)," p. 41.

from the Tokyo Chinese Association and the PRC government, it was impossible to dissociate themselves from this regime. This affiliation led to an antagonistic relationship with the Japanese police, who joined ROC representatives in investigating Chinese Communist meetings and pressuring their children to attend the Nationalist school.[50] The pro-PRC Chinese also suffered discrimination from Yokohama society. When school organizers first attempted to purchase land for the new school in the Futaba district of Yokohama, the owner balked when he heard they would be conducting "red" education there.[51] Even after they built the school in Yamate, the ROC consulate used its influence to prevent Kanagawa Prefecture from granting it authorization under Japan's 1947 School Education Law. From 1953 to 1957, the ROC consul repeatedly pressured Kanagawa Governor Uchiyama Iwatarō to delay and stonewall the application paperwork. In 1957, however, JCP politicians intervened, and the governor could no longer block the relevant committees from reviewing and approving the request.[52]

This division in the Yokohama Chinese community linked the performance of Chineseness with a choice between Cold War camps, which spawned two sets of community institutions. The parent meetings after the school incident gradually developed into the Yokohama Huaqiao Women's Association (Yokohama kakyō fujokai) in 1953.[53] The ROC consulate countered in 1955 by establishing the Yokohama Free Huaqiao Women's Association (Yokohama jiyū kakyō fujo kyōkai). Regarding the Yokohama Chinese Association, the pro-PRC faction would have won control of it in the May 1953 election, but the ROC consulate invalidated the election after votes had been cast. The consulate orchestrated a new election three months later that strongly favored their supporters.[54] Thwarted, the pro-PRC faction then established the Yokohama Huaqiao Federation (Hengbin huaqiao lianyihui) in July 1960 to replicate the same function as the other association.[55]

---

50. Sugawara, *Chainataun*, p. 153; *FNWS*, p. 112.

51. Konuma and Chin, "Nihon no kakyō gakkō (2)," p. 41.

52. Zhonghua minguo zhu-Hengbin lingshiguan, "Linian zhongda shijian baogao," pp. 78–87.

53. *FNWS*, pp. 34–36.

54. Zhonghua minguo zhu-Hengbin lingshiguan, "Linian zhongda shijian baogao," pp. 50–56.

55. Zeng, "Yokohama Yamate chūkagakkō rekishi nenpyō," p. 705; Yamashita Kiyomi, "Yokohama Chūkagai zairyū Chūgokujin," p. 45.

One could no longer passively remain in *huaqiao* society without taking a position within the political map of the community, a situation that threatened to turn any collective activity into a political contest. Immediately after the war, the Huaqiao Youth Association was active in organizing sports events, and led community participation in Yokohama City's annual Port Festival (Minato matsuri). But after the school incident, the Youth Association reduced its activities; as Li Fuquan (1926–2009) noted, it had a predominantly pro-Communist membership, so joining would make you red as well.[56] Flags were particularly inviting targets, and the source of much discord.[57] The issue of flags almost prevented Chinese participation in the 1958 celebration of the Hundred Year Anniversary of the Opening of the Port, which was organized by the Yokohama Chamber of Commerce and Industry (Shōkō kaigisho). Li Fuquan was then serving on the Yokohama Chinatown Development Association (Yokohama Chūkagai hattenkai; YDA), an institution founded in 1956 to facilitate economic cooperation between Chinese and Japanese businesses in the district. The YDA received a request from the Chamber to send lion and dragon dance teams to the celebration. Li found it difficult, however, to convince both sides to participate; even as separate troupes, both sides were troubled by the political symbolism of allowing their counterparts to fly their national flag. As Li later related,

> At the time, what worried me was the flag issue. What do we do about the fact that they have the "Blue Sky, White Sun" and we have the "Five-star Red Flag"? I told them, this is a Yokohama citizen's festival, and we're not national representatives. We don't need flags. They replied that this is an international parade, and everyone else, including the Koreans, would have flags, and so they should too. I told them, let's do this for the sake of business, as members of the Yokohama Chinatown Development Association. Can't we just be Chinatown A-team and Chinatown B-team?

---

56. CKK and YKS, *Yokohama kakyō no kioku*, p. 50.

57. Nihon Chūgoku yūkō kyōkai zenkoku honbu, *Nitchū yūkō undōshi*, pp. 96–97. The Oct. 1, 1958, edition of the *Yomiuri shinbun* newspaper reported the theft of a PRC flag from a restaurant hosting a party to celebrate the PRC's National Foundation Day. A higher-profile case occurred that same year in Nagasaki at an exhibition of products from the PRC at a department store. There, two youths yanked down the PRC flags, prompting protests by the PRC faction in Japan, the Sino-Japanese Friendship Association, and a Japanese trade delegation.

Li's argument carried the day, and the parade was a success. His solution, moreover, pointed toward a strategy for community reintegration that relied on economic imperatives and identification with Yokohama, rather than with *huaqiao* identity. This logic would gain influence over the succeeding decades. But at the time it was no breakthrough for the wider political schism. When the *Asahi shinbun* published an article describing this cooperation between Nationalist and Communist Chinese in Yokohama, a member of the pro-ROC faction came to warn Li that his involvement might displease the regime on Taiwan and make it difficult to travel there in the future.[58]

The Cold War also hobbled Yokohama's Chinese performing arts and holiday celebrations. Cantonese dramas and musical performances had been common at the yearly Guandi Festival, to honor the deified historical figure Guan Yu, and at Chinese New Year. Infighting now made it impossible to maintain these performance groups, and many communal celebrations and performances came to an end in the mid-1950s.[59] Commemorations and performances were more than an index of community cohesion; they helped define and maintain that community. Wing Chung Ng's analysis of Vancouver Chinatown points out that celebrations can serve as a "vivid non-written 'script' to work out an imagined community."[60] Their loss thus robbed the community, particularly its less vocal members, of another venue to live their Chinese identities.

This rivalry thus dealt a severe blow to the logic of ethnic unity. The children at school were particularly troubled by the contradiction between the ideology of ethnic pride and the reality of community division. Lu Jieliang was a member of the seventh graduating class of the pro-ROC school. He was so terrified by the attempts of pro-PRC students to disrupt his classes that his Japanese mother almost transferred him to a Japanese middle school.[61] Lü Xingxiong (Ro Yukio), son of Egawa Taka, switched to the pro-PRC school after the school incident, but in his young heart remained deeply

---

58. CKK and YKS, *Yokohama kakyō no kioku*, p. 52.

59. Wang Wei, *Nihon kakyō ni okeru dentō no saihen to esunishiti,*" pp. 256–57; Wang Wei, *Sugao no Chūkagai*, p. 170. The pro-ROC school formed a small lion-dance troupe of its own in 1966, but the pro-PRC school did not establish a comparable team until the 1980s.

60. Ng, "Collective Ritual and the Resilience of Traditional Organizations," p. 198.

61. Zhonghua xueyuan, *Bai zhou nian yuanqing jinian tekan*, p. 253.

troubled that "people of the same ethnicity could not get along."[62] The elders of the community too were divided, even as they passed from the scene. Wu Bokang supported the pro-PRC faction and returned to China in 1955.[63] Chen Dongting, on the other hand, remained with the pro-ROC Chinese Association until his retirement in 1958, even drawing denunciation in the February 2, 1953, edition of *Chūkagakkō nyūsu*, a pro-Communist newsletter.[64] Bao Bogong's last term as a supervisor of the Chinese Association ended in 1952, and it is unclear which side, if any, he took before he passed away in 1958.[65] The cultural and political unity of the *huaqiao* was gravely weakened by these clashes between pro-PRC and pro-ROC factions, a situation that was exacerbated by an economic crisis in Yokohama Chinatown during these same years.

Decline of the Huaqiao Economy and the Rise of Chinatown

Across Japan, *huaqiao* status became an economic liability after May 1952, when the San Francisco Peace Treaty came into effect and ended the Allied Occupation of Japan. Chinese in Japan lost their special advantages as Allied nationals just as Japan regained political and economic sovereignty. Rising competition from Japanese businesses, the loss of a middleman niche in international trade, and financial and currency exchange restrictions on foreign nationals resulted in an inexorable decline in the economic fortunes of Chinese in Japan. During the 1950s, Japanese corporations and individuals were able to buy back most of the stocks acquired by Chinese during the immediate postwar years.[66] This process was facilitated by government-enacted restrictions on foreign ownership of Japanese business assets through the 1949 Foreigner Assets Acquisition Ordinance (Gaikokujin zaisan shutoku seirei).[67]

Companies that had been eager to employ Chinese to help conduct foreign trade were now dispensing with their Chinese staff. In general,

---

62. Hirota, *Kakyō no ima*, p. 234.
63. *BX*, p. 90.
64. Wang Liang, *Zhonghua minguo liu-Ri Hengbin huaqiao zonghui*, pp. 106–8.
65. Fu Xunhe, "Hō Hakukō (Bao Bogong)," in *Kakyō-kajin jiten*, ed. Kani Hiroaki, Shiba Yoshinobu, and You Zhongxun (Tokyo: Kōbundō, 2002), p. 717.
66. Osada and Tanaka, "Ryūnichi kakyō keizai no dōkō (3)," 36–37; Osada and Tanaka, "Ryūnichi kakyō keizai no dōkō (1)," pp. 55–57.
67. Chūgoku kenkyūjo, *Gaikokujin zaisan shutoku seirei*, pp. 8–9.

Japanese corporations thereafter proved unwilling to hire non-Japanese, creating a situation where few Chinese entered university because they understood that higher education would not improve their career prospects.[68] This situation began to change somewhat after the Hitachi employment discrimination case of 1970–74, wherein a *zainichi* Korean named Pak Song-sok sued Hitachi for canceling his employment contract when the corporation learned he was not a Japanese national.[69] In a landmark ruling by the Yokohama District Court, Pak won the reinstatement of the contract and an acknowledgment that the company's hiring practices were discriminatory.[70] Nevertheless, Japanese companies did not hire many Chinese nationals until the 1980s, with the liberalization of trade and contact with the PRC.

Chinese and other foreign nationals also faced difficulties securing loans from Japanese commercial banks. In response to these financial obstacles, Chinese businessmen founded several small lending banks and credit unions. The Yokohama Chinese opened a Chinese commercial bank called the Shinyō kumiai Yokohama kagin in December 1952.[71] With more than ¥212 million in capitalization, it was the largest Chinese financial institution in Japan, though still below the scale of Japan's larger commercial banks.[72] Overall, it was nevertheless difficult for Chinese businesses to match the capital investments of Japanese businesses, which in Yokohama resulted in a lower rate of commercial renovation and expansion during the 1950s. This financial environment posed a specific problem for the traditional occupations of the Chinese in Japan, namely the "three knives" of barber, tailor, and chef. Chinese barbers did not have the capital to remodel their businesses in step with Japanese establishments, and tailors were facing stiff

---

68. Hayase, "Kakyō shakai kenkyū no shomondai (3)," pp. 5, 6–10; Hirota, *Kakyō no ima*, pp. 238–39. Many of the more affluent Chinese could afford to send their children to private Japanese schools, but this choice did not necessarily translate into higher job prospects.

69. Pak was living under the Japanese name Arai Shōji, and his application reflected this name.

70. Chapman, *Zainichi Korean Identity and Ethnicity*, pp. 33–36; Chung, *Immigration and Citizenship in Japan*, p. 127.

71. Shinyō kumiai Yokohama kagin, *Teikan*. The bank's bylaws restricted accounts to *huaqiao* who lived, worked, or operated businesses in Yokohama.

72. Osada and Tanaka, "Ryūnichi kakyō keizai no dōkō (3)," p. 36. In comparison, the Tokyo-based credit union Japan Huaqiao Economic Self-Help Corporation (Nihon kakyō keizai gassakusha) only raised ¥25 million.

competition from exporters in Hong Kong.[73] Japanese entrepreneurs with overwhelming amounts of capital challenged Chinese restaurateurs by building larger establishments and hiring away Chinese chefs.[74]

The 1950s thus brought political division but also an economic crisis, which worsened during the economic depression in Japan that followed the end of the Korean War in July 1953.[75] Unemployment and poverty became a serious issue, and one of the most urgent roles for Chinese associations during these years was providing economic assistance.[76] As in crises past, the Yokohama Chinese turned to their restaurants for economic survival, which proved to be the most resilient sector of the Chinatown economy. In that regard, Yokohama Chinatown relied on restaurants far more than other Chinese communities in Japan. According to an April 1959 survey, 40.9 percent of Yokohama's working Chinese were employed in the food-service industry, compared to 17.8 percent in Kobe, where occupations were evenly distributed between import-export (17.9%) and retail sales (19.5%).[77] The researchers remarked that after the closure of Chinatown's black markets, "if you were to exclude its Chinese restaurants, there would be little thriving there at all."[78] But, conditions in the postwar period were now more favorable than ever for these restaurants. Some Japanese analysts claimed that in the postwar era, Chinese restaurants expanded into the Japanese hinterland and indelibly altered the Japanese culinary palate.[79] Another related factor was the return of several million Japanese soldiers and settlers from the Chinese mainland; this population had grown accustomed to Chinese cuisine and contributed to its increased consumption in postwar Japan.[80] In

---

73. Osada and Tanaka, "Ryūnichi kakyō keizai no dōkō (1)," p. 54.

74. Yamaguchi, "Yokohama Chūkagai no seitai no kenkyū (3)," pp. 27–28; Osada and Tanaka, "Ryūnichi kakyō keizai no dōkō (1)," pp. 55–57; Osada and Tanaka, "Ryūnichi kakyō keizai no dōkō (3)," pp. 36–37. Most Chinese businesses in Yokohama were still operating from the same buildings they occupied since the immediate postwar period. In contrast, Japanese establishments built new and more modern facilities as they moved into the area.

75. Yamaguchi, "Yokohama Chūkagai no seitai kenkyū (1)," p. 2.

76. Osada and Tanaka, "Ryūnichi kakyō keizai no dōkō (1)," pp. 57–58.

77. Hayase, "Kakyō shakai kenkyū no shomondai (3)," p. 3.

78. Yamaguchi, "Yokohama Chūkagai no seitai no kenkyū (3)."

79. Osada and Tanaka, "Ryūnichi kakyō keizai no dōkō (1)," p. 55.

80. The owner of the *gyōza* (Chinese dumpling) shop Banri (Ten thousand miles) in downtown Yokohama, the oldest of its kind in Japan, claimed that his

addition, historian George Solt suggests that large-scale imports of American wheat flour to mitigate mass starvation after the war led to the substitution of Chinese-style ramen noodles for the traditional staple of rice.

The case of *shūmai* also serves as an exemplary case of how Japan's expanding mass media could boost the consumption of Chinese food. Although this steamed dumpling was introduced at the turn of the twentieth century by Bao Tang's Hakugatei, the Japanese-owned Kiyōken, which began selling *shūmai* in 1928, spearheaded the postwar popularization of the dish. In the 1920s, President Nonami Mokichi (1888–1965) sought a Yokohama specialty to entice travelers at Yokohama's train station to purchase lunch-box meals, a difficult proposition given the short length of the trip to Tokyo. He found his solution in Chinatown, where he recruited Cantonese chef Wu Yusun (1888–?) to make *shūmai* his company's flagship product. These were greeted with only moderate success, however, until after the war. In 1950, Mokichi struck upon the idea of sending girls in red uniforms to sell *shūmai* on the platforms of Yokohama station. These so-called *shūmai* girls (*shūmai musume*) then received national attention when novelist Shishi Bunroku featured them in a story titled *Yassa mossa* (Bustle), serialized in the *Mainichi shinbun*. Against the backdrop of a Yokohama recovering from the war, the story depicted the love affair between a *shūmai* girl and a baseball player who rode the train at Yokohama station. In this golden age of Japanese cinema, movie theater audiences also fell in love with the *shūmai* girl when the tale was released as a 1953 film directed by Shibuya Minoru.[81] Soon afterward, *shūmai* began appearing on menus and store shelves all over Japan.

With the sharp rise in popularity of Chinese cuisine, Chinatown's restaurant industry provided a source of economic vitality for the district's Chinese and Japanese residents alike. A door-to-door survey in 1962 revealed that these residents lived side by side: the survey found 95 Chinese and 108 Japanese homes and 204 Chinese and 312 Japanese businesses distributed around the district.[82] The businesses where Chinese operators dominated were Chinese restaurants (61 to 3) and bars and cabarets (81 to

---

father originally opened the restaurant to serve a clientele of demobilized soldiers who had been stationed in China and missed Chinese food.

81. Nonami, "Yokohama no shūsen wa Shōwa 30-nen," pp. 147–48.

82. Yamaguchi, "Yokohama Chūkagai no seitai no kenkyū (3)," pp. 11–12; Yamamuro and Kawamura, "Yokohama zairyū kakyō," p. 8. The proportion of Chinese

22). The businesses where Japanese operators dominated were food products (65 to 8) and trading companies (70 to 16).[83] These patterns suggest interconnected niches; Japanese vegetable, meat, and poultry wholesalers provided Chinese restaurants with their ingredients.[84]

Yokohama City's development plans reinforced these economic arrangements. Since the 1950s, city officials and local business owners had arrived at the consensus that Chinatown could be developed into a key, though subsidiary, node along an itinerary between the sights of Yamashita Park—including Marine Tower and the Hikawa-maru steamship—and the shopping and entertainment districts of Motomachi and Isezaki-chō.[85] Yokohama City and the Yokohama Chamber of Commerce and Industry concluded that they could revitalize Chinatown by widening its roads, restoring its distinctive sights, and promoting its famous restaurants.[86] In 1955, a group of Chinese and Japanese business owners from the neighboring districts of Chinatown and Motomachi erected a brilliantly colored Chinese-style gate emblazoned with the word "Chūkagai" (中華街) at the entrance of Chinatown.[87]

Thereafter, Chūkagai became the accepted named for Chinatown, replacing Nankinmachi. The change in name was a deliberate attempt by local residents and business owners to dislodge the public's long-held perception of Chinatown as filthy and dangerous. The following year, sixty Chinese and Japanese businesses in Chinatown banded together to establish the previously mentioned YDA, and improvements in the town were soon perceptible to visitors. Shishi Bunroku noted some dramatic changes between the 1963 and 1966 articles he contributed to the *Yomiuri shinbun*.[88] In 1966, he wrote: "Recently, I visited Chinatown for the first time in a while. I was

---

to Japanese homes and businesses stands in marked contrast to the Chinatown of Singapore, which was at the time more than 94 percent Chinese.

83. Yamaguchi, "Yokohama Chūkagai no seitai no kenkyū (3)," pp. 11–12.

84. Chūgoku kenkyūjo, *Gaikokujin zaisan shutoku seirei*, pp. 1–2; Yamaguchi, "Yokohama Chūkagai no seitai kenkyū (2)," p. 8.

85. Yamaguchi, "Yokohama Chūkagai no seitai kenkyū (1)," p. 1.

86. In 1953, the mayor of Yokohama led a delegation to investigate conditions in San Francisco's Chinatown in order to formulate their own development policies.

87. A Feb. 1, 1955, article in the *Yomiuri shinbun* claimed that the gate cost ¥1.3 million, a sum raised by "pro-China city residents."

88. Wang Wei, *Sugao no Chūkagai*, pp. 56–57; "Yokohama konjaku," *Yomiuri shinbun*, Jan. 17, 1963, evening edition, p. 5.

surprised at how clean it had become! . . . The Nankinmachi of old used to have a unique stench. Now it has become very hygienic, full of modern buildings and attractive restaurants no different from those in the Ginza [district of Tokyo]."[89] Chinatown—both its Chinese and Japanese residents—had in the 1950s adopted a model of economic development focused on Chinese cuisine and tourism, and by the 1960s the initiative was yielding concrete results.

SINO-JAPANESE NORMALIZATION AND THE PANDA BOOM

Through the united efforts of Chinese and Japanese, the district's reliance on restaurants was transmuted from a shortcoming to an exemplary developmental strategy that exploited the local and national identities of Yokohama Chinese. These processes accelerated after the normalization of diplomatic relations between Japan and the PRC in 1972.

Following American president Richard Nixon's visit to China in 1972, Japanese prime minister Tanaka Kakuei (1918–93) signed the Sino-Japanese Communiqué in September of that year, reestablishing diplomatic ties with the PRC and severing official ties with the ROC on Taiwan. This event restructured the relationships between Yokohama *huaqiao* and their host society, because Japanese recognition of the PRC legitimized the institutional efforts of the pro-PRC faction. The event also triggered an explosive growth of Japanese interest in things Chinese, a phenomenon that newspapers termed a "China boom" or "panda boom"—thanks to the pair of pandas sent by the PRC to the Ueno Zoo in Tokyo. This event led to two contradictory developments: the short-term revival of contestation over Yokohama's *huaqiao* institutions, and the long-term empowerment of inclusive efforts to develop Chinatown as a tourist destination.

To the Japanese public, the prime significance of normalization was the blossoming of cultural exchange between the two countries, reflected in a thirst for Chinese cultural products.[90] Moreover, the panda boom occurred at the end of nearly two decades of high-speed growth in the Japanese

---

89. "Chūkagai," *Yomiuri shinbun*, Feb. 5, 1966, evening edition, p. 2.

90. Ijiri, "Sino-Japanese Controversy," pp. 62–63. The wording of the communiqué closely followed the document signed by Nixon the previous year, and some scholars suggest that the Japanese policy makers of the time were not cognizant of its full significance. On the other hand, the Japanese newspaper *Yomiuri shinbun* ran forty-four articles in September, thirty-one in October, and fifteen in November

economy. Macrolevel economic changes promoted the development of a Japanese middle-class consumer consciousness; by the 1970s, 70 percent of the Japanese population considered itself middle class.[91]

The convergence of rising consumer buying power and the panda boom widened the customer base of Chinatown's businesses. Japanese memoirs indicate that before the 1970s, many local residents had only been able to eat at Chinatown's restaurants on major celebratory occasions, such as graduations, anniversaries, and holidays. For instance, actor Wataru Tetsuya customarily held staff dinners there during shoots in Yokohama; singer Yūki Saori recalled celebrating family birthdays and anniversaries since childhood in Chinatown restaurants.[92] Many other Yokohama residents considered its luxury restaurants out of financial reach. Horita Yūsuke recalled that he first came to Yokohama in 1958, but could not afford to eat in Chinatown until after he found a high-paying tutoring job. Even then he only could afford to dine there once or twice a month.[93] Japan's era of high growth changed all of that. Chinatown's sales of around ¥6.1 billion in 1976 rose to ¥12.5 billion by 1982, outstripping that of its neighbor and rival shopping district Motomachi.[94] Visitor data shows that Chinatown's consumer appeal broadened from the surrounding city and prefecture to all of Japan over the same period. In 1972, 63.7 percent of visitors were from within Yokohama City. In 1982, that segment made up 36.5 percent.[95]

Normalization also triggered grave anxieties among Chinese in Japan over their legal status, which led to a wave of naturalizations. Following the "one China policy," Japan's recognition of the PRC meant the withdrawal of

---

on the social impact of normalization, most of which were dedicated to the panda couple in Ueno Zoo.

91. By the time of the panda boom, Prime Minister Ikeda Hayato's Income Doubling Plan of 1960 had spectacularly hit its targets, allowing more Japanese to afford luxuries such as cars, televisions, washing machines, and travel. This plan sought to double both personal incomes and the gross national product through an expansion of investment, production, and exports.

92. Wataru et al., "Watashi no Chūkagai," pp. 8–9.

93. Horita, "Bigaku no machi."

94. Sugawara, *Chainataun*, p. 166.

95. Ibid., p. 162. City planning and infrastructure improvements made this growth possible, including the 1964 extension of the Japan National Railway Negishi Line, which allowed Tokyo residents easier access to Yokohama Chinatown.

recognition of the ROC.[96] Accordingly, the ROC permanently shuttered its diplomatic offices in Japan on December 28, 1972. Rumors also abounded that the property and assets of overseas Chinese would then be seized by the Communist government.[97] Some Taiwanese even advocated becoming stateless as a political protest of the impending invalidation of their ROC passports.[98] Despite psychic resistance to becoming Japanese, the number of Chinese who naturalized as Japanese citizens during these years leapt from 249 in 1971, to 1,303 in 1972, and 7,338 in 1973. The total for the years from 1972 to 1980 was 20,368 individuals, a figure representing 40 percent of the population of Chinese nationals in Japan at the start of the 1970s. In comparison, less than five thousand Chinese naturalized in the twenty years from 1952 to 1971.[99]

A change in ROC policy also eased the process of naturalization.[100] The ROC, following provisions deriving from the original 1909 Qing statute, maintained the prerogative to grant or deny the renunciation of Chinese nationality, which is a precondition for naturalization in some countries. Applicants were required to provide a personal history and specify the grounds for their renunciation. Although the ROC Ministry of Foreign Affairs appears to have accepted a variety of justifications, until normalization they did not take renunciation lightly; they seemed particularly unwilling to permit men to naturalize if it allowed them to evade their compulsory military service.[101] Moreover, the ministry enforced Article 6 of the nationality

---

96. Both the ROC and the PRC have officially declared that there is only one China, and that Taiwan should not be considered a separate sovereign entity. This "one China policy" has been accepted by all parties wishing to establish diplomatic relations with China, meaning the ROC *or* the PRC, but not both.

97. Nagano Takeshi, *Zainichi Chūgokujin*, p. 220; Zhu Huiling, *Kakyō shakai no henbō*, p. 34.

98. Jin Meiling, "Ketsui to shite 'mukokuseki' sengen," pp. 96–103; Chen Tien-shi, "Stateless Overseas Chinese," pp. 53–70. Although it is unclear how many Chinese elected to become stateless, Japan's Ministry of Justice noted that the number of stateless persons in Japan jumped from 930 in 1971 to 9,200 in 1974. For a personal memoir of life as a stateless person, see Chen Tien-shi, *Mukokuseki*.

99. Nagano Takeshi, *Zainichi Chūgokujin*, p. 220; Zhu Huiling, *Kakyō shakai no henbō*, pp. 29, 45–46.

100. Lin Tongchun, *Hashi wataru hito*, p. 230.

101. Waijiaobu, "Zhu-Ri dashiguan shouli huaqiao sangshi guoji," 1970–72, file 020000013282A, AH, pp. 15–16. The Ministry of Foreign Affairs granted applications for Chinese women who married Japanese men, Chinese who were born in

law enforcement regulations, which stated that "the fact of renunciation must be published in two newspapers in the community of residence."[102] Prior to 1972, naturalization thus involved a public rejection of one's bonds to the Chinese community—which perhaps dissuaded many from pursuing the procedure.[103] But after 1972, the ROC stopped enforcing Article 6, and many Chinese in Japan took the momentous step of giving up their nationality, the legal pillar of their Chinese identity.

Normalization also reignited violence between the two factions. The night after the signing of the Sino-Japanese Communiqué, a group of youths assaulted Wang Qingren, the former principal at the center of the 1952 school incident. Then, in 1974, the (pro-PRC) Yokohama Huaqiao Federation appropriated the name of the (pro-ROC) Yokohama Chinese Association in an unsuccessful attempt to settle the question of legitimacy.[104] In 1976, violence once again erupted between the two factions when the pro-PRC faction attempted to expropriate the Yokohama Chinese Association building complex, including school and temple. On May 22, they entered the Chinese Association building demanding its handover and triggered a wild brawl. Japanese police arrived and arrested nineteen interlopers. Undaunted, pro-PRC *huaqiao* and their Japanese supporters brought suit in July to evict the ROC faction from the building.[105] This lawsuit was not their first attempt to gain control of the facility. After the 1952 school incident, members of the pro-PRC faction initiated a lawsuit to force Wang Qingren and the new teachers to vacate the Chinese School.[106] At the time, Kanagawa

---

Japan and sought a more convenient legal status, those interested in improving their business opportunities, and those interested in securing their property in Japan. Some successful applicants were Japanese women who had acquired Chinese nationality after marrying Chinese men but sought to recover their Japanese nationality.

102. Waijiaobu, "Zhu-Ri dashiguan," p. 11.

103. Waijiaobu, "Lü Riben qiaomin shengqing sangshi woguo guoji," vol. 3, 11/27/1979–4/1/1980, ref. 020000013258A, AH; "Nitchū kokkō kaifuku no kage ni: Pekin ka Taiwan ka sentaku o semarareru Ō Sadaharu kara Ōyō Hihi made," *Asahi geinō*, Oct. 12, 1972, pp. 20–22.

104. Yomiuri shinbunsha, *Yokohama Chūkagai monogatari*, pp. 216–25.

105. Yokohama kakyō sōkai seijōka dan'atsu jiken saiban shiryōshū kankō iinkai, *Yokohama kakyō sōkai seijōka dan'atsu jiken*, p. 5.

106. "Hengbin zhonghua xuexiao guanli weiyuanhui fabiao, guanyu zhonghua xuexiao caipan jingguo baogao," *Huaqiao wenhua*, no. 47 (1952).

Prefectural courts ruled that the property was leased by the ROC, and thus came under the control of the Chinese Mission. Now that Japan no longer recognized the regime in Taiwan, pro-PRC *huaqiao* believed that the property should be transferred to their control. Japanese courts, however, refused to adjudicate, and the pro-PRC faction eventually dropped the suit in February 1994.[107] To this day there are two associations with identical names in the district, and Chinese representative authority remains divided.

In sum, the events following the normalization of ties with the PRC suggest a continuation of self-destructive rivalry between the two political foes. Neither association could make credible claims to political neutrality or representative authority, which led Tsukuba University professor Yamashita Kiyomi to conclude in 1979 that there were no institutions available to unify the Chinese in Chinatown.[108] Competing claims by the PRC and the ROC were effectively undoing the politically defined *huaqiao* community.

At the same time, however, cooperative commercial development was legitimating a different conception of community, one that could encompass political and ethnic differences. The YDA was eminently positioned to represent this local community.[109] In 1971, the organization's constituency comprised 71 Chinese and 43 Japanese business owners, but by 1977 its fee-paying membership had swelled to 203 businesses. As noted earlier, Japanese and Chinese occupied specific niches, with Chinese mainly operating restaurants, and Japanese supplying them with produce and meat. In fact, the first head trustee of the new YDA was Takahashi Teiyū, the Japanese owner of a large-scale meat distribution company.[110] In the 1970s, these business owners together erected several more Chinese-style gates and constructed a parking garage for visitors.

---

107. "Kakyō sōkai, kyōchō no jidai e," *Asahi shinbun*, Feb. 15, 1994, Kanagawa edition.

108. Yamashita, "Yokohama Chūkagai zairyū Chūgokujin," p. 45.

109. Wang Wei, *Sugao no Chūkagai*, p. 57. In 1971, the YDA was reorganized and registered with Kanagawa Prefecture's government under a slightly different name, the Yokohama Chinatown Development Cooperative Union (Yokohama Chūkagai hattenkai kyōdō kumiai).

110. Kanagawa-ken shōkō shidō sentā, "Saikaihatsu junkai sōgō shidō no jisshi ni tsuite (ukagai)," Mar. 1973, ref. 1200400086, KPA; Yamashita, "Yokohama Chūkagai zairyū Chūgokujin," p. 45.

Participation in the YDA also permitted greater interaction with wider administrative units, particularly Yokohama City and Kanagawa Prefecture, which led to infrastructure improvements. Takahashi Teiyū and Chinese trustee Sui Zhenbiao announced in 1973 that the YDA's objectives included redeveloping the zone along the south of Chinatown toward Motomachi and instituting a pedestrian-only policy on the main avenue.[111] Yokohama mayor Asukada Ichio cooperated with these efforts and also promised a subway station to serve Chinatown.[112] These various schemes were elaborated by Kanagawa Prefecture in 1975 as the YMI Redevelopment Plan, which sought to link Yamashita-chō, Motomachi, and Ishikawa-chō as one contiguous commercial center. This planning was conducted through the four main shopping street associations (*shōtengaikai*) representing business owners in these districts, of which the YDA was the largest.[113]

Most surprising, however, was the support of the Kaga-chō Police Station in the YDA's plans. Eliding the adversarial relationship that had existed between the police and the Chinese community, Police Chief Suzuki Tomizō happily remarked in a magazine interview that his colleagues were envious of his transfer to Chinatown because it gave him daily access to Chinese food. In terms of policy, Suzuki promised to support the YDA's efforts to designate pedestrian-only zones and to improve safety and convenience for visitors.[114] Although distrust of the police persisted among many Chinese through this period, the police and the YDA apparently enjoyed a constructive relationship.[115]

Since the 1970s, the YDA has increasingly taken a leadership role in the community, as befits its English-language slogan, "We are China Town." Its

---

111. Takahashi, "Kinkyō hōkoku"; Zui Shinpyō, "Yokohama Chūkagai o sekai no Chainataun ni."

112. Asukada, "Chūkagai to watashi."

113. Kanagawa-ken shōkō shidō sentā, "YMI kaihatsu renraku kyōgi kai no saikaihatsu junkai sōgō shidō," Feb. 1975, ref. 1199707393, KPA. Chinatown did not necessarily occupy a dominant position in this planning. The Motomachi Shopping Street Association only had 168 members, compared to 180 in the YDA, yet the aggregate sales for the Motomachi district were higher at this time. The Motomachi association in fact made the initial overtures to include the YDA.

114. Suzuki, "Chūkagai to watashi."

115. Tsukuba University professor Yamashita Kiyomi claimed that when he began his research in Yokohama Chinatown in the late 1970s, many residents suspected that he was an undercover policeman.

economic orientation has moreover enabled it to occupy a neutral space between the two rival factions—much the same strategy that Li Fuquan had articulated in the 1950s. The YDA leveraged Li's approach in a bid to revive the annual Chinese New Year's celebration in 1986.[116] This plan was orchestrated by Hayashi Kensei, a Yokohama-born ethnic Chinese who had naturalized as Japanese.[117] He recalled that Japanese police strongly counseled him to abort the plan because of the potential for violent conflict.[118] Nevertheless, the event was carried off peacefully through delicate planning of the order of the procession and the thorough removal of flags.[119] This successful reconciliation of the two factions, if only for a day, was all the more momentous considering that someone—presumably a pro-PRC agitator—had set fire to the Guandi Temple adjacent to the pro-ROC Chinese Association one month earlier.[120]

Through these achievements, Yokohama Chinatown's economic development and local integration have become a model for other Chinese communities in Japan. Kobe's Chinatown, still known as Nankinmachi, followed a similar course when local Chinese and Japanese business owners established the Nankinmachi Shopping Street Promotion Association (Nankinmachi shōtengai shinkō kumiai) in 1977. The organization sought to revamp the district's infrastructure, expanding roads and installing public bathrooms. Although the area was not historically a cluster of Chinese settlements but rather a Chinese and Japanese market, it began marketing itself in earnest as a gourmet republic (*gurume no kyōwakoku*) during its first public Chinese New Year's festival in 1987. As in Yokohama nearly a decade earlier,

---

116. Wang Wei, *Sugao no Chūkagai*, p. 203. The lunar new year festival was abandoned in the 1950s because of political divisions. The revived festival cost the YDA's members a total of ¥10 million.

117. Hayashi Kensei is a Japanese name he adopted when he naturalized, a practice that was strongly encouraged by the Japanese Ministry of Justice until 1985. As of the writing of this book, Hayashi is serving as both head trustee of the YDA and representative of the pro-PRC Chinese Association.

118. This factional tension is typical of almost all overseas Chinese communities. Wayne Wang's 1982 film *Chan Is Missing* depicts a similar rivalry between pro-PRC and pro-ROC factions in San Francisco Chinatown.

119. Wang Wei, *Nihon Kakyō ni okeru dentō no saihen to esunishiti*, pp. 257–58.

120. "Yokohama Chūkagai no Kanteibyō ga zenshō," *Asahi shinbun*, Jan. 3, 1986, p. 23.

this effort to promote one of Kobe's districts through its international past was undertaken by the municipal government, business community, and Chinese organizations.[121] Nagasaki's New Territory Chinatown (Shinchi Chūkagai) inaugurated a similar development scheme in 1983. But given the dwindling Chinese population in the city, leadership has more often come from the local government rather than the Chinese community. After local Chinese residents revived the Chinese lantern festival (Yuanxiaojie) in 1987, Nagasaki City co-opted the event in 1994 as an official city festival and contributed significant financial support.[122]

From Diaspora to Minority

Amid these economic and institutional developments, the meaning of Chinese identity in Yokohama began shifting once again. From the 1950s to the 1970s, the participation of the Yokohama Chinese in political struggles proved the importance of homeland issues to their community. A Japan-wide survey of *huaqiao* in 1966 confirmed that an overwhelming majority (93%) showed deep concern for the homeland, and 81 percent answered that they were concerned with the state of affairs in either Chinese regime.[123] Although the study skewed the numbers upward by sampling only those who chose to participate in Chinese organizations or maintain economic relations with either homeland, it nevertheless suggests that for many, a diasporic affiliation was a strong component of their Chinese identity.[124]

Another survey from the 1960s suggested, however, that the diasporic orientation of Chinese identity was gradually being superseded by what might be best described as a minority orientation. Regardless of nationality, the widespread acculturation of the Chinese in Yokohama meant that their

---

121. Wang Wei, *Sugao no Chūkagai*, pp. 37, 74; Tsu, "From Ethnic Ghetto to 'Gourmet Republic,'" pp. 18–19.

122. Wang Wei, *Sugao no Chūkagai*, pp. 29, 178, 185. Chinese institutions in Nagasaki have atrophied as a result of a decline in the Chinese population, which is now only in the hundreds. As reported in a Mar. 23, 1988, *Nagasaki shinbun* article, Nagasaki's Chinese school closed after the graduation of its last two students that spring.

123. Tull Chu, *Political Attitudes of the Overseas Chinese in Japan*, p. 31.

124. Ibid., pp. v–vi.

commonly assumed Chineseness was not the aggregation of cultural traits shared with Chinese in the homeland, but rather, defined by markers of difference from the Japanese. A 1967 survey of graduates of the pro-ROC school indicated that in 61.7 percent of their households, Japanese was the primary language, with only 18.3 percent and 14.5 percent using Mandarin and Cantonese, respectively. Most Chinese by then had also adopted Japanese-style funerals, replacing the more extravagant Chinese traditional rites. On the other hand, a clear majority (72.9%) responded that they primarily ate Chinese food at home, compared with 13.9 percent who predominantly ate Japanese food. On the other hand, only 10 percent of respondents claimed that they would choose a Japanese as a marriage partner.[125] Despite these attitudes toward marriage, Chinese apparently encountered few social impediments in their daily life in Yokohama; one survey respondent expressed his satisfaction with his treatment by local society, which had allowed his family to "live here without feeling like a foreigner and with many Japanese friends."[126]

The diasporic orientation was also weakened by Cold War attenuation of direct links to hometowns in the mainland, persistent political division, and naturalization. Conversely, their relationship with the host society gained in importance through economic interdependence with their Japanese neighbors and alliances with city planners and administrators. In the process, Yokohama Chinatown came to figure more noticeably in the local historical consciousness. From the late 1950s, the magazine *Kyōdo Yokohama* (Hometown Yokohama), like the later magazine *Shimin to bunka*, prominently featured memoirs of Chinatown from the 1930s and before.[127] The inclusion

---

125. Yamashita, "Yokohama Chūkagai zairyū Chūgokujin," pp. 43, 46–48; Sugawara, *Nihon no kakyō*, p. 191; *BX*, p. 110. These expressed preferences notwithstanding, anecdotal evidence indicates Chinese-Japanese couples were common in Yokohama.

126. Hayase, "Kakyō shakai kenkyū no shomondai (3)," pp. 6–10. This anonymous *huaqiao* from Zhejiang Province was married to a Japanese woman and was a member of both the pro-ROC Chinese Association and the Yamashita-chō Association (Yamashita-chō chōnaikai). Among his closest associates, he listed one Chinese uncle living in Osaka and five Japanese friends living in the Tokyo-Yokohama area.

127. Hiramatsu, "Yokohama meibutsu"; Arahata, "Meiji sanjūnendai no Yokohama o kataru"; Kayama, "Nankinmachi o egaku."

of Yokohama Chinese in local histories substantiates the gradual acknowledgment of their role in local culture and identity.[128]

The integrity of the Yokohama community, therefore, derived less from
intrinsic Chineseness than their position of alterity within Japanese society.[129] In that sense, their Chinese ethnicity approached the ethnicity of
American usage, defined by marginality and otherness as well as peoplehood. Yokohama Chinatown now bore more in common with the Chinatowns of San Francisco and New York, where scholars have noted that
Chinese minority identity has been determined more by ethnic discrimination from outside than by actual cultural unity or economic solidarity.[130]
Interestingly, the 1967 survey of Chinese graduates suggests that the markers that mattered were not language, ritual observances, or social distance.
Clothing and physical appearance were likewise indistinguishable. The
predilection toward Chinese food was one of the clearest markers that dis-
tinguished the Chinese from the Japanese. The minority status was also
fundamentally unstable, because this dimension of their identity was sustained by its commodification into an economic niche and relied on Japanese
consumption. Its commercial success would undermine the very distinctiveness of this gastronomic choice. But more importantly, the status was entirely local in scope. The pull of local society made these Chinese more ready
to identify as Yokohama-ites; but this identification did not imply belonging
to the Japanese nation, as many still maintained Chinese nationality.

Concurrently, the rigid notion of Japanese citizenship premised on ethnicity was being challenged across Japan during these years, as demonstrated by activism and identity debates led by *zainichi* Koreans. In 1970,
zainichi Koreans comprised the largest foreigner group in Japan, by far,
numbering 614,202 in comparison to 51,481 Chinese nationals.[131] The

---

128. Kimura, "Kyōdoshi, chihōshi, chiikishi," p. 12. As Kimura Motoi argues,
the term *kyōdo* (hometown) has been used to describe local history projects associated with emperor-centric nationalism and hence attempts to define a Japanese national tradition as deriving from authentic local cultures. There is thus some irony
in the recognition of *huaqiao* contributions to Yokohama's *kyōdo* history, but it implies their participation in creating an essential, affective attachment to the local
space.

129. Sollors, "Theories of American Ethnicity," p. xi; Crossley, "Thinking about
Ethnicity in Early Modern China," p. 13.

130. Kwong, *New Chinatown*; Nee and de Bary Nee, *Longtime Californ'*.

131. Guo, *Zainichi kakyō*, p. 49.

Cold War similarly divided Koreans into opposed camps, which coalesced around rival organizations: the South Korea–affiliated Mindan (est. 1946), and Chongryun (est. 1955) with ties to the North.[132] These organizations endeavored to sustain community cohesion through a diasporic nationalism that discouraged naturalization and denied the possibility of living as an ethnic minority. However, by the 1970s, some *zainichi* Koreans were advocating identities that moved beyond diaspora by rejecting homeland politics, emphasizing permanent settlement, and demanding greater rights and equality with the Japanese majority.[133] One major breakthrough was the previously mentioned Hitachi employment discrimination case. During the case, Pak's supporters, mainly second- and third-generation Korean activists and their Japanese allies, formed a group called the National Council for Combating Discrimination against Ethnic Peoples in Japan (Mintōren). In the 1970s, this group spearheaded a movement to secure rights and better treatment for resident aliens, and employed the concept of local citizenship to secure those rights. At the end of the decade, the concept of a minority status for *zainichi* Koreans was given forceful, controversial expression by Kim Tong-myung in his concept of a "third way (*daisan no michi*)" between diaspora and assimilation, that is, "living as ethnic Koreans and, at the same time, as citizens of Japan."[134]

The *zainichi* Korean third way differed somewhat from expressions of Yokohama Chinese identity in both content and effects. *Zainichi* Korean activism possessed national clout and triggered a national dialogue on the status of permanent foreign residents in Japan, particularly former colonial subjects. In contrast, Yokohama Chinese identified specifically with the local community of their city. They found refuge in a profitable economic niche that expressed both their Chinese and Yokohama identities, a situation without parallel among *zainichi* Koreans at that time. Nevertheless, the Mintōren appeal for equality according to local citizenship rights would be familiar to the Yokohama Chinese; it was premised on patterns of national

---

132. C. Lee, "Organizational Division and Conflict," pp. 112, 123.

133. Ryang, *North Koreans in Japan*, pp. 196–99; Lie, *Zainichi*, pp. 95–96, 118. Subsequent developments in *zainichi* Korean communities and further elaboration of the concept of local citizenship will be discussed in the concluding chapter.

134. Chung, *Immigration and Citizenship in Japan*, pp. 99–100, 127; Chapman, *Zainichi Korean Identity and Ethnicity*, p. 48.

difference and local incorporation that the Yokohama Chinese had experienced since the nineteenth century.

Conclusion

The importance of a *huaqiao* political identity among Yokohama Chinese peaked and subsequently declined during the years from 1945 to 1972. Initially, there were advantages to this category that set them apart from their Japanese neighbors. *Huaqiao* status was encouraged by preferential treatment under the Allied Occupation and was mobilized by patriotic calls to support either the ROC or the PRC. Moreover, among Chinatowns of the "free world," the pro-PRC partisans had greater resilience, owing to the protection they received as resident foreigners; the price to be paid for this autonomy was exclusion from the Japanese national community. Sustained political division between the two factions, however, undercut the ideology of ethnic unity and even impelled many to renounce their Chinese nationality. Economic imperatives over the same period fostered attitudes open to integration with Yokohama society, and the promotion of the district's Chinese restaurants became a commercial strategy that benefited both Chinese and Japanese residents. During these decades, Chinese food performed a dual function: first, as an inclusive commercial enterprise for Chinese and Japanese residents, and second, as an important ethnic marker defining Chineseness. The YDA has exemplified these inclusive economic and social arrangements.

Chineseness was thus reconstituted not through substantive political, cultural, or ethnic ties with the homeland, but as a minority status defined in relation to the Japanese majority. Chinese were no longer unified by political loyalty to a homeland, nor were they a bounded social or language group. Ties of blood were weakened as many of the Yokohama Chinese were children of Chinese-Japanese parentage.[135] Maintenance of Chinese citizenship

---

135. C. B. Tan, "People of Chinese Descent"; L. Pan, *Sons of the Yellow Emperor*, pp. 168–69. This situation is not unique. The maintenance of Chineseness as a local relationship with other social groups can also be seen in Malaysia where the Baba Chinese, also known as the Peranakan or Straits Chinese, have preserved a consciousness of their ethnic identity without retaining the Chinese language. Their culture has been localized and is a hybrid of Fujian Chinese and Javanese influences.

in a *jus sanguinis* context had perpetuated legal distinctions between Chinese and Japanese, but large-scale naturalization after 1972 mitigated this aspect as well. Naturalization, however, did not necessarily reduce the subjective sense of Chinese identity among Yokohama Chinese; many of the leaders of the pro-ROC Chinese Association have naturalized but keep separate business cards for their Chinese and Japanese names, to be used in different contexts.[136] Thus over time the objective determinants of Chineseness became fewer in comparison to the many contextual and subjective links with Japanese society.

In that sense, economics can explain the persistence of a Chinese community in Yokohama as much as nationalist ideology or *jus sanguinis* nationality laws. The commercialization of Chinese culture during the decades since 1945 allowed acculturation and integration even as it impelled the expansion of its most marketable dimension, Chinese cuisine. The case of Yokohama Chinatown thus provides an example of how Chinese culture could be construed as cultural foreignness from a national perspective but simultaneously incorporated into Yokohama's cosmopolitan local identity.

Yokohama localism was moreover being defined through a dialectic between central authority and regional autonomy. It entered into policy making at the same moment that many other provincial towns were engaged in revitalization (*machi okoshi*) projects similarly based in their cultural distinctiveness.[137] Local identity, like national identity, is always relational. While national consciousness and global competition were driving the boom in Nihonjinron writings during these decades, domestic competition was giving rise to local differentiation. In Yokohama's case, its local cosmopolitanism was based on the marketability of its treaty-port past, which had long set it apart from Tokyo and other Japanese cities.

This local identity was more than a mere economic instrument, however, since it continued to encompass social, cultural, and political dimensions. The Yokohama Chinese had become minorities in Yokohama society,

---

136. Until 1985, the Japanese Ministry of Justice strongly urged naturalization applicants to adopt Japanese names; this did not entail a hard-and-fast rule, but in practice it led nearly all naturalizers to legally change their name.

137. Knight, "Rural Revitalization in Japan." For instance, Ōita Prefecture on the southern island of Kyushu developed a "one village–one product (*isson ippin*)" plan in the late 1970s, associating each village with an emblematic product, such as mandarin oranges or tomatoes, in order to build brand awareness of its products.

though not necessarily in Japan as a whole. In spite of the postwar myth of Japanese ethnic homogeneity, the journal *Shimin to bunka* included Chinese in the category of *shimin*, suggesting the acceptance of Yokohama Chinese as members of the local community. Together with the similar term *jūmin*, this conception of belonging has since come to legitimate an advocacy for local political rights for non-Japanese. The political instrumentality of these overlapping identities, the oft-invoked presence of "the local in the global," will be examined in more depth in the concluding chapter.

Conclusion:

Minorities in a Monoethnic State and the

Micropolitics of Everyday Life

The story of how the Yokohama Chinese maintained their community from the late nineteenth to the late twentieth century reveals radical transformations in their collective identities beneath apparent continuities. Broadly speaking, interactions in local society and geopolitical developments allowed the rise of a unified sense of Chineseness, while at the same time, these Chinese also developed a strong sense of Yokohama localism. This concluding chapter examines how the Yokohama Chinese have understood their relationships with China, Japan, and Yokohama in more recent years, as well as the implications of the Yokohama Chinese identity position. The first section reflects on the historical development of an identity as Chinese Yokohama-ites. It examines how this identity position challenges the exclusivity of Chineseness and Japaneseness as terminal and ethnic identifications, and bears significance for Sino-Japanese reconciliation. The second will relate these collective identities to social movements seeking to fundamentally alter the meaning of Japanese citizenship, and consider the community's role in shaping the contours of a future Japanese society.

Yokohama Chinese Identities in Historical Perspective

Chinatown's spatial coherence has displayed a remarkable amount of continuity across the twentieth century. Its dimensions and layout have not changed significantly, and despite near complete destruction in 1923 and

1945, its streets and alleys maintain their distinctive tilted orientation relative to the surrounding city (maps 2A and 2B). At the same time, historical developments have remapped the social position of the Chinese in Yokohama. Until the nineteenth century, immigrants from China were affiliated primarily with their native place rather than the dynasties that ruled China. When not continually replenished by immigration, these communities were gradually absorbed into Japanese society. The rise of modern nation-states worldwide changed this situation. The ideologies and institutions of a nascent Chinese nation-state extended their influence to Yokohama Chinatown in the late 1890s and successfully promoted a diasporic *huaqiao* identity after the founding of the Republic of China (ROC) in 1912. In the same years, Chinese identity gained a cross-generational persistence through ideas of shared ethnicity and the *jus sanguinis* nationality laws of both China and Japan. Rising conflict between China and Japan then mobilized Chinese residents in support of the political causes of their Chinese homeland. The devastating Asia-Pacific War of 1937–45 and its immediate aftermath under the Allied Occupation completed this process of diasporic nation building by making *huaqiao* identity obligatory for all Chinese in Yokohama, even as the Cold War divided the political allegiances of that community.

However, in the decades since, the Chinese in Yokohama have increasingly expressed their social and economic integration in an inclusive discourse of local identity, as Yokohama-ites, or *hamakko*. In this period of peace, the need for Chinese and Japanese to demonstrate loyalty to their respective countries was diminished, and local solidarities became more relevant in daily life. Along the way, the socioeconomic role of Chinatown itself also changed. With increasing work opportunities in mainstream Japanese society, the cohesiveness of the ethnic enclave has lost some of its pull. This shift has been more a product of economic forces than the social and legal developments like the Hitachi employment discrimination case. Since the 1970s, Japanese companies have shown more willingness to hire Chinese, particularly companies involved in trade with China, Taiwan, or Hong Kong.[1] And with the availability of jobs outside the traditional family-owned enterprises of Chinatown, many of the older shops have closed. One of the most missed is Hakugatei—originator of the Yokohama *shūmai*—which

---

1. Hirota, *Kakyō no ima,* p. 239.

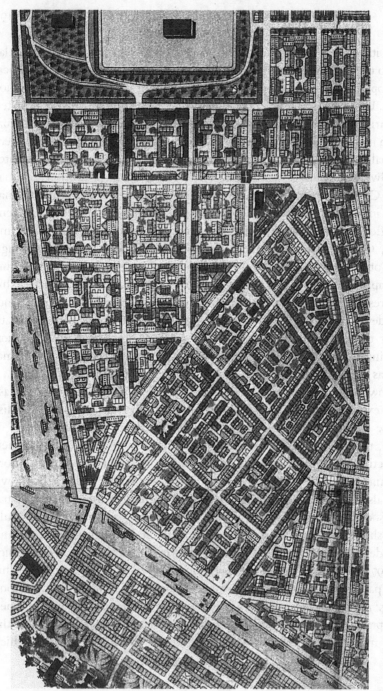

MAP 2A. An 1891 print titled *Yokohama shinkei ichiran zue*. Courtesy of Yokohama kaikō shiryōkan.

MAP 2B. A 2013 satellite image. *Sources:* Imagery ©2013 Cnes/Spot Image, Digital Earth Technology, Digital Globe; map data ©2013 Google, ZENRIN.

closed its doors in the early 1980s.[2] The final proprietor was Mai Yinyu, the wife of one of Bao Tang's grandsons. Each of her sons went to medical school and became doctors, and her daughters married and moved away, leaving no one to inherit the shop.[3]

The district now serves less as an ethnic enclave and more a pillar of Yokohama's cultural distinctiveness. Recent developments clearly demonstrate that Yokohama Chinatown is no longer solely for the Chinese, if it ever was. Chinatown appears prominently in Yokohama's official publicity materials, both the city's tourist literature and its website. It has also achieved a presence in the regional mass transportation infrastructure. Although the promised Chinatown station on the Yokohama City subway system did not come to fruition, a Motomachi-Chūkagai (Motomachi-Chinatown) station opened as the terminus of the Minatomirai (Port of the future) train line in February 2004. There has also been greater public acknowledgment of the role Chinese play in shaping local culture. According to a 2001 survey commissioned by Kanagawa Prefecture, Yokohama Chinatown topped the list of the prefecture's one hundred most important "treasures that should be maintained for eternity."[4] And as mentioned in the introduction, Yokohama Chinatown today draws approximately 18.6 million visits a year, a figure that makes it Japan's second-most popular tourist destination after Tokyo Disneyland.[5]

Yokohama's Chinese schools also serve as an index of the cross-generational integration of Chinese into local life. From its origins in the late nineteenth century, Chinese education in Yokohama primarily sought to instill and to maintain a sense of Chinese cultural identity and diasporic patriotism. Today, however, both Yokohama Chinese schools enroll significant numbers of Japanese students; as a December 29, 2003, *Aera* article noted, the schools'

---

2. Although the original restaurant closed, the brand was revived in 2011 as a mail-order business selling *shūmai*. See "Hakuga: Kôshiki saito," accessed May 6, 2013, http://hakuga.net.

3. Sugawara, *Chainataun,* pp. 102–7. Mai Yinyu naturalized and took the name Hori Tamako, and though she speaks Japanese far better than Chinese, still prefers her Chinese name.

4. "Anata ga eranda Kanagawa mirai isan 100," Kanagawa Prefecture, accessed Nov. 6, 2007, http://www.pref.kanagawa.jp/osirase/tosiseibi/machi/keikan/50sen_100sen/mirai100.

5. Yokohama Chūkagai machi zukuri dantai rengō kyōgikai, *Yokohama Chūkagai no gurando dezain,* pp. 7–8.

increasingly diverse student bodies have necessitated changes in their curricular emphases.

Japanese nationals are now the majority in both schools—in 2010 comprising 73.3 percent (381) of the students at the pro-ROC Yokohama chūkagakuin, and 67.6 percent (526) at the pro-PRC Yamate chūkagakkō. This is a marked shift from the late 1980s and early 1990s, when more than 75 percent of students in both schools held Chinese nationality. It bears mentioning that most of the Japanese nationals at the schools today are ethnic Chinese or of Chinese-Japanese parentage, but a significant percentage—29.8 percent at the Yokohama chūkagakuin and 5.3 percent at the Yamate chūkagakkō—are Japanese without any Chinese heritage.[6] The diverse ethnic and cultural backgrounds of these students reflect the shift toward intermarriage and Japanese naturalization among Chinese, as well as internationalization of the wider community.

Both schools are currently at full capacity, which is no small feat considering Japan's declining birth rate. Moreover, the Yamate chūkagakkō has recently expanded. In April 2010, the school moved from the Yamate district, and while retaining its original name, currently occupies a modern and spacious building in central Yokohama near the Ishikawa-chō Japan Rail station. Despite this new capacity, the number of Japanese students remains low because the school offers priority first to the children of graduates, and next, to newcomer Chinese. The latent demand among Japanese for enrollment is, however, quite high, in spite of significant institutional obstacles created by Japanese educational policy. Japan's Ministry of Education, Culture, Sports, Science and Technology (MEXT) has not accredited either school as a middle or high school. MEXT has only certified them as miscellaneous schools (kakushu gakkō), on a par with vocational, language, and driving schools, as well as zainichi Korean schools. As a result, degrees granted by the Yokohama Chinese schools do not qualify graduates to sit for most entrance exams, so the range of high schools and universities to which they can apply is quite limited.[7] Nevertheless, the appeal of the unique cur-

---

6. Chen Tien-shi, "Kajin to wa dare ka," pp. 46–47; Zhu Huiling, Kakyō shakai no henbō, p. 31.

7. Pan Minsheng, "Yokohama Yamate chūkagakkō no kako, genzai, mirai," p. 58. The two Chinese schools in Yokohama have received permission from public and private schools within Kanagawa Prefecture to let their graduates sit for entrance exams. In most other cases, however, graduates must first take an

ricula offered by the two schools is strong enough to keep their classes filled for the forseeable future.

The principals of the two schools explain that whereas Chinese language and cultural traditions continue to be cornerstones of their curricula, the schools also aim for an international education, one that is oriented toward a future—and multicultural—Japanese society. Pan Minsheng, the first Japan-born principal of the Yamate chūkagakkō, points out that since 1993 the school has not taught Chinese as a native language, but rather as a second language to better suit students born and raised in Japan. Citing a historically resonant phrase, Pan stated that the school's purpose is "to cultivate persons who can contribute to Sino-Japanese friendship."[8] Lee Tzsu Maan of the Yokohama chūkagakuin explained that his school teaches a trilingual curriculum and uses Taiwanese texts alongside ones authorized by MEXT, in order to pass down Chinese tradition as well as impart an "international consciousness." The school is not seeking to mechanically reproduce Chineseness; as Lee argues, "identity is up to the individual."[9] Both schools provide an education with a strong emphasis on Chinese culture, but which also recognizes the ethnic diversity of the student body and its members' permanent settlement in Yokohama or Japan.

Taken together, these developments in commerce and education suggest the ways that mutual acculturation between Chinese and Japanese have helped constitute a multiethnic society in this local space, one with its own legitimating discourses and institutions. By expressing their identity as Yokohama-ites, Yokohama Chinese were acknowledging their belonging in the local community even as they maintained a *huaqiao* identity. Not a matter of capricious self-ascription, their identity is enabled and reinforced by widespread acceptance from their Japanese neighbors. This form of external affirmation functioned in postwar Japan just as it did during the Asia-Pacific

---

equivalency exam. Tokyo, on the other hand, has a much more restrictive policy that forbids Japanese nationals who have attended the Chinese schools to take Tokyo-area entrance exams. This policy seems to be based on the notion that these children have evaded their compulsory education under Japanese law. The Chinese schools themselves are moreover disadvantaged by the miscellaneous school classification because they receive a fraction of the usual government subsidy per student and are not eligible for government support for textbooks and insurance.

8. Ibid., pp. 57–59.

9. Lee Tzsu Maan, "Hyakunen no kakyō gakkō no kenshō," pp. 62, 69.

war. Recall that Chen Dongting's newspaper interview in 1940 lauded him as a "pure Yokohama-ite." In more recent years, Lü Xingxiong, son of Egawa Taka, has used that exact expression, *"kissui no hamakko,"* to describe his Sino-Japanese commitments. In 1990–99, he managed a Cantonese restaurant and was president of the pro-PRC Chinese Association; at the same time, he worked on the programming board of the Japanese Yokohama FM Radio Broadcasting and the consultation committee of the Yokohama Hometown History Foundation (Yokohama furusato rekishi zaidan).[10] These examples show that the pure Yokohama character has been constructed as nationally hybrid and cosmopolitan.[11]

Acquiring Japanese nationality is not incompatible with a hybrid consciousness, and naturalization for Yokohama Chinese has often been a matter of legal expedience. For instance, the naturalized head trustee of the YDA, Hayashi Kensei, has written that "Gaoming Prefecture, Guangdong Province is my 'father,' while Yokohama is my 'mother.'" Identifying with either China or Japan is inadequate, while identifying with both—in light of prevailing conceptions of peoplehood—is still considered oxymoronic.[12] Under similar constraints, the resident Chinese of other Japanese cities have adopted analogous idioms of local identity: "child of Kobe" (*Kobekko*) for Kobe residents, and "person of Satsuma" (*Satsuma no hito*) for residents of Kagoshima.[13] There is still nothing approaching a widely held Chinese Japanese identity.

The burgeoning influence of local identity discourses among Yokohama Chinese correlates as well with waning psychological identification with the homeland. A 1991–92 survey of long-term Chinese residents of Japan confirmed a degree of alienation from a Chineseness anchored in China. The respondent pool was limited to those who immigrated to Japan before 1972 and their descendants; when asked with which country they identified, 81 percent of those aged fifty-five and above answered China, whereas only 43

---

10. Hirota, *Kakyō no ima*, pp. 230, 236, 238–40.
11. On this point, I follow David Hollinger's approach to the significance of the cosmopolitanism, which "promotes multiple identities, emphasizes the dynamic and changing character of many groups, and is responsive to the potential for creating new cultural combinations" (Hollinger, *Postethnic America*, pp. 3–4).
12. Tan and Liu, *Shinkakyō rōkakyō*, p. 144.
13. Hayashi Masashige, "Kōbe kakyō no kokoro o tsutaeru." Satsuma Domain is the historical name of the western portion of modern-day Kagoshima Prefecture.

percent of those aged thirty and under did so. On the contrary, 11 percent of the latter group claimed to be Japanese, 38 percent claimed to be persons in-between (chūkanjin), and 6 percent answered that they did not know what they should be called.[14] International sport can also reveal psychological alignments. A 2004 survey conducted at the Yamate chūkagakkō asked respondents whom they would support in international competition. The survey found that between the PRC and Japan, 46 percent would root for the PRC, compared to 14 percent for Japan. In contrast, in the case of Taiwan and Japan, 54 percent would root for Japan, and only 18 percent would root for Taiwan.[15] We may presume that there were reciprocal feelings on the pro-ROC side. Affective attachment to Japan appears to have supplanted feelings of ethnic solidarity with their political rivals.

Sociologist Guo Fang corroborates this dilution of national consciousness; her findings indicate that young Chinese share a pattern of "transnational identity" at variance with the "ethnic identity" of their grandparents and the "national identity" of their parents. Members of the younger generation consider their Chineseness to be only one of their identities, which include links with Japan and the world.[16] Their transnational identity derives not from a homogenizing globalization, but one that in its local registers produces what might be termed cultural bricolage: a mixing, particularization, and fragmentation of existing identities.[17] The commodification of Chinese culture in Yokohama Chinatown may appear to undermine the bricolage thesis because, as the logic goes, this process reinforces and institutionalizes differences between Chinese and Japanese. However, the lives of the Chinese in Yokohama consisted of more than selling shūmai to Japanese consumers. Individuals in Yokohama, both Chinese and Japanese, de-

---

14. Zhu Huiling, Kakyō shakai no henbō, pp. 61, 65. Those who claimed to be Japanese did not necessarily have Japanese nationality. Only 8.1 percent of those aged 30 and under were naturalized.

15. BX, p. 496.

16. Guo, Zainichi kakyō, pp. 171–73, 183. The "ethnic identity" of Chinese who came of age before 1945 was attached foremost to their native-place associations; the "national identity" of the middle-aged Chinese was fostered by political associations from 1945 and 1972.

17. Dijkstra, Geuijen, and de Ruijter, "Multiculturalism and Social Integration in Europe," pp. 60–62. This phenomenon has also been known by the awkward neologism "glocalization."

veloped a range of solidarities over the past century through mutual participation in a shared community.

   In addition, from the 1980s the arrival of large numbers of immigrants
from the People's Republic of China also weakened identification with the
Chinese homeland by introducing a new local-national axis of differentiation. The liberalization of foreign travel by the PRC, combined with Japanese
visa policies welcoming foreign students and trainees, led to a near tripling
of the population of Chinese nationals in Japan during this decade.[18] In 1980,
there were 52,896 Chinese in Japan, but in 1989 that number had grown to
150,339. By 2007, the total number of Chinese in Japan reached 606,889,
finally surpassing the Korean population, which was then 593,489.[19] Ostensible compatriots of the older community, these "new *huaqiao*" (*xin huaqiao*)
are distinct in a number of subjective and objective dimensions. First, their
primary areas of settlement are not the old Chinatown communities of
Yokohama, Kobe, or Nagasaki. As noted in the introduction, the registered
Chinese population of Naka Ward, including Chinatown, was 9,085 in
2011. This is a stark jump from pre-1980 figures, but not proportional to the
rise in the overall Chinese population. The number of Chinese in Naka
Ward rose a modest 35 percent from 1980 to 1989—from 2,882 to 3,892—
over a decade when the Chinese population in Japan tripled.[20]

   The intelligibility of the acculturated Yokohama Chinese identity has
derived in part from differentiation from the newcomers. On this point, the
previously mentioned 2004 survey among graduates of the Yamate
chūkagakkō found that 36.4 percent of respondents claimed they felt themselves *less* Chinese when meeting Chinese fresh from the mainland; in comparison, only 5.7 percent claimed that they got along smoothly with the

---

   18. Liu-Farrer, "Creating a Transnational Community," pp. 119–21; Guo,
Zainichi kakyō, p. 49; Zhu Huiling, *Kakyō shakai no henbō*, p. 29; Oda, *Nihon ni zairyū
suru Chūgokujin*, p. 39. Official educational exchange programs between the PRC
and Japan were inaugurated in 1979. Chinese began arriving in larger numbers in
1984, when the PRC initiated a policy to allow self-funded students to travel
abroad. The Japanese government created the category of trainee through its 1981
Industrial Training Program for Non-Japanese, which permitted Japanese industries to sponsor and to train workers from developing countries. It has since largely
functioned as a "side door" for low-wage, semi-skilled labor migration into Japan.
   19. Statistics Bureau, *Registered Aliens by Nationality*.
   20. Yokohama-shi, *Tōkei sho*, 60:32, 69:36.

newcomers, and 11.0 percent felt their Chineseness confirmed by such encounters.[21]

Moreover, the newcomers enjoy a much less harmonious relationship with Japanese society than the older community. Whereas Andrea Vasishth characterizes the Chinese community in Japan in the 1990s as a "model minority," her emphasis lies on the historical *huaqiao* communities.[22] Other scholars, as well as the Japanese press, portray the newcomer Chinese as anything but. Recapitulating anxieties about Chinese labor and mixed residence from the end of the nineteenth century, much writing in recent years focuses on unauthorized Chinese migrants, the crimes they commit, the role of human smugglers that provide them entry, and the various forms of identity theft and deception that make this possible.[23] These negative popular perceptions among Japanese have made the historical Chinese communities much less likely to identify with the new arrivals, even if the newcomers are not merely or even principally composed of unskilled labor migrants. Less visible in media reports, but demographically significant, are returned Japanese war orphans from China, wives of Japanese nationals, students, and transnational entrepreneurs.

Though the newcomers do not constitute a singular community, in aggregate they now outnumber the old Chinatown communities by tenfold. Nevertheless, the latter still carry analytical significance for the newcomers because earlier experiences in Japan suggest potential future social positions. The terminology used to define the new arrivals is itself not new. "New *huaqiao*" at one time referred to the Taiwanese who became Chinese nationals at the end of the Asia-Pacific War; in the face of new newcomers, however, all those who arrived prior to Sino-Japanese normalization are now thought of as "old *huaqiao*."[24] In other words, the sheer number of the more recent arrivals is unprecedented, but their position in relation to existing Chinese communities and Japanese society is not.

---

21. *BX*, p. 496.

22. Vasishth, "Model Minority."

23. Friman, "Evading the Divine Wind through the Side Door," pp. 9–34; Friman, "Immigrants, Smuggling, and Threats to Social Order in Japan," pp. 294–317; Zha, "Chinese Migrant Workers in Japan." These studies critique, as well as exemplify, this tendency.

24. Guo, *Zainichi kakyō*, p. 9; Nagano Takeshi, *Zainichi Chūgokujin*, p. 184; Zhu Huiling, *Kakyō shakai no henbō*, p. 56.

A historical perspective also contributes a good deal to our understanding of newcomers' transnational lives. In a recent study of Chinese newcomers, Gracia Liu-Farrer argues that their life choices "maintain a closely-knit transnational social field and preserve their social and cultural roots in the home country." She notes the salience of border-crossing child rearing, reliance on the booming economic ties between Japan and their homeland, and instrumental acquisition of Japanese nationality and permanent residency.[25] These facets of life in Japan for Chinese, however, adhere closely to patterns established in the late nineteenth century and are typical of historical communities of overseas Chinese in general. As a September 22, 1893, *Mainichi shinbun* article observed, Chinese in Japan often sent their children, even those of mixed Sino-Japanese parentage, back to China to be raised by family members and educated there for a time. Writer and artist Su Manshu, described in chapter 2, was an exemplary case; he was sent to his ancestral home in China at age five before returning to Yokohama at age fourteen.[26] Naturalization for pragmatic reasons was also a common practice among the earlier arrivals to Japan.[27] Under the 1899 Japanese nationality law, Chinese made up more than half of the 303 individuals who acquired Japanese nationality before June 1950.[28] Many others took an easier route to Japanese imperial citizenship by establishing residency in Taiwan. In 1930, the number of Fujianese who completed the process and gained extraterritoriality in China and exemption from Chinese taxes was 1,318.[29] These former Chinese nationals, however, did not sever their relationships with China, but

---

25. Liu-Farrer, "Creating a Transnational Community," pp. 116, 129. This builds upon explorations of transnationalism by Linda Basch, Nina Glick Schiller, and Cristina Szanton Blanc, who define it as "processes by which immigrants forge and sustain multi-stranded social relations that link together their societies of origin and settlement" (Basch, Glick Schiller, and Szanton Blanc, *Nations Unbound*, p. 7).

26. Liu Wuji, *Su Man-shu*, pp. 17, 20.

27. Liu-Farrer, "Creating a Transnational Community," p. 129. Many Chinese consider permanent residency superior to Japanese nationality; although more difficult to acquire, the status grants access to benefits in both societies without giving up Chinese nationality.

28. Guo, *Zainichi kakyō*, p. 75.

29. M. Lin, "Overseas Chinese Merchants and Multiple Nationality," pp. 992, 995, 1006. One specific case was Guo Chunyang; after he took Japanese nationality, he donated money to the Qing dynasty, to various pan-Asianist causes, and for disaster relief after the Kantō Earthquake of 1923.

rather sought Japanese nationality to ease their entry into Japan and travel to other countries.[30]

The role of bilateral trade in shaping the lives of Chinese in Japan is also far from unprecedented. As described earlier, the Chinese communities in Japan's treaty ports were first settled by Chinese merchants and compradores. Although the volume of trade between China and Japan has grown explosively in the past few decades, the prewar volume of trade and investment between China and Japan was also considerable.[31] In the 1920s, Japan was China's most important trade partner. Chinese in Japan handled much of this commerce, contributing to the prosperity of their various communities.[32]

The more recent newcomers, to date, have only superficially integrated into Japanese schools, workplaces, and communities. This situation has caused Chinese journalist and twenty-year Tokyo resident Mo Bangfu to lament that Chinese are receiving scant social acceptance or recognition as local residents in Tokyo.[33] However, this outcome should be considered neither inevitable nor immutable. Considering historical continuities with the social, legal, and economic practices of earlier waves of Chinese migrants, newcomer communities may indeed integrate in ways homologous with Yokohama Chinatown. The creation of an inclusive local identity, however, will likely require the perseverance of a second generation—like Bao Bogong, Chen Dongting, and Wu Bokang—with all the attendant struggles to reconcile their national and local identifications.

_____

30. To cite one example, Tan Lioe Liem, a Fujianese merchant in Nagasaki, expressed his desire to naturalize in 1906 in an English-language letter to the Foreign Minister of Japan: "Owing to my commercial business I have to travel about very much and moreover as I intend commencing [sic] an import and commission business that would oblige me to visit Japan, China, Europe" (Tan Lioe Liem to Minister of Foreign Affairs of Japan, "Naigaijin kika kankei zakken," vol. 1, Oct. 1906, 3:8:7:5, JMFA, pp. 1–2).

31. Wan, *Sino-Japanese Relations*, p. 47. From 1994 to 2003, Japan was China's most important trade partner, before being overtaken by the European Union and the United States. Conversely, in 2004, Japan's trade with China was second only to the United States.

32. Iriye, *China and Japan in the Global Setting*, pp. 56–57. The United States was Japan's most important trade partner during this decade, but exports to China were closing the gap.

33. Mo Bangfu, "'Shin Tōkyōjin' itsu tanjō?," *Asahi shinbun*, Feb. 2, 2008, p. B3. Mo Bangfu has argued that, in contrast to the more open cities of New York, Shanghai, Singapore, and Hong Kong, Tokyo's reception of its Chinese residents indicates a society still marked by a "traditional Japanese exclusivity."

Their struggle for self-definition is perhaps typical of transnational or globalized communities worldwide, but in this case has intriguing implications for Sino-Japanese relations. Mutual acculturation in Yokohama has softened perceived hard boundaries between Chineseness and Japaneseness. And as they distanced themselves from one-dimensional affiliations, Yokohama Chinese have been reversing the process of national difference making itself. As shown in chapter 4, identifying as Yokohama-ites disrupted the intended function of collaborationist rhetoric because it diminished their status as representatives of the Chinese nation. In the postwar period as well, such a position has entailed affiliation with a community outside the nested set of subcommunities that comprise the nation. To live as *huaqiao* and Yokohama-ite is to implicitly reject the hierarchical relation between Yokohama and Japan, and between the Chinese diaspora and China. With the complicity of local governments, the Yokohama Chinese have engaged in cultural practices that undermine the acceptance of the nation as an individual's terminal community.

This history of cooperative interactions at the local level also demonstrates that relations between Chinese and Japanese were not inevitably conflictual and dissociative. The shared Yokohama local identity has enabled commercial cooperation between rival Chinese political factions as well as their Japanese neighbors. But it might have broader implications as well. Inasmuch as the Yokohama Chinese have not repudiated their innate Chineseness, their efforts at crafting solidarities across ethnic and national boundaries with their Japanese neighbors signify a process of national reconciliation. Such efforts echo a paradigm for conflict resolution offered by the Commonwealth Secretariat in 2007. Its report, entitled *Civil Paths to Peace: Report of the Commonwealth Commission on Respect and Understanding*, argues that persistent antagonisms are difficult to resolve when one-dimensional identities—for instance, Chinese and Japanese—are treated as absolute and essential. The authors of this report consider this approach to identity counterproductive because it militates against mutuality, empathy, and solidarity with others. One of the most hopeful conclusions they draw is that individuals can recognize, in the multiplicity of their identifications, elements of commonality with their erstwhile enemies which can help broker reconciliation.[34]

---

34. Commonwealth Commission on Respect and Understanding, *Civil Paths to Peace*, pp. 10, 29.

It would, however, be overly optimistic to read in the history of Yokohama Chinatown lasting contibutions to Sino-Japanese friendship, at least
on the national level. Calls for pan-Asianism and Sino-Japanese cooperation
by men such as Sun Yatsen, Inukai Tsuyoshi, and Ōkuma Shigenobu demonstrate, perversely, how easily such ideas could be subordinated to aggressive national interests. Likewise, bromides of Sino-Japanese friendship during the Asia-Pacific War served foremost as rhetorical cover for Japan's
invasion of the Chinese homeland. Such examples suggest that invocations
of *national* friendship have often been cynical, instrumental, and easily be-
trayed, compromised, or discarded. In contrast, this book has examined social transactions at the *local* level that propose an alternate history of modern
Sino-Japanese relations, one that transcends national problematics. The
friendships that emerged between Chinese and Japanese in Yokohama were
lived, local, and personal; they arose in spite of the palpable animus that has
developed between the two countries since the late nineteenth century, and
that has reemerged in recent years. The narrative presented in this work
points to cases in which Sino-Japanese friendship was not merely a euphe-
mism for collaboration and to the times when Chinese and Japanese played
baseball together, twice rebuilt their city from the ashes, and cooperated to
make its Chinatown, in the words of Japanese mystery novelist Saitō Sakae,
"the best Chinatown in the world."[35]

Yokohama Chinese Identities in Comparative Context

Yokohama Chinese identities also raise issues germane to recent discussions
on citizenship in Japan and the social position of foreigners. Yokohama Chinatown can serve as a prominent example of the foreigner as local citizen
(*gaikokujin shimin*) concept, which since the 1970s has become a vehicle for
foreign residents to acquire political rights in Japan. These initiatives are
based on solid legal foundations. Under the postwar constitution, the Japanese political community is defined as *Nihon kokumin* (nationals), but the
Local Government Act assures rights to *jūmin* (local residents), which includes Chinese and other foreign residents.[36] The pursuit of local citizenship rights for foreigners, however, may lead to deeper transformations;
if followed to their logical conclusion, it may lead to a reevalation of both

---

35. Saitō, *Chūkagai satsujin jiken*, p. 21.
36. Tegtmeyer Pak, "Foreigners Are Local Citizens Too," p. 252.

Japan's identity as a monoethnic political community and the central government's exclusive right to determine inclusion and exclusion in that community.

The activism and identities of Koreans in Japan is a highly important comparative case; for most of the half century since the end of the Asia-Pacific War, Koreans were the largest group of foreigners in Japan. Like the Chinese in Japan, they contributed significantly to the globalization of Japan's local spaces, and *zainichi* Korean organizations have wielded considerable political clout in that regard. Since the 1970s, *zainichi* Korean leaders and intellectuals have led debates over immigrant incorporation, multiculturalism, and the rights of resident aliens. They have been particularly active in articulating local identities and leading movements to offer citizenship rights to foreigners.[37]

Zainichi Koreans have experienced many of the same identity transformations as the Yokohama Chinese, though in a more compressed time frame. As described in chapter 5, the Japanese government stripped Koreans of their Japanese imperial citizenship following the end of the Asia-Pacific War. Until the 1970s, the cohesiveness of Korean identity in Japan depended on this legal exclusion from the Japanese community and subject positions as temporary residents awaiting return to the homeland. Discrimination by Japanese society was also extreme; as John Lie argues, Koreans experienced a mixture of "discrimination and sympathy" while under colonial dominance, but then open hatred and vilification after liberation in 1945. Japanese associated Koreans with both black markets and labor militancy, which led to a collective characterization of Koreans as "sly, rustic, poor, pathetic, and barbaric."[38] This was one point of difference with Chinese in the postwar years. As Lie argues, Japanese found Chinese relatively more acceptable because "Japan defeated and colonized Korea, but not China" and because of a greater appreciation of Chinese civilization.[39]

---

37. Chung, *Immigration and Citizenship in Japan*, pp. 25, 121–23.

38. Lie, *Zainichi*, pp. 9, 147. Lie cites surveys in 1939 and 1949 to substantiate this shift in Japanese public attitudes. In 1939, Japanese ranked Koreans fifth out of fifteen peoples, when asked for their preference order. In 1949, Koreans were ranked fifteen out of fifteen.

39. Ibid., p. 24. This characterization applies best to the years since 1945. Japanese society openly and vehemently denigrated Chinese at other times, particularly as described in chap. 1, during the Sino-Japanese War of 1894–95.

Nevertheless, the some 600,000 Koreans who remained in Japan after 1945 did not oppose the revocation of their Japanese nationality. Koreans, like Chinese, keenly felt that Japanese nationality implied complete assimilation to Japan and a rejection of their essential identity. According to ethnic-nationalist assumptions, the Korean representative organizations Mindan and Chongryun promoted competing versions of Korean nationalism and established a policy of mutual noninterference with Japanese authorities. In the face of strong discrimination from Japanese, these associations crafted separate social spheres for their constituencies by providing financial services, education, welfare, and a sense of cultural pride.[40]

These ethnic organizations did not seek to expand rights for their constituencies in the host country, but rather espoused an ideology that rejected full participation in Japanese society. Some Koreans, however, began taking up domestic rights issues from the 1970s as their communities transitioned from a migrant first generation to a diasporic second generation. The relevant generational difference lay in their relationships to homeland and host land. In contrast to the first generation, the second accepted the permanence of their settlement in Japan, even while maintaining a stable identification with a largely unknown homeland. This diasporic form of identity, Lie argues, derived from a combination of "Korean descent and Japanese livelihood" amid "the persistence of Japanese discrimination."[41]

By the 1970s, however, Koreans had become a settled minority within their *local* communities even if most maintained foreign nationality. Over three-fourths of *zainichi* Koreans were born in Japan by then, and greater than half of their marriages were with Japanese nationals. Like Chinese in Japan, language was no longer a distinguishing and unifying factor between co-ethnics. Nor was there an obvious or foolproof test to tell Koreans from Japanese; *zainichi* Koreans spoke Japanese without a Korean accent, and Japanese now regularly ate many Korean foods like kimchi and barbecued meat. And also like the Yokohama Chinese, *zainichi* Koreans began openly expressing hybrid identities as both local residents and foreign nationals. In this context, new organizations with significant *zainichi* Korean leadership arose to take up issues of discrimination and equality for foreigners. One example was Mintōren, discussed in chapter 5. A range of institutions also

---

40. Ryang, *North Koreans in Japan*, p. 121; Chapman, *Zainichi Korean Identity and Ethnicity*, p. 25; Lie, *Zainichi*, pp. 41–43.

41. Lie, *Zainichi*, p. 128.

promoted the integration of *zainichi* Koreans into their local communities, including the nonprofit Kawasaki Fureai Hall (Fureaikan), which serves as a venue for cultural exchange between Japanese and Korean residents of Kawasaki City. Nevertheless, these efforts and the related "third-way" advocacy still rejected naturalization as a legitimate option. These were noncitizen civil rights movements, and still reflected the ethnic-nationalist assumptions under which most Koreans, Japanese, and Chinese lived.[42]

The third way, however, did not merely reaffirm ethnic-nationalism; like the fragmentation and bricolage of Chinese identities, the debates it triggered opened up a space for the further elaboration of identity discourses.[43] In the wake of these debates, third- and fourth-generation ethnic Koreans, variously characterized as transnational, post-*zainichi*, or post-diaspora, have become more willing to reject the ethnic-nationalism of their forebears. From the 1990s, two emerging developments—a gradual *zainichi* Korean acceptance of naturalization, and a Japanese advocacy of multicultural coexistence (*tabunka kyōsei*)—have led some among the new generations to call for a Korean-Japanese hyphenated identity, something not yet seen among Chinese in Japan. These activists have presented this as a "fourth choice" which entails naturalization as Japanese while openly maintaining Korean names and identity.[44] If widely accepted, such a choice promises to delink ethnicity from Japanese nationality and to fundamentally transform the nature of belonging in Japanese society. It is predicated, however, on a transformation of the social meaning of Japanese naturalization: from a process understood as cultural conformity, political passivity, a "privilege" granted to foreigners, and erasure of heritage, to an active means of acquiring citizenship rights premised on equality and the acknowledgment of group differences.[45]

---

42. Ibid., pp. 18, 32, 84, 118; Chung, *Immigration and Citizenship in Japan*, pp. 96, 127. In 1974, three-fourths of ethnic Koreans in Osaka opposed naturalization. This option was widely considered a form of passing, not a gateway to full and equal membership in Japanese society.

43. Chapman, *Zainichi Korean Identity and Ethnicity*, p. 56; Hester, "*Datsu Zainichi-ron*," p. 139.

44. Lie, *Zainichi*, p. 167; Hester, "*Datsu Zainichi-ron*," pp. 145–46. These Korean activists have used the terms *Kankoku-kei nihonjin* (Japanese of Korean descent) or *Korian Japanīzu* (Korean Japanese).

45. Chapman, *Zainichi Korean Identity and Ethnicity*, pp. 131–35; Chung, *Immigration and Citizenship in Japan*, pp. 140–43.

These debates among activists over *zainichi* Korean identities should not be read as direct evidence of social change. To be sure, the number of ethnic Koreans naturalizing as Japanese in recent years has increased from two to three thousand per year in the 1950s and 1960s to over ten thousand per year today. The new generation has apparently come to regard naturalization as an individual choice and is less concerned about its implications for collective identity or national loyalty.[46] Naturalization, however, is still fiercely rejected by many in ethnic Korean communities, particularly the older generations who struggled for decades to maintain community cohesion and cultural expression. Moreover, little evidence shows that overall Japanese attitudes have changed much regarding the ethnic or descent basis of Japanese identity.[47] The reality of discrimination and the dilemmas of passing as Japanese suggest that naturalization can still lead to a second-class citizenship status, one that falls far short of full acceptance as members of Japanese society.[48] As long as these conditions obtain, the fourth choice will remain an intellectual position more than a living option.

The *zainichi* Korean third-way and fourth-choice debates also point to a dramatic difference between Koreans and Chinese in Japan in their levels of explicit political activism. Recall that during the Asia-Pacific War, *huaqiao* leaders from Yokohama expressed to Japanese government officials that they wanted to be treated as "Japanese, broadly defined" or that their children were "practically the same as Japanese." However, they stopped short of claiming that they *were* Japanese, and thus did not directly challenge existing ideas of Japaneseness. On the contrary, their private statements aimed to ingratiate them with Japanese leaders and affirm their trustworthiness. Likewise, in the postwar era, the Chinese of Yokohama have demonstrated a commitment to their local community, but have not advocated a more expansive and inclusive understanding of Japaneseness. They have not significantly contributed to *zainichi* Korean-led debates or actions for foreigners' rights on the national level, such as the Hitachi employment discrimination case and the antifingerprinting movement of the 1980s.[49]

---

46. Lie, *Zainichi*, pp. 144–46; Ryang, *North Koreans in Japan*, pp. 196–200.
47. Ryang, "Visible and Vulnerable," p. 62; Hester, "*Datsu Zainichi-ron*," p. 148.
48. Chapman, *Zainichi Korean Identity and Ethnicity*, p. 135.
49. Ibid., pp. 73–74. The Hitachi case was discussed in chap. 5. The antifingerprinting movement was taken up by the *zainichi* Korean community in the 1980s. It contested Japan's requirement since 1955 for all resident aliens to be fingerprinted.

Several explanations may be made for this difference, ranging from demographics, circumstances of migration, and experiences postmigration. The role of Chinatown as a cultural and economic nexus is also highly significant. The most obvious explanation for the relative dearth of intellectual leadership and direct activism among Chinese derives from population size. *Zainichi* Koreans comprised the largest foreigner group in Japan from the end of the Asia-Pacific War until 2007, with a larger pool of activists willing to contest the ideologies and policies of both their diasporic organizations and the Japanese government. However, demonstrable differences in attitudes also exist between the two communities. One indicator is the gap between the proportions of Chinese and Koreans who live under Japanese aliases (*tsūmei*). A 1986 survey concluded that only 17.4 percent of Chinese did so, compared to 91.3 percent of Koreans.[50] This discrepancy helps substantiate John Lie's assertion that Chinese have experienced comparatively milder discrimination in Japan.

Another major factor is certainly the concentration of Kanagawa Prefecture's Chinese into the relatively insulated Chinatown, where Chinese culture has been packaged for Japanese consumers. This freedom to express their heritage is therefore a particular feature of the Chinese economic niche and does not offer much of a model for *zainichi* Koreans or any other minority group in Japan. In fact, Chinese cultural expression is accepted most readily in the context of Chinatown's commercial ventures, not among the Chinese newcomer communities in working-class districts of Tokyo and other metropolitan centers. The Japanese demand for Chinese food is also unmatched by anything on the Korean side; a 2007 survey found that the most common thing that Japanese think of when hearing the word "China" was Chinese food, appearing in 61.6 percent of responses.[51] It remains to be seen whether a recent boom in Japanese interest in Korean movies, television dramas, and popular music will translate into a similar economic niche. Early observations indicate that this consumer fad has altered the image of Korea more than the image of Koreans in Japan, and that

---

Under *zainichi* Korean leadership, by 1985 over ten thousand foreign residents were refusing to be fingerprinted in protest of the requirement. As a result, fingerprinting of permanent residents ended in 1999.

50. Kanagawa-kennai zaijū gaikokujin jittai chōsa iinkai, *Nihon no naka no Kankoku-Chōsenjin, Chūgokujin*, pp. 175–78.

51. Genron NPO, *Japan-China Joint Opinion Polls*.

working-class Korean communities around Japan still suffer various forms of discrimination.

Finally, differing experiences of migration and settlement may also have led to divergent psychological orientations toward integration. The community of Chinese in Yokohama coalesced from a history of voluntary migration, in contrast to *zainichi* Koreans, many of whom were forcibly brought to Japan as laborers during the colonial period. This forced migration politicized the origins of the community in Japan, and also was an important state-to-state issue. The 1965 treaty normalizing relations between the Republic of Korea and Japan included provisions to guarantee rights for Koreans in Japan.[52] There were no comparable provisions in treaties signed by either the PRC or the ROC with Japan; the status of *huaqiao* was seen as a private matter, based on the volition of the individual and under the purview of the Japanese state. Similar differences of attitude have also emerged between Korean newcomers and the earlier arrivals, the so-called "oldcomers," for this very reason. As oldcomer activist Pak Yong Ho related, "newcomers are voluntary immigrants who don't relate to our history as immigrants who were forced to come to Japan" and endured forced Japanization policies. Untouched by such experiences, voluntary immigrants have been less interested in the politics of Korean identity and instead "focus on economic success."[53] Such a description would be apt for the Yokohama Chinese as well.

It seems then that Yokohama Chinese have not joined to any great extent the *zainichi*-led "battle of ideas" with mainstream Japanese society to transform the nature of Japanese citizenship. However, the ways in which they have integrated into their local community point to wider social processes that are indeed transforming Japan. Even without prominent intellectual leadership, the foregoing narrative illustrates attempts to reconcile diasporic identities with local belonging. This history illustrates the transformative potentials of what cultural studies scholar Ien Ang terms the "micropolitics of everyday life." Ang has written about the "identity blues" of globalization; she argues that although globalization has introduced a social and economic web that supersedes local and national boundaries, it has also engendered fundamentalisms in response to the erosion of certainties of place and

---

52. Ryang, *North Koreans in Japan*, p. 124.
53. Chung, *Immigration and Citizenship in Japan*, p. 131.

belonging. In order to resolve this tension, Ang advocates a social praxis; living and communicating among our neighbors would "facilitate the creation of a sense of commonality, a togetherness in difference," which both grounds the migrant and transforms the host culture.[54] The Chinese community came to identify with Yokohama in precisely this fashion. They gained wide acceptance as Yokohama-ites through daily encounters, bridging ethnic differences with other crosscutting affiliations. The Yokohama Chinese have been engaged in building, through a non-elite micropolitics, the cultural conditions of possibility for the fourth choice articulated by *zainichi* Korean activists.

The historical emergence of a Yokohama-ite identity for the Yokohama Chinese anticipated the discourses on local citizenship that have gained salience over the past three decades. Citizenship, local or national, is a complex concept, and on this point I employ Katherine Tegtmeyer Pak's analysis of its four dimensions: juridical, which denotes formal legal status; substantive, which comprises rights and obligations under a state; cultural, which describes an individual's sense of social and cultural belonging; and participatory, which entails active engagement with communal life.[55] Accordingly, expressions of Yokohama-ite identity by the resident Chinese are claims to local cultural citizenship.

Today, the idea of local citizenship is shaping the way local municipalities are dealing with a rapidly expanding population of foreigners. The number of registered aliens, which does not count a substantial population of unauthorized immigrants, rose from 984,000 in 1989 to over 2.1 million in 2009.[56] A large number of these immigrants are unskilled or semi-skilled, and have immigrated to Japan via the trainee-status visa "side door" and a number of other specialized visas. They are drawn by the labor needs of the host society; because of an aging population and declining birthrate, Japan requires substantial labor migration to maintain the size of its economy. Officially, however, Japan's immigration policies ban unskilled foreign workers.[57] The national government, moreover, has largely left to local

---

54. Ang, "Identity Blues," p. 11.
55. Tegtmeyer Pak, "Cities and Local Citizenship in Japan," pp. 81–83.
56. Statistics Bureau, *Registered Aliens by Nationality*.
57. Tsuda, "Localities and the Struggle for Immigrant Rights," pp. 12–15, 20–21. Writing in 2006, Takeyuki Tsuda has estimated that 800,000 authorized and unauthorized immigrants are participating in Japan's economy as unskilled or

governments the responsibility to manage the globalization of their communities. As a result, since the 1970s, local governments have granted foreign residents access to the substantive citizenship rights of education, public housing, child support, and eligibility for national health insurance.[58] Cities with large foreigner populations such as Yokohama, Kobe, Osaka, Kyoto, Sapporo, and Nagoya have also taken up the rhetoric of local citizenship to craft additional policies to serve the needs of their foreigner citizens, which range from "language classes, translation services, information pamphlets, consultation services, public housing, health insurance and emergency medical coverage, and limited political representation."[59]

Among these initiatives, the participation of foreigners in local government is perhaps the most provocative and controversial. The groundwork was laid by progressive local governments in the 1960s and 1970s that sought to foster what they called "people's diplomacy" (*minsei gaikō*), meaning a role for civil society in international policy making.[60] Kawasaki, a city in Kanagawa Prefecture with a large population of ethnic Koreans, established a foreigner's assembly in 1996.[61] Kanagawa Prefecture as a whole followed with the Kanagawa Foreigners' Assembly in 1998. These assemblies are not invested with any decision-making power but function as consensus-building or investigative-deliberative councils (*shingikai*). Nevertheless, they are legitimated by a communitarian ideal holding that all *jūmin* or *shimin* deserve a voice in policy making.[62]

---

semi-skilled workers. Besides the trainee status, these laborers also arrive under entertainer visas (often used by bar hostesses and prostitutes), pre-college (*shūgakusei*) visas (exploited by students registered for language schools), and special visas for Latin Americans of Japanese ancestry.

58. Chung, *Immigration and Citizenship in Japan*, pp. 101–103, 164–165. Many of these services were thereafter guaranteed nationwide through reforms implemented after Japan ratified a number of international conventions: the International Covenant on Economic, Social and Cultural Rights and on Civil and Political Rights in 1979; and the Convention Relating to the Status of Refugees in 1982.

59. Tegtmeyer Pak, "Cities and Local Citizenship in Japan," pp. 80–81. Tegtmeyer Pak notes as well that these trends are visible in cities in advanced democracies around the world.

60. Avenell, "Regional Egoism as the Public Good"; Tegtmeyer Pak, "Foreigners Are Local Citizens Too," p. 261.

61. Komai, *Foreign Migrants in Contemporary Japan*, pp. 121–22.

62. This strategy is based on an ideal of a "*territorially based* local community that encompasses *all* residents within its boundary, as a powerful image to set against the

The acceptance of local citizenship in Japan bears the potential to open up more comprehensive political rights for foreign residents, especially denizens, meaning noncitizen permanent residents. It has also been argued that policies by municipalities to recognize local citizenship constitute a trend toward the decoupling of substantive citizenship, that is, rights and obligations, from juridical citizenship.[63] This trend might appear to be a logical resolution of the contradictions between local and national identities presented by communities such as the Yokohama Chinese. However, at present its limitations are evident. The cultural and ethnic content of national citizenship remains strong in Japan. As common sense, Japan's monoethnic myth has survived vigorous efforts at debunking, and accords with most Japanese citizens' everyday perceptions. Policies that permit foreigner political participation at the local level are persuasive precisely because they avoid contradicting the ethnic definition of the national community. Locally based social welfare programs for foreign nationals may in fact help *preserve* exclusionary policies at the national level, because they reduce the need to modify existing nationality laws or to challenge notions of Japanese identity.[64]

Advocacy for local suffrage rights for foreigners (*gaikokujin chihō sanseiken*) is a major venue for the articulation of local citizenship rights. But the ongoing political debate over this issue also demonstrates how moral and economic arguments for foreigners' rights can lose traction when balanced against national identity and sovereignty. *Zainichi* Koreans and British living in Japan began raising the issue of voting rights in local elections around 1990; citing the precedent of European countries, they described it as a matter of human rights and argued that it would give foreign residents a stronger stake in their communities. In October 1994, the Fukui District Court ruled that granting local suffrage did not violate the Japanese constitution, and the Supreme Court issued an opinion in 1995 that supported this stance.[65] Many municipalities in Japan have since offered local voting rights

concept of the *ethnically based* community" (Han, "From the Communitarian Ideal to the Public Sphere," pp. 43–45).

63. Tegtmeyer Pak, "Cities and Local Citizenship in Japan," pp. 80–81.

64. Ibid., pp. 88–89; Burgess, "The 'Illusion' of Homogeneous Japan and National Character."

65. Taniguchi, "Senkyo wa dare ga surumono nano deshōka," pp. 70–71; Tegtmeyer Pak, "Cities and Local Citizenship in Japan," p. 79. There is debate over not

to foreign residents, beginning in 2002 with the decision by the former town of Maibarachō in Shiga Prefecture to permit foreigners to vote in a town-merger referendum. By 2005, some two hundred municipalities had authorized foreigners to vote in local elections.[66]

However, as of the writing of this book, no national policy governing local foreign suffrage has been established. From the late 1990s, the Clean Government Party (Kōmeitō), the Democratic Party of Japan (DPJ), and the Japan Communist Party have repeatedly proposed bills to grant suffrage to foreigners in local elections. By 2000, the political climate appeared quite favorable. A November 2000 survey conducted by the *Asahi shinbun* indicated that 80 percent of prefectural governors and a selected group of twelve mayors supported the local suffrage bill. One month earlier, Yokohama mayor Takahisa Hisanobu stated he believed that from a human rights perspective, Japan should grant this form of limited suffrage.[67]

The DPJ came to power in 2009 and made local voting rights for foreigners a part of its platform. On November 5, 2009, DPJ prime minister Hatoyama Yukio publicly stated that the government could grant that right as long as it did not conflict with the constitution. The issue, however, became a lightning rod for opposition from the conservative Liberal Democratic Party (LDP). At the start of 2010, fourteen prefectural assemblies passed resolutions opposing local suffrage for foreigners, including seven that reversed their earlier support for such a law.[68] Prime Minister Hatoyama generated a

---

only the advisability or constitutionality of foreigner suffrage rights, but also its specific form. A variety of precedents is available. Sweden offers the right to vote in local elections to all foreigner residents, whereas France and Germany have a reciprocal system that recognizes mutual rights for nationals of certain European Union countries. South Korea offers local suffrage to those who have had permanent residency for three years.

66. Green, "Local Foreign Suffrage in Kawasaki City."

67. "Gaikokujin sanseiken chijira ankēto: 'fuyo' jūnin, hantai hitori, hachi wari wa 'kokkai mimaoru,'" *Asahi shinbun*, Nov. 12, 2000, morning edition, p. 38; "Gaikokujin sanseiken 'kuni ga ketsuron o': Takahisa, Yokohama shichō," *Asahi shinbun*, Oct. 3, 2000, morning edition, p. 35.

68. "Gaikokujin chihō sanseiken, fūfu besshō: shushō giron mimamoru kangae," *Asahi shinbun*, Nov. 6, 2009, morning edition, p. 4; "Gaikokujin sanseiken ni 14 kengikai 'hantai,'" *Asahi shinbun*, Jan. 8, 2010, morning edition, p. 1; Fukui, "Eijū gaikokujin chihō sanseiken mondai," p. 35. The DPJ bill would grant suffrage in local elections to an estimated 900,000 permanent residents.

particularly angry response in April 2009 when he stated in an argument in favor of local suffrage that "the Japanese isles are not solely for the Japanese." The bluntness of his terms framed the issue in a way that seemingly favored rights for non-Japanese at the expense of national sovereignty, an intolerable trade-off in national politics. By relying on a facile distinction between Japanese and non-Japanese, Hatoyama foreclosed ongoing and fundamental debates over citizenship in Japan, that is, who counts as Japanese, and whether Japaneseness can be redefined as a civic and nonethnic form of identity.

In opposing the DPJ bill, Japanese conservatives rallied around the defense of Japan's sovereignty. Slogans unfurled at opposition demonstrations included the remarkably hyperbolic "We firmly oppose selling Tsushima, Yonagunijima, or Okinawa to North Korea, South Korea, or China!" Others have revived the venerable fear of being dominated by a flood of Chinese migrants, should Chinese permanent residents be politically empowered. A more sober opinion was offered by Kimura Mitsuhiro, representative of the Japanist group Issuikai, who stated that on an emotional level he understands the desire to grant suffrage to those foreigners who have lived in Japan a long time, but worries whether they will really commit to Japan "when the chips are down" (*iza to iu toki ni*).[69] The DPJ ultimately removed the issue of local foreign suffrage from its legislative agenda in July 2010.[70] In spite of globalizing trends that are making mobility and transnational communities more of a norm, the nation is still held to be an individual's terminal community in the political realm.

This political controversy suggests some hard limits to local citizenship initiatives. In the current political landscape, many seem to agree with conservative former Tokyo governor Ishihara Shintarō, who has asserted that "suffrage is an exclusive right of people who hold nationality in that country; it is illogical to consider the local as completely separate from the nation."[71] The prerogatives of the nation-state and its assumed priority over local spaces have yet to be overcome. At least for the foreseeable future, citizenship in Japan is unlikely to be broadened by local suffrage movements.

However, as this book has attempted to show, the definition of an authentic national community is itself a historical process, and ethnic exclusivity

---

69. Fukui, "Eijū gaikokujin chihō sanseiken mondai," p. 35.
70. Green, "Local Foreign Suffrage in Kawasaki City."
71. "Gaikokujin sanseiken chijira ankēto," *Asahi shinbun*, Nov. 12, 2000, morning edition, p. 38.

should not be seen as a fixed feature of Japaneseness. Ishihara is quite correct that local and national spaces are linked, but the logic should work both ways. Expressions of local cultural citizenship carry the potential to reconfigure national citizenship by altering underlying understandings of Japanese identity. Yokohama Chinatown, as a globalized local community, is a key example in this regard; it confounds the assumed priority of national over local spaces by demonstrating the viability of multiethnic communities within a presumptively monoethnic state. Resolving this paradox of local inclusion and national exclusion may augur deeper changes in Japanese society. As noted in the introduction, it is now more difficult to dismiss Yokohama as exceptional because of international migration flows to ever wider parts of Japan, and the result, in time, may be a more thorough rejection of the ethnic basis of Japanese identity. Indications of such changes are already discernible in contemporary political debates and media expressions, and this book has chronicled the role of Yokohama's Chinese sons and daughters in this long-term historical trend.[72]

---

72. Morris-Suzuki, "'Welcome to Our Family'"; Lie, *Zainichi*, p. 152.

Appendix

Bok Choy and Braised Whole Chicken (Bokchoy pagai), by Bao Bogong

INGREDIENTS

    two scallions
    ginger
    two shiitake mushrooms
    a splash of *laojiu* (aged rice wine)
    soup (stock, preferably chicken)
    four or five bok choy cabbage leaves
    salt and black pepper
    soy sauce
    potato starch (*katakuriko*)
    one slice of dry-cured Chinese ham (Jinhua huotui)

DIRECTIONS

Remove the head and slit the chicken down the back. Soak in soy sauce and fry in heated lard on high heat until browned. Remove and rinse in water to remove oil, and place in a bowl with one scallion, sliced into 15cm (six-inch) pieces, on each side; then add two slices of ginger, two shiitake mushrooms, *laojiu*, and enough soup (or water) to cover the ingredients. Steam in a bamboo steamer for two hours. After steaming, carefully remove the bones from the chicken, retaining the shape of the chicken as much as possible.

Arrange shiitake in a deep bowl and place the chicken on top. Blanch the bok choy and cut into large pieces and place on top. Invert and transfer to a flat dish and steam once more. Make a sauce from the previously used soup, salt, *laojiu*, black pepper, soy sauce, and potato starch (dissolved in some water). Liberally coat the chicken, and the dish is finished with a thin slice of ham on top.[1]

---

1. Bao, "Fuyu ni oishii shina ryōri," pp. 24–25.

Bibliography

Archival Sources

Academia Historica, Taipei (AH)
Diplomatic Archives of Japanese Ministry of Foreign Affairs (JMFA), Tokyo
Japan Center for Asian Historical Records (JACAR), Tokyo
    Diplomatic Records of the Ministry of Foreign Affairs (DRMFA)
    Records of the former Home Ministry (RHM)
Kanagawa Prefectural Archives (KPA), Yokohama
National Archives and Record Administration, College Park, MD (NACP)
    RG 59: General Records of the Department of State, Consular Despatches, Record Group 59
    RG 331: Records of Allied Operational and Occupation Headquarters, World War II, Record Group 331
    RG 554: Records of General Headquarters, Far East Command, Supreme Commander Allied Powers, and United Nations Command, 1945–60, Record Group 554
Tōyō bunko, Tokyo

Newspapers and Periodicals

Asahi geinō, Tokyo
Asahi shinbun, Tokyo
Huawen Daban meiri, Osaka
Japan Weekly Mail, Yokohama
Jiji shinpō, Tokyo
Kanagawa shinbun, Yokohama
Kobe Weekly Chronicle
Mainichi shinbun, Tokyo
Nagasaki shinbun
Nippon, Tokyo
Ōsaka mainichi
Shiwu bao, Shanghai

Tokyo nichinichi shinbun
Yokohama bōeki shinbun/shinpō
Yokohama maichō shinbun
Yomiuri shinbun, Tokyo
Yorozu chōhō, Tokyo
Zhejiang chao, Tokyo

Books and Articles

Abrams, Philip. "History, Sociology, Historical Sociology." *Past and Present* 87 (May 1980): 3–16.

Anderson, Benedict R. *Imagined Communities: Reflections on the Origin and Spread of Nationalism*. New York: Verso, 1991.

Anderson, Kay J. "The Idea of Chinatown: The Power of Place and Institutional Practice in the Making of a Racial Category." *Annals of the Association of American Geographers* 77, no. 4 (1987): 580–98.

Ang, Ien. "Identity Blues." In *Without Guarantees: In Honour of Stuart Hall*, edited by Paul Gilroy, Lawrence Grossberg, and Angela McRobbie, pp. 1–13. London: Verso, 2000.

Arahata Kanson. "Meiji sanjūnendai no Yokohama o kataru." *Kyōdo Yokohama* 4, no. 2 (1959): 7–14.

Asao Naohiro, Amino Yoshihiko, Ishii Susumu, Kano Masanao, Hayakawa Shōhachi, and Yasumaru Yoshio, eds. *Iwanami kōza Nihon tsūshi*. 21 vols. 4 suppl. vols. Tokyo: Iwanami shoten, 1993–96.

Asukada Kazuo. "Chūkagai to watashi." *Gekkan Chūkagai* 2 (1973): 8.

Avenell, Simon. "Regional Egoism as the Public Good: Residents' Movements in Japan during the 1960s and 1970s." *Japan Forum* 18, no. 1 (2006): 89–113.

Balibar, Etienne. "The Nation Form: History and Ideology." In *Becoming National: A Reader*, edited by Geoff and Suny Eley and Ronald Gregot, pp. 132–49. New York: Oxford University Press, 1996.

Bao Bogong. "Fuyu ni oishii shina ryōri no iroiro." *Eiyō to ryōri* 2, no. 2 (Feb. 1936): 23–26.

Bao Guanming, Bao Hui'e, Bao Huiqiu, Bao Huixiang, and Chen Xiaoqun. "Jiti zonghe jishi." In *Hengbin zhonghua xueyuan bai zhou nian yuanqing jinian tekan*, edited by Zhonghua xueyuan, pp. 230–31. Yokohama: Zhonghua xueyuan, 2000.

Basch, Linda, Nina Glick Schiller, and Cristina Szanton Blanc. *Nations Unbound: Transnational Projects, Postcolonial Predicaments, and Deterritorialized Nation-States*. Basel: Gordon and Breach, 1994.

Befu, Harumi. *Hegemony of Homogeneity: An Anthropological Analysis of Nihonjinron*. Melbourne: Trans Pacific Press, 2001.

Berger, Louis J. W. *The Overseas Chinese in Seventeenth Century Nagasaki*. PhD diss., Harvard University, 2003.

Bourdieu, Pierre. "Systems of Education and Systems of Thought." In *Knowledge and Control*, edited by Michael F. D. Young, pp. 198–207. Sydney: Collier Macmillan, 1971.

Boyle, John Hunter. *China and Japan at War, 1937–1945: The Politics of Collaboration*. Stanford, CA: Stanford University Press, 1972.

Brook, Timothy. *Collaboration: Japanese Agents and Local Elites in Wartime China*. Cambridge: Harvard University Press, 2007.

Brubaker, Rogers. *Citizenship and Nationhood in France and Germany.* Cambridge, MA: Harvard University Press, 1992.

Burgess, Chris. "The 'Illusion' of Homogeneous Japan and National Character: Discourse as a Tool to Transcend the 'Myth' vs. 'Reality' Binary." *Asia-Pacific Journal,* March 1, 2010. Accessed May 20, 2013. http://japanfocus.org/-chris-burgess/3310.

Caprio, Mark. *Japanese Assimilation Policies in Colonial Korea, 1910–1945.* Seattle: University of Washington Press, 2009.

Carter, Sean. "The Geopolitics of Diaspora." *Area* 37, no. 1 (Mar. 2005): 54–63.

Cassell, Pär. *Grounds of Judgment: Extraterritoriality and Imperial Power in Nineteenth-Century China and Japan.* New York: Oxford University Press, 2012.

Ceng Fengying. "Ou." Chūkagai de nīhao!, *Tousai* 9 (1998): 7.

———. "Yukari." Chūkagai de nīhao!, *Tousai* 6 (1997): 7.

Chapman, David. *Zainichi Korean Identity and Ethnicity.* New York: Routledge, 2008.

Chen Changhao. "Huiyi yu qipan: yiwei lao guiqiao de xinsheng." In *Huiguo wushi nian,* edited by "Huiguo wushi nian" bianxie zubian, pp. 276–85. Beijing: Taihai chubanshe, 2003.

Chen Efang. "Zainichi kakyō genron shuppan kai no genjō." *Chūgoku kōron,* no. 1 (1948): 16–20.

Chen Jicheng. "Qiaowu gongzuo zhi jinzhan xianzhuang jiqi jihua." *Kabun Ōsaka mainichi* 7, no. 10 (1941): 11–13.

Chen Kunwang. *Nihon kakyō, ryūgakusei undōshi.* Tokyo: Nihon kakyōhō, 2004.

Chen Shaobai. *Xingzhonghui geming shiyao.* Nanjing: Jianguo yuekanshe, 1935.

Chen Tien-shi. "Kajin to wa dare ka: kyōiku to aidentiti." *Kakyō kajin kenkyū,* no. 8 (2011): 43–48.

———. *Mukokuseki.* Tokyo: Shinchōsha, 2005.

———. "Stateless Overseas Chinese: Nationality and Identity of Overseas Chinese in Japan." In *Shidai bianju yu haiwai huaren de zuguo rentong,* edited by Zhang Qixiong, pp. 53–70. Taipei: Zhonghua minguo haiwai huaren yanjiu xuehui, 2005.

Chen Xiaoyin. "Yokohama Chūka kōritsu shōgakkō no omoide." In *Yokohama Yamate chūkagakkō hyakunen kōshi,* edited by Yokohama Yamate chūkagakkō hyakunen kōshi henshū iinkai, p. 143. Yokohama: Yokohama Yamate chūkagakuen, 2005.

Ching, Leo. *Becoming "Japanese": Colonial Taiwan and the Politics of Identity Formation.* Berkeley: University of California Press, 2001.

Chu, Samuel C. "China's Attitudes toward Japan at the Time of the Sino-Japanese War." In *The Chinese and the Japanese: Essays in Political and Cultural Interactions,* edited by Akira Iriye. Princeton, NJ: Princeton University Press, 1980.

Chu, Tull. *Political Attitudes of the Overseas Chinese in Japan.* Hong Kong: Union Research Institute, 1967.

Chūgoku kenkyūjo, ed. *Zainichi kakyō to "gaikokujin zaisan shutoku seirei" ni kansuru ikensho.* Tokyo: Chūgoku kenkyūjo, 1949.

Chūkakaikan and Yokohama kaikō shiryōkan, eds. *Yokohama kakyō no kioku: Yokohama kakyō kōjutsu rekiski kiroku shū.* Yokohama: Chūkakaikan, 2010.

Chung, Erin Aeran. *Immigration and Citizenship in Japan.* New York: Cambridge, 2010.

Church Missionary Society. *Mission to Chinese Students and Merchants in Japan.* Church Missionary Society, n.d. [ca. 1916–23].

Clifford, James. *Routes: Travel and Translation in the Late Twentieth Century.* Cambridge, MA: Harvard University Press, 1997.

Commonwealth Commission on Respect and Understanding. *Civil Paths to Peace: Report of the Commonwealth Commission on Respect and Understanding.* London: Commonwealth Secretariat, 2007.

Creighton, Millie. "*Soto* Others and *Uchi* Others: Imaging Racial Diversity, Imagining Homogeneous Japan." In *Japan's Minorities: The Illusion of Homogeneity*, edited by Michael Weiner, pp. 211–38. New York: Routledge, 1997.

Crossley, Pamela Kyle. "Nationality and Difference in China: The Post-Imperial Dilemma." In *The Teleology of the Modern Nation-State: Japan and China*, edited by Joshua Fogel, pp. 138–58. Philadelphia: University of Pennsylvania Press, 2004.

———. "Thinking about Ethnicity in Early Modern China." *Late Imperial China* 11, no. 1 (June 1990): 1–35.

Cwiertka, Katarzyna J. "Eating the World: Restaurant Culture in Early Twentieth Century Japan." *European Journal of East Asian Studies* 2, no. 1 (Mar. 2003): 89–116.

———. *Modern Japanese Cuisine: Food, Power and National Identity.* London: Reaktion Books, 2006.

Daitōashō Shina jimukyoku sōmuka. *Gen jikyoku ka ni okeru Nihon kakyō no katsuyō men.* Tokyo, 1944.

De Bary, William Theodore, and Richard John Lufrano. *Sources of Chinese Tradition: From 1600 through the Twentieth Century.* 2nd ed. Vol. 2. New York: Columbia University Press, 2000.

Devereux, George. "Ethnic Identity: Its Logical Foundations and Its Dysfunctions." In *Theories of Ethnicity: A Classical Reader*, edited by Werner Sollors, pp. 385–414. New York: New York University Press, 1996.

Dijkstra, Steven, Karin Geuijen, and Arie de Ruijter. "Multiculturalism and Social Integration in Europe." *International Political Science Review* 22, no. 1 (2001): 55–83.

Dikötter, Frank. *The Discourse of Race in Modern China.* London: C. Hurst, 1992.

Doak, Kevin M. "The Concept of Ethnic Nationality and Its Role in Pan-Asianism in Imperial Japan." In *Pan-Asianism in Modern Japanese History: Colonialism, Regionalism and Borders,* edited by Sven Saaler and J. Victor Koschmann, pp. 168–82. London: Routledge.

———. *A History of Nationalism in Modern Japan: Placing the People.* Boston: Brill, 2007.

———. "What Is a Nation and Who Belongs? National Narratives and the Ethnic Imagination in Twentieth-Century Japan." *American Historical Review* 102, no. 2 (1997): 283–309.

Duara, Prasenjit. *Rescuing History from the Nation.* Chicago: University of Chicago Press, 1995.

———. *Sovereignty and Authenticity: Manchukuo and the East Asian Modern.* Lanham, MD: Rowman & Littlefield, 2003.

———. "Transnationalism and the Predicament of Sovereignty: China, 1900–1945." *American Historical Review* 102, no. 4 (1997): 1030–51.

Farris, William Wayne. *Sacred Texts and Buried Treasures: Issues in the Historical Archaeology of Ancient Japan.* Honolulu: University of Hawai'i Press, 1998.

Feng Jinglong, ed. *Datong tongxue lu.* Yokohama: Ōhashi insatsusho, 1909.

Feng Ruiyu. "Yokohama Yamate chūkagakkō 'hyakunen kōshi' hakkan ni yosete: Yokohama Daidō gakkō to Feng Jingru." In *Yokohama Yamate chūkagakkō hyakunen kōshi*, edited by Yokohama Yamate chūkagakkō hyakunen kōshi henshū iinkai, pp. 35–38. Yokohama: Yokohama Yamate chūkagakuen, 2005.

Feng Ziyou. *Geming yishi*. 6 vols. Chongqing: Shangwu yinshuguan, 1939–48. Reprint, Beijing: Zhonghua shuju, 1981.

Fitzgerald, Stephen. *China and the Overseas Chinese: A Study of Peking's Changing Policy, 1949–1970*. Cambridge: Cambridge University Press, 1972.

Fowler, Edward. "Minorities in a 'Homogeneous' State: Japan." In *What's in a Rim: Critical Perspectives on the Pacific Region Idea*, edited by Arif Dirlik, pp. 211–33. Boulder, CO: Westview Press, 1993.

Friman, H. Richard. "Evading the Divine Wind through the Side Door: The Transformation of Chinese Migration to Japan." In *Globalizing Chinese Migration: Trends in Europe and Asia*, edited by Pál Nyíri and Igor Savaliev, pp. 9–34. Burlington, VT: Ashgate, 2002.

———. "Immigrants, Smuggling, and Threats to Social Order in Japan." In *Global Human Smuggling: Comparative Perspectives*, edited by David Kyle and Rey Koslowski, pp. 294–317. Baltimore, MD: Johns Hopkins University Press, 2001.

Fujino Yutaka. *Kyōsei sareta kenkō: Nihon fashizumu-ka no seimei to shintai*. Tokyo: Yoshikawa kōbunkan, 2000.

Fujisawa Fumiko. "Yokohama umare." Dokusha no koe, *Shimin to bunka*, no. 9 (1982): 39.

Fukuda, Shozo, and L. R. Oates. *With Sweat & Abacus: Economic Roles of Southeast Asian Chinese on the Eve of World War II*. Singapore: Select Books, 1995.

Fukui Yōhei. "Eijū gaikokujin chihō sanseiken mondai: genki ni natta Nihon no hoshu." *Aera* 22, no. 57 (Nov. 30, 2009): 35.

Fukushima Yū. "Shōwa-ki Chūkagai no seisui." Chūkagai shijitsu roku, *Gekkan Chūkagai* 6 (1973): 16–18.

Fukuzawa Yukichi. "On De-Asianization by Fukuzawa Yukichi, March 16, 1885." In *Meiji Japan through Contemporary Sources* 1:129–33. Tokyo: Center for East Asian Cultural Studies, 1969.

Gellner, Ernest. *Nations and Nationalism*. Ithaca: Cornell University Press, 1983.

Genron NPO. *Japan-China Joint Opinion Polls*. Tokyo: Genron NPO, 2007.

Gerth, Karl. *China Made: Consumer Culture and the Creation of the Nation*. Cambridge: Harvard University Press, 2003.

Gill, Tom. "Review: *Multiethnic Japan*." *Monumenta Nipponica* 56, no. 4 (Winter 2001): 574–77.

Glazer, Nathan. "The Universalisation of Ethnicity: Peoples in the Boiling Pot." *Encounter* 44, no. 2 (1975): 8–17.

Gluck, Carol. *Japan's Modern Myths: Ideology in the Late Meiji Period*. Princeton, NJ: Princeton University Press, 1985.

Goodman, Bryna. "New Culture, Old Habits: Native-Place Organization and the May Fourth Movement." In *Shanghai Sojourners*, edited by Frederic Wakeman Jr. and Wen-hsin Yeh, pp. 76–107. Berkeley: University of California Press, 1992.

Gordon, Andrew. *The Modern History of Japan: From Tokugawa Times to the Present*. New York: Oxford University Press, 2003.

Green, David. "Local Foreign Suffrage in Kawasaki City: The Changing State of Voting Rights in Japan." *Electronic Journal of Contemporary Japanese Studies* 13, no. 1 (2013). Accessed May 30, 2013. http://www.japanesestudies.org.uk/ejcjs/vol13/iss1/green.html.

Guo Fang. *Zainichi kakyō no aidenttiti no henyō*. Tokyo: Tōshindō, 1999.

Guoli bianyiguan. *Gaoji xiaoxue guoyu keben*. Vol. 4. Tokyo: Zhonghua minguo liu-Ri huaqiao jiaoyuhui, 1947.

Haga Hideo. "Yomigaeru kioku: Yokohama chūka kōritsu shōgakkō 1942-nen." *Yokohama Yamate chūkagakkō hyakunen kōshi henshū iinkai*, edited by Yokohama Yamate chūkagakkō hyakunen kōshi henshū iinkai, pp. 137–40. Yokohama: Yokohama Yamate chūkagakuen, 2005.

Hammar, Tomas. *Democracy and the Nation State*. Brookfield, VT: Gower, 1990.

Han, Seung-Mi. "From the Communitarian Ideal to the Public Sphere: The Making of Foreigners' Assemblies in Kawasaki City and Kanagawa Prefecture." *Social Science Japan Journal* 7, no. 1 (2004): 41–60.

Harrell, Paula. "The Meiji 'New Woman' and China." In *Late-Qing China and Meiji Japan: Political and Cultural Aspects*, edited by Joshua Fogel, pp. 109–50. Norwalk, CT: EastBridge, 2004.

Hayase Toshio. "Kakyō shakai kenkyū no shomondai (3): Sengo honpō kakyō no jittai ni kansuru chōsa no tame ni." *Keizai to bōeki*, no. 82 (Mar. 1963): 1–10.

Hayashi Masashige. "Kōbe kakyō no kokoro o tsutaeru." *Kōbe kakyō rekishi hakubutsukan tsūshin*, no. 5 (2005): 1.

Hayashi, Takeshi. *The Japanese Experience in Technology: From Transfer to Self-Reliance*. Tokyo: United Nations University Press, 1990.

Hayashi Teishirō. *Tōa kyōeiken to kakyō no ugoki*. Otaru: Hokkai kokuminsha, 1942.

"Hengbin huaqiao funühui wushinian shi" bianji weiyuanhui, ed. *Hengbin huaqiao funühui wushinian shi*. Yokohama: Hengbin huaqiao funühui, 2004.

"Hengbin zhonghua xuexiao guanli weiyuanhui fabiao, guanyu zhonghua xuexiao caipan jingguo baogao." *Huaqiao wenhua*, no. 47 (1952): 10.

Herzog, Peter. "Minorities." In *The Making of Modern Japan: A Reader*, edited by Tim Megarry, pp. 552–72. Dartford, UK: Greenwich University Press, 1995.

Hester, Jeffry T. "*Datsu Zainichi-ron*: An Emerging Discourse of Belonging among Ethnic Koreans in Japan." In *Multiculturalism in the New Japan: Crossing the Boundaries Within*, edited by Nelson H. H. Graburn, John Ertle, and R. Kenji Tierney, pp. 139–50. New York: Berghahn Books, 2008.

Higuchi Hiroshi. "Nagasaki hanga no kigen." In *Nagasaki ukiyoe*, edited by Higuchi Hiroshi, pp. 1–6. Tokyo: Mitō shooku, 1971.

———, ed. *Nagasaki ukiyoe*. Tokyo: Mitō shooku, 1971.

Hiramatsu Shikō. "Meiji nijūninen koro no Yokohama meibutsu." *Kyōdo Yokohama* 2, no. 2 (1958): 20.

Hirota Kazuko. *Kakyō no ima: Nitchū no bunka no hazama de*. Tokyo: Shinhyōron, 2003.

Hoare, James. *Japan's Treaty Ports and Foreign Settlements: The Uninvited Guests, 1858–1899*. Folkestone, Kent, UK: Japan Library, 1994.

Holcombe, Charles. *Genesis of East Asia: 221 B.C.–A.D. 907*. Honolulu: Association for Asian Studies and University of Hawai'i Press, 2001.

Hollinger, David A. *Postethnic America: Beyond Multiculturalism*. New York: Basic Books, 2000.

Horita Yūsuke. "Ā, kono 'bigaku no machi.'" *Watashi to Chūkagai, Gekkan Chūkagai* 11 (1973): 4–6.

Huang Chengwu. "Kō sensei ga tsukuru, 'furusato no aji' ippin." *Shimin to bunka*, no. 6 (1981): 48–49.

Ide Tokutarō, ed. *Nihon shōkō eigyō roku*. Tokyo: Nihon shōkō eigyō roku hakkōsho, 1902.

Ijiri, Hidenori. "Sino-Japanese Controversy since the 1972 Diplomatic Normalization." In *China and Japan: History, Trends, and Prospects*, edited by Christopher Howe, pp. 60–82. New York: Oxford University Press, 1996.

Iriyama Taiichi. "Honpō ni okeru kakyō o ronzu." *Hikone kōshō ronsō* 30 (1941): 195–225.

Iriye, Akira. *China and Japan in the Global Setting*. Cambridge, MA: Harvard University Press, 1992.

Itagaki, Seishirō. "Supplement: Japan to Assist, Not Oppress, China." In *China and Japan: Natural Friends, Unnatural Enemies*, edited by Liangli Tang, pp. 153–66. Shanghai: China United Press, 1941.

Itō Izumi. "1920-nendai nakagoro no Yokohama kakyō shakai: Shodantai no dōkō o chūshin ni." *Yokohama kaikō shiryōkan kiyō* 24 (2006): 1–44.

———. "Ryō-ke: Chūgoku ni yakyū o hiromeru." In *Yokohama Chūkagai 150-nen: Rakuchi seikon no saigetsu*, edited by Yokohama kaikō shiryōkan, pp. 52–53. Yokohama: Yokohama kaikō shiryōkan, 2009.

———. "'Yokohama daishinsai chū no kakyō jōkyō' ni miru Kantō daishinsai zengo no Yokohama kakyō shakai." *Yokohama kaikō shiryōkan kiyō*, no. 20 (2002): 1–49.

———. "Yokohama kaikō to Chūkagai." In *Yokohama Chūkagai no sekai: Yokohama shōka daigaku Chūkagai machi naka kyanpasu*, edited by Yokohama shōka daigaku, pp. 14–30. Yokohama: Yokohama shōka daigaku, 2012.

———. "Yokohama kakyō shakai no keisei." *Yokohama kaikō shiryōkan kiyō*, no. 9 (1991): 1–28.

Itō Tatsujirō. *Yokohama bōeki shōkei*. Yokohama: Yokohama kyōdo kenkyūkai, 1893.

Iwakabe Yoshimitsu. "Nisshin sensō to kyoryūchi Shinkokujin mondai." *Hōsei shigaku* 36 (1984): 61–79.

Jansen, Marius B. *China in the Tokugawa World*. Cambridge, MA: Harvard University Press, 1992.

———. *The Japanese and Sun Yat-sen*. Stanford, CA: Stanford University Press, 1970.

Jin Meiling. "Ketsui to shite 'mukokuseki' sengen." *Gendai no gan* (Mar. 1973): 96–103.

Judge, Joan. "Talent, Virtue, and the Nation: Chinese Nationalisms and Female Subjectivities in the Early Twentieth Century." *American Historical Review* (June 2001): 765–803.

Kagawa Aya. "Sōkan ni atatte." *Eiyō to ryōri* 1, no. 1 (June 1935): 2–4.

Kagotani, Naoto. "The Chinese Merchant Community in Kobe and the Development of the Japanese Cotton Industry, 1890–1941." In *Japan, China, and the Growth of the Asian International Economy, 1850–1949*, edited by Kaori Sugihara, 1:49–72. New York: Oxford University Press, 2005.

Kamachi, Noriko. "The Chinese in Meiji Japan: Their Interactions with the Japanese before the Sino-Japanese War." In *The Chinese and the Japanese*, edited by Akira Iriye, pp. 58–73. Princeton, NJ: Princeton University Press, 1980.

Kanagawa kenchō. *Kanagawa-ken tōkeisho: Meiji sanjū nen.* Vol. 1. Yokohama: Kanagawa Kenchō, 1899.

———. *Warera no Kanagawa-ken.* Yokohama: Ōhashi kappan insatsusho, 1928.

Kanagawa-ken keisatsu shi hensan iinkai, ed. *Kanagawa-ken keisatsu shi.* Vol. 1. Yokohama: Kanagawa-ken keisatsu honbu, 1940.

Kanagawa-kennai zaijū gaikokujin jittai chōsa iinkai. *Nihon no naka no Kankoku-Chōsenjin, Chūgokujin: Kanagawa-kennai zaijū gaikokujin jittai chōsa yori.* Tokyo: Meiseki shoten, 1986.

Kani Hiroaki, Shiba Yoshinobu, and You Zhongxun, eds. *Kakyō-kajin jiten.* Tokyo: Kōbundō, 2002.

Kanome Shōzō. *Nankinmachi.* Tokyo: Asahi, 1924.

Karl, Rebecca. *Staging the World: Chinese Nationalism at the Turn of the Twentieth Century.* Durham, NC: Duke University Press, 2002.

Kawahara Misako. *Karachin ōhi to watashi.* Tokyo: Fuyō shobō, 1969.

Kayama Kazan. "Nankinmachi o egaku." *Kyōdo Yokohama,* no. 40 (1964): 17–20.

Keene, Donald. "The Sino-Japanese War of 1894–95 and Its Cultural Effects in Japan." In *Tradition and Modernization in Japanese Culture,* edited by Donald H. Shively, pp. 121–75. Princeton, NJ: Princeton University Press, 1971.

Kikuchi Kazutaka. *Sensō to kakyō: Nihon, kokumin seifu kōkan, kairai seiken, kakyō kan no seiji rikigaku.* Tokyo: Kyuko shoin, 2011.

Kimura Motoi. "Kyōdoshi, chihōshi, chiikishi kenkyū no rekishi to kadai." In *Iwanami kōza Nihon tsūshi, betsumaki 2, Chiikishi kenkyū no genjō to kadai,* edited by Asao Naohiro, pp. 3–31. Tokyo: Iwanami shoten, 1994.

Kipling, Rudyard. "The Rhyme of the Three Sealers (1892)." In *Kipling on Japan: Collected Writings,* edited by Hugh Cortazzi and George Webb, p. 258. London: Athlone, 1988.

Knight, John. "Rural Revitalization in Japan: Spirit of the Village and Taste of the Country." *Asian Survey* 34, no. 7 (1994): 634–46.

Kobayashi Shinsaku. *Kakyō no kenkyū.* Tokyo: Gaimushō tsūshōkyoku, 1929.

———. *Shina minzoku no kaigai hatten: Kakyō no kenkyū.* Tokyo: Kaigaisha, 1931.

Komai, Hiroshi. *Foreign Migrants in Contemporary Japan.* Melbourne: Trans Pacific Press, 2001.

Konuma Arata and Chin Masao. "Nihon no kakyō gakkō (2): Kōka shōgakkō (Kyoto) to Yamate chūkagakkō (Yokohama)." *Miyazaki daigaku kyōikubu kiyō, shakai kagaku* 57 (1985): 27–43.

Kotani Kyōsuke. *Yokohama Chūkagai satsujin jiken.* Tokyo: Kadokawa Haruki jimusho, 2001.

Kuhn, Philip A. *Chinese among Others: Emigration in Modern Times.* Lanham, MD: Rowman & Littlefield, 2008.

Kushner, Barak. "Imperial Cuisines in Taishō Foodways." In *Japanese Foodways, Past, and Present,* edited by Eric C. Rath and Stephanie Assmann, pp. 145–65. Champaign: University of Illinois Press, 2010.

———. *Slurp! A Social and Culinary History of Ramen—Japan's Favorite Noodle Soup.* Boston: Brill, 2012.

Kwong, Peter. *The New Chinatown.* New York: Hill & Wang, 1996.

Lai, Him Mark. "Teaching Chinese Americans to Be Chinese." In *Chinese American Transnationalism: The Flow of People, Resources, and Ideas between China and America during the Exclusion Era*, edited by Sucheng Chan, pp. 194–210. Philadelphia: Temple University Press, 2006.

Lavrov, George. *Yokohama Gaijin: Memoir of a Foreigner Born in Japan*. Bloomington, IN: AuthorHouse, 2011.

Lebra-Chapman, Joyce. *Ōkuma Shigenobu: Statesman of Meiji Japan*. Canberra: Australian National University Press, 1973.

Lee, Changsoo. "The Legal Status of Koreans in Japan." In *Koreans in Japan: Ethnic Conflict and Accommodation*, edited by Changsoo Lee and George De Vos, pp. 133–58. Berkeley: University of California Press, 1981.

———. "Organizational Division and Conflict: Ch'ongnyon and Mindan." In *Koreans in Japan: Ethnic Conflict and Accommodation*, edited by Changsoo Lee and George De Vos, pp. 110–30. Berkeley: University of California Press, 1981.

Lee Tzsu Maan. "Hyakunen no kakyō gakkō no kenshō." *Kakyō kajin kenkyū*, no. 8 (2011): 62–70.

Li Chunjia. "Shisso de kenjitsu na shōgakkō." In *Yokohama Yamate chūkagakkō hyakunen kōshi*, edited by Yokohama Yamate chūkagakkō hyakunen kōshi henshū iinkai, pp. 141–43. Yokohama: Yokohama Yamate chūkagakuen, 2005.

Liang Fuchu. *Bangqiu yundong*. Edited by Liang Youde. Beijing, 1986.

Liang Youwen. "Yi xianfu." In *Bangqiu yundong*, edited by Liang Youde, pp. 22–29. Beijing, 1986.

Lie, John. *Multiethnic Japan*. Cambridge, MA: Harvard University Press, 2001.

———. *Zainichi (Koreans in Japan): Diasporic Nationalism and Postcolonial Identity*. Berkeley: University of California Press, 2008.

Lin Huiru, ed. *Xiaoxue xinduben*. 6 vols. Yokohama: Zhisheng hao, 1903.

Lin, Man-Houng. "Overseas Chinese Merchants and Multiple Nationality: A Means for Reducing Commercial Risk (1895–1935)." *Modern Asian Studies* 35, no. 4 (2001): 985–1010.

Lin Tongchun. *Hashi wataru hito: Kakyō haran banjō shishi*. Kobe: Epikku, 1997.

Lincicome, Mark E. *Imperial Subjects as Global Citizens: Nationalism, Internationalism, and Education in Japan*. Lanham, MD: Lexington Books, 2009.

Liu, Wuji. *Su Man-shu*. New York: Twayne, 1972.

Liu Yi, "Ji xianbei Liang Fuchu xiansheng de bangleiqiu shengya." In *Bangqiu yundong*, edited by Liang Youde, pp. 8–16. Beijing, 1986.

Liu-Farrer, Gracia. "Creating a Transnational Community: Chinese Newcomers in Japan." In *Japan's Minorities: The Illusion of Homogeneity*, 2nd ed., edited by Michael Weiner, pp. 116–38. New York: Routledge, 2009.

Lu Feng. "Quan Riben huaqiao zonghui, dierjie dahui canjia ji." *Kabun Ōsaka mainichi* 6, no. 12 (1941): 23–25.

Lu, Yan. *Re-understanding Japan: Chinese Perspectives, 1895–1945*. Honolulu: Association for Asian Studies and University of Hawai'i, 2004.

Matsumoto Gaku. "Kokumin taii kōjō to kenkoku taisō." *Kōsei jidai* 1, no. 2 (1939): 1.

Matsumoto Otō. "Nanyang huaqiao wenti yu zairi huaqiao de shiming." *Kabun Ōsaka mainichi* 8, no. 8 (1942): 11.

McKeown, Adam. *Chinese Migrant Networks and Cultural Change: Peru, Chicago, and Hawaii, 1900–1936.* Chicago: University of Chicago Press, 2001.

———. "Conceptualizing Chinese Diasporas, 1842 to 1949." *Journal of Asian Studies* 58, no. 2 (May 1999): 303–37.

Meyer, Karl E., and Shareen Blair Brysac. *Pax Ethnica: Where and How Diversity Succeeds.* New York: PublicAffairs, 2012.

Minami Manshū tetsudō Tōa keizai chōsakyoku. *Kakyō.* Tokyo: Minami Manshū tetsudō tōa keizai chōsa kyoku, 1927.

Miyazaki, Tōten. *My Thirty-Three Years' Dream: The Autobiography of Miyazaki Tōten.* Translated by Etō Shinkichi and Marius B. Jansen. Princeton, NJ: Princeton University Press, 1982.

Miyozaki Ryū "Hitsugi bune, shi wa ryūshū ni ari." *Shimin to bunka,* no. 6 (1981): 30–31.

Morris-Suzuki, Tessa. *Re-inventing Japan: Time, Space, Nation.* Armonk, NY: M. E. Sharpe, 1998.

———. "'Welcome to Our Family.'" *Traces* 2 (2001): 197–203.

Münz, Rainer, and Rainer Ohliger. "Diasporas and Ethnic Minorities in Twentieth-Century Europe: A Comparative Perspective." In *Diasporas and Ethnic Migrants: Germany, Israel and Russia in Comparative Perspective,* edited by Rainer Münz and Rainer Ohliger, pp. 3–17. Portland, OR: Frank Cass, 2003.

Murakami Rei'ichi. *Yokohama Chūkagaiteki kakyōden.* Tokyo: Shinpūsha, 1997.

Muraoka Keizō. "Yukikau benpatsu sugata." In *Yokohama konjaku,* edited by Mainichi shinbun Yokohama shikyoku, pp. 64–65. Yokohama: Mainichi shinbun Yokohama shikyoku, 1957.

Murayama Izuru. *Yamanoue Okura no kenkyū.* Tokyo: Ōfūsha, 1976.

Murphy-Shigematsu, Stephen. "Multiethnic Japan and the Monoethnic Myth." *Melus* 18, no. 4 (1993): 63–80.

Nagano Akira. *Kakyō: Shina minzoku no kaigai hatten.* Tokyo: Shina mondai kenkyūjo, 1928.

Nagano Takeshi. *Zainichi Chūgokujin: Rekishi to aidentiti.* Tokyo: Akashi shoten, 1994.

Naimushō. "Shin seiken to zairyū kakyō." *Shūhō* 76 (1938): 26–29.

Naimushō keihōkyoku, ed. *Gaiji keisatsu gaikyō.* 9 vols. (1935–43). Tokyo: Ryūkei shosha, 1980.

Najita, Tetsuo. "Inukai Tsuyoshi: Some Dilemmas in Party Development in Pre–World War II Japan." *American Historical Review* 74, no. 2 (1968): 492–510.

Naka-ku 50 shūnen kinen jigyō jikkō iinkai, ed. *Yokohama Naka-ku shi: Hitobito ga kataru gekidō no rekishi.* Yokohama: Naka-ku 50 shūnen kinen jigyō jikkō iinkai, 1985.

Nakamura Toshiko. *Katei de dekiru shina ryōri.* Tokyo: Fubunkan, 1927.

Nee, Victor, and Brett de Bary Nee. *Longtime Californ': A Documentary Study of an American Chinatown.* Boston: Houghton Mifflin, 1974.

Ng, Wing Chung. *The Chinese in Vancouver, 1945–80: The Pursuit of Identity and Power.* Vancouver: University of British Columbia Press, 1999.

———. "Collective Ritual and the Resilience of Traditional Organizations: A Case Study of Vancouver since the Second World War." In *The Chinese Diaspora: Selected Essays,* edited by Ling-Chi Wang and Gungwu Wang, 1:195–227. Singapore: Times Academic Press, 1998.

Ngai, Mae. "Legacies of Exclusion: Illegal Chinese Immigration during the Cold War Years." *Journal of American Ethnic History* 18, no. 1 (Fall 1998): 3–35.

Nihon Chūgoku yūkō kyōkai zenkoku honbu, ed. *Nitchū yūkō undōshi.* Rev. ed. Tokyo: Seinen shuppansha, 1980.

Niki Fumiko. *Shinsaika no Chūgokujin gyakusatsu.* Tokyo: Aoki shoten, 1993.

Nish, Ian Hill. *Japanese Foreign Policy, 1869–1942: Kasumigaseki to Miyakezaka* (Foreign policies of the great powers). London: Routledge & K. Paul, 1977.

Nonami Yutaka. "Yokohama no shūsen wa Shōwa 30-nen: Shiumai shōshi." In *Sengo 50-nen Yokohama saigen: Futari de utsushita haisen sutōrī,* edited by Okumura Taikō and Tokiwa Toyoko, pp. 146–48. Tokyo: Heibonsha, 1996.

Nozoe Kenji. *Hanaoka jiken to Chūgokujin: Daitaichō Kō Jun no hōki.* Tokyo: San'ichi shobō, 1997.

Oda Kazuhiko. *Nihon ni zairyū suru Chūgokujin no rekishiteki henyō.* Osaka: Fūeisha, 2010.

Ogasawara Kenzō. *Sonbun o sasaeta Yokohama kakyō On Heichin (Wen Bingchen)/Keichin (Huichen) kyōdai.* Tokyo: Yasaka shobō, 2009.

Ogata Kunio. "Kakyō no shinbun: 'Kansai kakyō hō' o chūshin ni." *Kobe to gaikoku bunka,* no. 10 (2004): 92–118.

Oguma, Eiji. *A Genealogy of "Japanese" Self-Images.* Translated by David Askew. Melbourne: Trans Pacific Press, 2002.

Okamatsu Kazuo. "Chūgokujin no bochi." *Shinchō* 86, no. 11 (Nov. 1989): 158–59.

———. *Umi no toride.* Tokyo: Shinchōsha, 1988.

Osada Gorō and Tanaka Masumi. "Ryūnichi kakyō keizai no dōkō (1): 'Kakyō keizai nenkan' o chūshin to shite." *Keizai to bōeki* 79 (Mar. 1962): 53–61.

———. "Ryūnichi kakyō keizai no dōkō (3)," *Keizai to bōeki* 81 (February 1963): 34–41.

Ōsato Hiroaki. "'Yokohama bōeki shinpō' o tōshite miru zairyū Chūgokujin no ariyō." *Jinbun kenkyū* 112 (1992): 101–23.

———. "Zainichi Chūgokujin rōdōsha, gyōshōnin: Senzen no keisatsu shiryō ni miru." In *Chūgoku minshū-shi he no shiza: Shin shinoroji, rekishi,* edited by Kanagawa daigaku Chūgokugo gakka, pp. 203–35. Tokyo: Tōhō shoten, 1998.

Otobe Junko. "Yokohama kyoryūchi ni okeru Chūgokujin shūjūchiku no kūkan kōzō." *Journal of Chinese Overseas Studies* 2 (2005): 79–92.

Paine, S. C. M. *The Sino-Japanese War of 1894–1895: Perceptions, Power, and Primacy.* Cambridge: Cambridge University Press, 2003.

Pan, Lynn. *Sons of the Yellow Emperor: A History of the Chinese Diaspora.* New York: Kodansha International, 1994.

Pan Minsheng. "Yokohama Yamate chūkagakkō no kako, genzai, mirai." *Kakyō kajin kenkyū* 8 (2011): 55–61.

Poole, Otis Manchester. *The Death of Old Yokohama in the Great Japanese Earthquake of September 1, 1923.* London: Allen & Unwin, 1968.

Purcell, Victor. *Problems of Chinese Education.* London: Kegan Paul, Trench, Trübner, 1936.

Qiaowu weiyuanhui, ed. *Qiaowu wushinian.* Taipei: Qiaowu weiyuanhui, 1982.

Qingyi bao. 12 vols. (1898–1901). Reprint, Taipei: Chengwen chubanshe, 1967.

Reaves, Joseph A. *Taking in a Game: A History of Baseball in Asia.* Lincoln: University of Nebraska Press, 2002.

Roden, Donald. "Baseball and the Quest for National Dignity in Meiji Japan." *American Historical Review* 85, no. 3 (June 1980): 511–34.

Ryang, Sonia. *North Koreans in Japan: Language, Ideology, and Identity.* Boulder, CO: Westview Press, 1997.

———. "The Tongue That Divided Life and Death: The 1923 Tokyo Earthquake and the Massacre of Koreans." *Asia-Pacific Journal*, Sept. 3, 2007. Accessed May 21, 2013. http://japanfocus.org/-Sonia-Ryang/2513.

———. "Visible and Vulnerable: The Predicament of Koreans in Japan." In *Diaspora Without Homeland: Being Korean in Japan*, edited by Sonia Ryang and John Lie, pp. 62–80. Berkeley: University of California Press, 2009.

Safran, William. "Diasporas in Modern Societies: Myths of Homeland and Return." *Diaspora* 5, no. 1 (1996): 83–99.

Saitō Sakae. *Yokohama Chūkagai satsujin jiken.* Tokyo: Kōbunsha, 1993.

Scott, James C. *Domination and the Arts of Resistance: Hidden Transcripts.* New Haven, CT: Yale University Press, 1990.

Seki Akira. *Kodai no kikajin.* Tokyo: Yoshikawa kōbunsha, 1996.

Seraphim, Franziska. *War Memory and Social Politics in Japan, 1945–2005.* Cambridge, MA: Harvard University Press, 2006.

Shibata Yoshimasa. "Tekisan shori to tokushu zaisan shikin tokubetsu kaikei." In *Yokohama no kindai: Toshi no keisei to tenkai*, edited by Yokohama kindaishi kenkyūkai and Yokohama kaikō shiryōkan, pp. 423–48. Tokyo: Nihon keizai hyōronsha, 1997.

Shinyō kumiai Yokohama kagin. *Teikan: Gyōmu no shurui oyobi hōhōsho.* Yokohama: Shinyō kumiai Yokohama kagin, n.d.

Shiragami Yoshio. *Yokohama no aji.* Osaka: Hoikusha, 1976.

Silverberg, Miriam. "The Modern Girl as Militant." In *Recreating Japanese Women, 1600–1945*, edited by Gail Lee Bernstein, pp. 239–66. Berkeley: University of California Press, 1991.

Siu, Lok. *Memories of a Future Home: Diasporic Citizenship of Chinese in Panama.* Stanford, CA: Stanford University Press, 2005.

Sohoni, Deenesh. "Unsuitable Suitors: Anti-Miscegenation Laws, Naturalization Laws, and the Construction of Asian Identities." *Law and Society Review* 41, no. 3 (Sept. 2007): 587–618.

Sollors, Werner. "Foreword: Theories of American Ethnicity." In *Theories of Ethnicity: A Classical Reader*, edited by Werner Sollors, pp. xxii–xxv. New York: New York University Press, 1996.

Spence, Jonathan D. *The Gate of Heavenly Peace: The Chinese and Their Revolution, 1895–1980.* New York: Penguin Books, 1982.

Statistics Bureau. *Registered Aliens by Nationality and Status of Residence (Permanent Residents, Non-permanent Residents) (1948–2009).* Tokyo: Ministry of Internal Affairs and Communications, 2009. Accessed Mar. 7, 2013. http://www.stat.go.jp/english/data-chouki/02.htm.

Sugawara, Kōsuke. *Chainataun, henbō suru Yokohama Chūkagai.* Tokyo: Yōzensha, 1987.

———. *Nihon no kakyō.* Tokyo: Asahi shinbunsha, 1991.

Sun Shijie. *Hengbin da zhenzai zhong zhi huaqiao zhuangkuang.* Yokohama: Consulate General of the Republic of China, 1924.

Suzuki Tomizō. "Chūkagai to watashi." *Gekkan Chūkagai* 11 (1973): 17.

Swislocki, Mark. *Culinary Nostalgia: Regional Food Culture and the Urban Experience in Shanghai.* Stanford, CA: Stanford University Press, 2009.

Takahashi Teiyū. "Kinkyō hōkoku." Kongetsu hitokoto aisatsu: Chūkagai jinbutsu shi, *Gekkan Chūkagai* 1 (1973): 14–15.

Tan, Chee Beng. "People of Chinese Descent: Language, Nationality and Identity." In *The Chinese Diaspora: Selected Essays,* edited by Ling-chi Wang and Gungwu Wang, pp. 337–58. Singapore: Academic Press, 1998.

Tan Lumei (Tan Romi) and Liu Jie (Ryū Ketsu). *Shinkakyō rōkakyō: Henbō suru Nihon no Chūgokujin shakai.* Tokyo: Bungei shunjū, 2008.

Taniguchi Tsukane. "Senkyo wa dare ga surumono nano deshōka." One Word. *Aera* 13, no. 48 (Nov. 13, 2000): 70–71.

Tatewaki Kazuo, ed. *Japan Directory: Bakumatsu Meiji zainichi gaikokujin, kikan meikan.* 48 vols. (1861–1912). Reprint, Tokyo: Yumani shobō, 1996–97.

Tegtmeyer Pak, Katherine. "Cities and Local Citizenship in Japan: Overcoming Nationality?" In *Local Citizenship in Recent Countries of Immigration,* edited by Takeyuki Tsuda. Lanham, MD: Lexington Books, 2006.

———. "Foreigners Are Local Citizens Too: Local Governments Respond to International Migration in Japan." In *Japan and Global Migration: Foreign Workers and the Advent of a Multicultural Society,* edited by Michael Douglass and Glenda S. Roberts, pp. 244–74. New York: Routledge, 2000.

Tōa keizai chōsakyoku, ed. *Shina kokutei hainichi dokuhon.* Tokyo: Tōa keizai chōsa kyoku, 1929.

Tölölyan, Khachig. "The American Model of Diasporic Discourse." In *Diasporas and Ethnic Migrants: Germany, Israel and Russia in Comparative Perspective,* edited by Rainer Münz and Rainer Ohliger, pp. 56–73. Portland, OR: Frank Cass, 2003.

———. "Rethinking Diaspora(s): Stateless Power in the Transnational Moment." *Diaspora* 5, no. 1 (1996): 3–36.

Toyama Shōichi. *Chūzan zonkō.* Vol. 2. Tokyo: Maruzen, 1909.

Tsai, Chutung. "The Chinese Nationality Law, 1909." *American Journal of International Law* 4, no. 2 (1910): 404–11.

Tsang, Chiu-sam. *Nationalism in School Education in China.* Hong Kong: Progressive Education, 1967.

Tsu, Timothy Y. "From Ethnic Ghetto to 'Gourmet Republic': The Changing Image of Kobe's Chinatown in Modern Japan." *Japanese Studies* 19, no. 1 (1999): 17–32.

Tsuda, Takeyuki. "Localities and the Struggle for Immigrant Rights: The Significance of Local Citizenship in Recent Countries of Immigration." In *Local Citizenship in Recent Countries of Immigration: Japan in Comparative Perspective,* edited by Takeyuki Tsuda, pp. 3–36. Lanham, MD: Lexington Books, 2006.

Tsūshō kyoku dainika, ed. *Kakyō no gensei.* Tokyo: Gaimushō tsūshō kyoku, 1935.

Uchida Naosaku. *Nihon kakyō shakai no kenkyū.* Tokyo: Dōbunkan, 1949.

Ueda Toshio. "Nihon ni okeru Chūgokujin no hōritsuteki chii: Bakumatsu yori konji taisen ni itaru." *Ajia kenkyū* 1, no. 3 (1955): 1–19.

U.S. Bureau of Navigation. *U.S. Navy Ports of the World: Yokohama.* Washington, DC: Government Printing Office, 1920.

Vasishth, Andrea. "A Model Minority: The Chinese Community in Japan." In *Japan's Minorities: The Illusion of Homogeneity*, edited by Michael Weiner, pp. 108–39. New York: Routledge, 1997.

Wan, Ming. *Sino-Japanese Relations: Interaction, Logic, and Transformation.* Stanford, CA: Stanford University Press, 2005.

Wang, Gungwu. *The Chinese Overseas: From Earth-bound China to the Quest for Autonomy.* Cambridge, MA: Harvard University Press, 2000.

———. "The Limits of Nanyang Chinese Nationalism: 1912–1937." In *Community and Nation: Essays on Southeast Asia and the Chinese,* edited by Wang Gungwu, pp. 142–58. Singapore: Heinemann, 1981.

———. "A Note on the Origins of *Hua-Ch'iao*." In *Community and Nation: Essays on Southeast Asia and the Chinese,* pp. 118–27. Singapore: Heinemann, 1981.

Wang Liang, ed. *Zhonghua minguo liu-Ri Hengbin huaqiao zonghui maixiang liushi nian jinian tekan.* Yokohama: Zhonghua minguo liu-Ri Hengbin huaqiao zonghui, 2002.

Wang Wei. *Nihon kakyō ni okeru dentō no saihen to esunishiti: Saishi to geinō o chūshin ni.* Tokyo: Fūkyōsha, 2001.

———. *Sugao no Chūkagai.* Tokyo: Yōzensha, 2003.

Watanabe Takahiro. "1920-nendai no 'shina ryōri' (1), Yamada Masahei no chosaku kara." *Shokuseikatsu kenkyū* 28, no. 6 (2008): 21–31.

———. "Zasshi 'Eiyō to ryōri' ni Yamada Masahei ga ki shita mono: 1935-nen kara 1940-nen no 'shina ryōri'," *Shoku seikatsu kenkyū* 30, no. 4 (2010): 11–23.

Wataru Tetsuya, Yūki Saori, Itsuki Hiroshi,Tanaka Mari, Fujiwara Shinji, Sakaki Hiromi, Sonoi Keisuke, Hidari Sachiko, Sugawara Kenji, and Takita Yūsuke. "Watashi no Chūkagai." *Gekkan Chūkagai* 1 (1973): 8–12.

Weiner, Michael. "Editor's Introduction." In *Japan's Minorities: The Illusion of Homogeneity,* edited by Michael Weiner, 2nd ed., pp. xiv–xxi. New York: Routledge, 2009.

———. "Invention of Identity: Race and Nation in Pre-War Japan." In *The Construction of Racial Identities in China and Japan,* edited by Frank Dikötter, pp. 99–117. Honolulu: University of Hawai'i Press, 1997.

Whiting, Robert. *You Gotta Have Wa.* New York: Vintage, 1989.

Williams, Harold S. *Tales of the Foreign Settlements in Japan.* Tokyo: Charles E. Tuttle, 1958.

Wu Bokang. "Enkaichū hitokoto mōshiagemasu." *Kōsei jidai* 1, no. 2 (1939): 8.

———. "Yi Hengbin huaqiao xuexiao." In *Yokohama Yamate chūkagakkō hyakunen kōshi,* edited by Yokohama Yamate chūkagakkō hyakunen kōshi henshū iinkai, pp. 133–35. Yokohama: Yokohama Yamate chūkagakuen. 2005.

Xu Shuzhen (Kyo Shukushin). "Ryūnichi kakyō sōkai no seiritsu ni tsuite (1945–1952)." In *Nihon kakyō to bunka masatsu,* edited by Yamada Nobuo, pp. 119–87. Tokyo: Gennandō, 1983.

Yamada Masahei. "Shūmai to shinasoba no tsukurikata." *Eiyō to ryōri* 2, no. 12 (Dec. 1936): 22–25.

Yamaguchi Tokio. "Yokohama Chūkagai no seitai kenkyū (1): Yokohama ni okeru kankō shōtengai to shite no tokuisei." *Keizai to bōeki* 79 (Mar. 1962): 1–32.

———. "Yokohama Chūkagai no seitai kenkyū (2)." *Keizai to bōeki* 80 (Aug. 1962): 8–35.

———. "Yokohama Chūkagai no seitai no kenkyū (3)." *Keizai to bōeki* 81 (Feb. 1963): 9–33.

Yamamuro Shūhei, and Kawamura Masuo. "Yokohama zairyū kakyō no tokushitsu ni kansuru jakkan no kōsatsu (sono 1)." *Yokohama kokuritsu daigaku jinbun kiyō, daiichirui tetsugaku shakai gaku* 9 (1963): 1–40.

Yamashita Kiyomi. "Yokohama Chūkagai zairyū Chūgokujin no seikatsu yōshiki." *Jinbun chiri* 31, no. 4 (1979): 33–50.

Yang Murray, Alice. *Historical Memories of Japanese American Internment and the Struggle for Redress*. Stanford, CA: Stanford University Press 2008.

Yasui Sankichi, Chen Laixing, and Guo Fang. *Hanshin dai shinsai to kakyō*. Kobe: Authors, 1996.

Ye Mingcheng. "Chūgoku daidō gakkō-shi." In *Yokohama Yamate chūkagakkō hyakunen kōshi*, edited by Yokohama Yamate chūkagakkō hyakunen kōshi henshū iinkai, pp. 505–656. Yokohama: Yokohama Yamate chūkagakuen, 2005.

Yokohama Chūkagai hattenkai kyōdō kumiai. *Yokohama Chūkagai machizukuri kihon kōsō*. Yokohama: Yokohama Chūkagai hattenkai kyōdō kumiai, 1992.

Yokohama Chūkagai machi zukuri dantai rengō kyōgikai. *Yokohama Chūkagai no gurando dezain*. Yokohama: Yokohama Chūkagai machi zukuri dantai rengō kyōgikai, 2005.

Yokohama kaikō shiryōkan, ed. *Yokohama Chūkagai, kaikō kara shinsai made: Rakuyō kikon kara rakuchi seikon e*. Yokohama: Yokohama kaikō shiryōkan, 1994.

———. *Shisei shikō to Yokohama no hitobito: Meiji nijū-nendai no Yokohama*. Yokohama: Yokohama kaikō shiryōkan, 1988.

———. *Yokohama Chūkagai 150-nen: Rakuchi seikon no saigetsu*. Yokohama: Yokohama kaikō shiryōkan, 2009.

Yokohama kakyō sōkai seijōka dan'atsu jiken saiban shiryōshū kankō iinkai, ed. *Yokohama kakyō sōkai seijōka dan'atsu jiken saiban shiryōshū: Nitchū yūkō no uragawa de*. Yokohama: Yokohama kakyō sōkai seijōka dan'atsu jiken saiban shiryōshū kankō iinkai, 1977.

Yokohama-shi, ed. *Yokohama shishi*. 21 vols. Yokohama: Yokohama-shi, 1958–82.

———. *Yokohama-shi tōkei sho*. Multiple volumes. Yokohama: Yokohama-shi, 1903–.

Yokohama-shi chūō toshokan kaikan kinenshi henshū iinkai, ed. *Yokohama no hon to bunka: Yokohama-shi chūō toshokan kaikan kinenshi*. Vol. 1. Yokohama: Yokohama-shi chūō toshokan, 1994.

Yokohama-shi sōmukyoku shishi henshūshitsu, ed. *Yokohama shishi II*. Vol. 1. Yokohama: Yokohama-shi, 1996.

Yokohama-shi tōkei jōhōka. *Chiiki-kokusekibetsu gaikokujin tōroku jinkō*. Accessed May 8, 2013. http://www.city.yokohama.lg.jp/ex/stat.

———. *Daitoshi hikaku tōkei nenpyō (Heisei 22-nen)*. Accessed May 8, 2013. http://www.city.yokohama.lg.jp/ex/stat.

Yokohama shinpōsha. *Yokohama hanjō ki*. Yokohama: Yokohama shinpōsha, 1903.

Yokohama shiyakusho, ed. *Yokohama shishi kō, fūzoku hen*. Reprint, Kyoto: Rinkawa shoten, 1985.

———. *Yokohama shishi kō, kyōiku hen*. Reprint, Kyoto: Rinkawa shoten, 1985.

Yokohama shiyakusho shishi hensangakari, ed. *Yokohama-shi shinsai shi*. Vol. 5. Yokohama: Yokohama shiyakusho shishi hensangakari, 1926.

Yokohama Yamate chūkagakkō hyakunen kōshi henshū iinkai. "Bainian xiaoshi." In *Yokohama Yamate chūkagakkō hyakunen kōshi*, edited by Yokohama Yamate chūkagakkō hyakunen kōshi henshū iinkai, pp. 41–130. Yokohama: Yokohama Yamate chūkagakuen, 2005.

Yomiuri shinbunsha, ed. *Yokohama Chūkagai monogatari*. Tokyo: Yomiuri, 1998.

Yoshinao Washio, ed. *Inukai Bokudō den*. Vol. 2. Tokyo: Tōyō keizai shinpōsha, 1939.

Yoshino, Kosaku. "Rethinking Theories of Nationalism: Japan's Nationalism in a Marketplace Perspective." In *Consuming Ethnicity and Nationalism: Asian Experiences*, edited by Kosaku Yoshino, pp. 8–28. Honolulu: University of Hawai'i Press, 1999.

Zanasi, Margherita. "New Perspectives on Chinese Collaboration." *Asia Pacific Journal*, July 24, 2008. Accessed Apr. 29, 2013. http://japanfocus.org/-Margherita-Zanasi/2828.

Zarrow, Peter. "Introduction: Citizenship in China and the West." In *Imagining the People: Chinese Intellectuals and the Concept of Citizenship, 1890–1920*, edited by Joshua A. Fogel and Peter G. Zarrow, pp. 3–38. Armonk, NY: M. E. Sharpe, 1997.

Zeng Deshen. "Yokohama Yamate chūkagakkō rekishi nenpyō." In *Yokohama Yamate chūkagakkō hyakunen kōshi*, edited by Yokohama Yamate chūkagakkō hyakunen kōshi henshū iinkai, 687–724. Yokohama: Yokohama Yamate chūkagakuen, 2005.

Zha, Daojiong. "Chinese Migrant Workers in Japan: Policies, Institutions and Civil Society." In *Globalizing Chinese Migration: Trends in Europe and Asia*, edited by Pál Nyíri and Igor Savaliev, pp. 129–57. Burlington, VT: Ashgate, 2002.

Zhang Shu. *Hengbin zhonghua xueyuan qianqi xiaoshi gao*. Yokohama: Hengbin zhonghua xueyuan, 1989.

Zhang Xuejing. "Datong xuexiao lueshi." In *Datong tongxue lu*, edited by Feng Jinglong, pp. 3–7. Yokohama: Ōhashi insatsusho, 1909.

Zhonghua minguo liu-Ri lingshiguan. *Riben zhenzai cansha huaqiao an*. Yokohama: Consulate General of the Republic of China, 1925.

Zhonghua xueyuan, ed. *Hengbin zhonghua xueyuan bai zhou nian yuanqing jinian tekan*. Yokohama: Zhonghua xueyuan, 2000.

Zhou Yu'e. "Riben huaqiao jiaoyu lüekuang." *Huaqiao jiaoyu* 1 (1983): 179–87.

Zhu Huiling. *Kakyō shakai no henbō to sono shōrai*. Tokyo: Nihon kahōsha, 1999.

Zhu Jingxian, ed. *Huaqiao jiaoyu*. Taipei: Taiwan zhonghua shuju, 1973.

Zui Shinpyō. "Yokohama Chūkagai o sekai no Chainataun ni." Kongetsu hitokoto goaisatsu: Chūkagai jinbutsu shi, *Gekkan Chūkagai* 2 (1973): 14–15.

Index

Pages on which figures appear are in *italics*.